Prai

NIGHT

"Jared Dillian's last book, *No Worries*, was about how to live a stress-free financial life. Good thing Dillian's fictional characters don't take his real-life advice. Their stories would be safe and boring. The characters in *Night Moves* aren't stress free; they're stress full. In all the best ways, like all the best fiction. This collection sizzles."

—JOE OESTREICH
Author of *Hitless Wonder*

"Jared Dillian crunches numbers by day, but his *Night Moves* are gloriously unquantifiable. Equal parts dangerous and delicious, this bold collection from Dillian explores the darkest corners of the human heart and revels in its characters' wildest impulses—thrilling, often destructive, and always gripping."

—BILL SCHWEIGART
Author of *The Guilty One*

"In *Night Moves*, Jared Dillian masterfully crafts stories that grip you with the force of unexpected plot twists. His storytelling is as uncomfortably riveting as flying coach, hungover, in the middle seat back from Vegas after losing twenty-five grand. Prepare yourself for a rollercoaster of emotions that will leave you questioning your life choices and the thin line between self-destruction and redemption."

—TURNEY DUFF
Author of *The Buy Side*

"*Night Moves* is a haunting mix of emotionally-charged, character-driven stories that cover the darker side of life's experiences—mental illness, greed, fidelity and sex. I dare you to stop reading after one story."

—BARBARA CLAYPOLE WHITE
Bestselling author of *The Perfect Son*

"In *Night Moves*, Jared Dillian delivers a raw and consistent book full of tightly-wound short stories that feel like arthouse films. The stories linger on in your mind and each one forces you to think long and hard about what the hell just happened. Dillian poses interesting questions and then cleverly supplies just enough answers to satisfy. I give *Night Moves* five out of five stars."

—JACK MOORE
Author of *The Reset: The Final Days of the Last American Bubble*

"To the canon of great fiction writers who came late to the party— Henry Miller, the Marquis de Sade, Charles Bukowski among them—please add Jared Dillian. In *Night Moves*, Dillian combines a massive imagination with the delicate ability to let the reader think for themselves. In doing so, he's revitalized the art of short literary fiction."

—BRIAN MCDONALD
Author of *Last Call At Elaine's* and *Five Floors Up: The Heroic Family Story of Four Generations in the FDNY*

"With his previous work, Jared Dillian brought us insights into the collapse of Lehman Brothers and the nature of creativity, but now with *Night Moves* he expands his canvas to the short story, and presents us with a cavalcade of American Dreamers: philandering husbands, Vicodin-dealing doctors, cocky finance bros, trophy wives, teenage runaways, prostitutes, suburban sports dads, and musicians, all striving for the basic necessities—love, sex, and money—with their mortality looming in the rear-view mirror. Dillian knows better than to judge his characters and isn't afraid to follow them down the rabbit hole of their bad decisions. Even better, this is a story collection with a capital 'S,' in that these are plotted stories with big emotions and even bigger stakes. You'll either snort with laughter or throw this book across the room, but either way you'll be entertained, and I reckon you'll feel something for this cast of recognizable and flawed human beings."

—MATTHEW MERCIER
Author of *POE & I*

"A cold chill makes its way through Jared Dillian's story collection, *Night Moves*. A girl innocently becomes a voyeur, musicians are embattled, a woman unravels in a separation, a newscaster gets creeped on. Written in a simple prose style, both succinct and pointed, Dillian deftly crafts plot-driven narratives that move effortlessly toward their intended target—poignant dismay. Set in modern-day America among middle to high income-earning characters, *Night Moves* nods toward the techno age while giving us real people with real problems—and a few text messages thrown in for good measure."

—K. P. GIORDANO
Poet and author of the forthcoming novel *Freelancer*

"More than anything, *Night Moves* chronicles the struggles of insider-outsiders: A lottery winner who is determined to lose. A successful dentist who can't get out of his own way—or out of his bag of Vicodin. A DJ adrift in women, but sunk in loneliness. An economics PhD student streaking towards the Fed—whether it's the Reserve or Pen is TBD. All of Dillian's characters writhe with intensity, and the insights he brings to their struggles thump like CO_2 cannons firing from the dancefloor of their souls."

—LEE GRIFFITH
Professor of Writing, and Member of the National Book Critics Circle

"Recklessness and depraved scenarios underpin Dillian's short stories ... a somewhat brash volume of uncomfortable stories ... The author's writing is at its strongest when he situates readers in settings or delivers moments of absurdity."

—*KIRKUS REVIEWS*

First published in 2024.

Paperback ISBN: 979-8-9909447-0-1

eBook ISBN: 979-8-9909447-1-8

JAREDDILLIAN.COM

NIGHT MOVES

And other stories

Jared Dillian

Available by the same author

CONTENTS

INTRODUCTION

TWENTY-EIGHT years ago, I walked into a used bookstore and spied the latest issue of *Granta*, a British literary magazine, though I had never heard of *Granta* and I didn't know what a literary magazine was. It was a "Best of Young American Novelists" issue. I fancied myself a writer, and I was really interested to read about these great young American novelists. They were: Sherman Alexie, Madison Smartt Bell, Ethan Canin, Edwidge Danticat, Tom Drury, Tony Earley, Jeffrey Eugenides, Jonathan Franzen, David Guterson, David Haynes, Allen Kurzweil, Elizabeth McCracken, Lorrie Moore, Fae Myenne Ng, Robert O'Connor, Chris Offutt, Stewart O'Nan, Mona Simpson, Melanie Rae Thon and Kate Wheeler They had these lush black-and-white portraits among trees, in cityscapes, or riding subways, looking like... writers. Some of them have gone on to become *very* famous (Alexie, Franzen, Eugenides), others middling famous (Canin, Danticat, and Mona Simpson, who is probably best known for her obituary of her brother, Steve Jobs), and some have dropped off the face of the earth. I wanted to be a Best Young American Novelist, right then and there, in my twenty-two-year-old body and brain, in sunny and optimistic Port Angeles, Washington.

I bought the magazine and took it home and read the stories. I bought a bunch of other literary magazines, too. And I was reading a lot of Barry Hannah, a Southern Gothic writer I discovered in my creative writing class at the Coast Guard Academy. One day, I thought, I would be publishing short stories in these literary magazines. Well, my life went a different direction, to say the least. I got an MBA from the University of San Francisco, had a successful career as a trader on Wall Street, and ultimately did become a writer—of newsletters and op-eds and memoirs and novels and essay collections—but not short stories. I was in my late forties, and I had missed my chance to become a Best Young Writer. So I applied to an MFA program at the Savannah College of Art and Design, got accepted, and took a few fiction classes in the context of a larger nonfiction program. I began to write short stories—it was the most fun I had had writing in years. And I wrote lots of them. I would send them out for feedback to friends and family, and the feedback was universally positive; but, of course, I was sending them to friends and family, so of course it was going to be positive. Yet it seemed like people really liked these stories. I started submitting to literary journals.

I submitted sixteen stories to over one hundred literary journals. I was rejected by all of them, except one where I had a personal relationship with the editor. There were a few close calls as well. In these situations, where it seems like you suck at something, you do some introspection. *What am I doing wrong*? There has been much written about the sharp left turn in the literary world, and here I was, a straight, white, (and rich!) male trying to get published when most of the writers getting published were members of some underrepresented minority. But by this point in history, the underrepresented had become overrepresented. In the list of writers from *Granta* above, many of them were straight, and white, and male—that doesn't happen anymore.

So that was a possibility. But it was also possible that I sucked, and sucked bad, so I asked my literary agent about it. And he spent some time reading my stuff, and came back and told me that my stories were very *plot-heavy*, and that people tend to read novels for plot, and stories for something else. What is that something else? The line-by-line richness of the writing, I guess. So I bought more literary journals and read the stories, and found that most of them were not just plot-light but completely devoid of plot, meandering aimlessly in the authors' consciousness. Shoegazer stuff. I don't know if you've ever had this experience, but sometimes when I read a story in the *New Yorker*, I say to myself, "What the fuck did I just read?" It would be completely nonsensical.

It wasn't always this way. I grew up on literary fiction in the 1990s, and back then stories had plot. The was a protagonist, an arc, and a resolution. There was a beginning, middle, and an end. The endings didn't always have to be satisfying, but there were endings. Literary fiction has become very postmodern, and as a result the only consumers of literary fiction are typically writers of literary fiction. Last I heard, about five years ago, sales of literary fiction were down 40% from the highs—and that was five years ago. It is a dying art, and the reason it is dying is because people are writing things that nobody wants to read. But that is the standard by which most literary fiction is judged—if someone wants to read it, it is bad. And I am not kidding. The art world went through this postmodern convulsion sixty years ago, but the difference is that some hedge fund poseur will spend $80 million to install that crap in his lobby. The art world is filled with fart-smelling tastemaker critics, and the literary world is now no different, but you can't install a word salad in your corporate headquarters.

Taste is a funny thing. Even the uninitiated can tell the

difference between highbrow art (Beuys) and lowbrow art (happy little trees). The same is true of literature, with the Iowa Writers' Workshop on one end and James Patterson on the other. And so I asked myself: Are my stories *lowbrow*? Or at least *middlebrow*? Perhaps they were not getting published because they were not highbrow enough. But I simply am incapable of writing a story without a story. Maybe I don't have line-by-line richness in my writing, but I *can* tell a story. I can tell you a story that makes you *feel* something. Writing isn't an intellectual exercise, and I know some writers who over-intellectualize it, and then it sounds over-intellectualized. They call it craft. Instead, I write from the heart. I have actually cried while writing my stories. I write about sex, death, life, success, money, anxiety, spirituality, the self-conscious desire for self-sabotage, bad relationships, good relationships, substance abuse, mental illness, poverty, wealth, and God. But mostly sex and death, because often we have to choose between the two at some crucial moment in our lives. And you will never, ever see one of these mustache-twirling academics write about money. How can it be art if there is money in it? Oh, it absolutely can be.

What I am saying is that I am doing it right, and everyone else is doing it wrong. I want to start a revolution, of sorts—I want to go back to the literary fiction of thirty years ago. In that sense, I am a conservative, standing athwart literature, yelling "Stop!" But I really just want to save literature from its most nihilistic tendencies. The MFAs want you to read their stuff and feel smart. *I just read some weird highbrow shit and I'm an intellectual.* I want you to feel something, all right, but "smart" is not what I'm after. A good story will stick with you for days after you read it. It will be in your heart and mind. A collection of such stories will stick with you for a lifetime.

This revolution I am starting requires your participation. If you agree with me that this is what literature should be, talk about this book to your friends. Even better, buy copies and hand them out. This book is Jerry Maguire's manifesto. Of course, Jerry Maguire was excommunicated before being vindicated in the end. First, they ignore you, then they laugh at you, then they fight you, then you win.

Clement Greenberg once said that socialism was required to raise the taste of the masses. Nothing could be less true. I will say this: Patterson's writing isn't good because millions of people buy it. But he's doing something right. And maybe it is art, in the way that industrial, mass-produced art is art. But the true believers think that if something is commercially successful, it can't be art. Go out there and prove them wrong.

JARED DILLIAN
January 2024

THE WALLET

I MATCHED the first number and I said oh and I matched the second number and I said OH and I matched the third number and I said OH OH OH. My heart skipped about seventeen beats. The rest of the numbers were a foregone conclusion:

I won the Powerball.

I couldn't breathe. I felt the excitement hit me like an impatient rush of wind, starting at my head, down through my body and culminating in a pain in my penis, like when you clear the first hill of a roller coaster and start heading down, down, down. *This changes everything*, I thought. I hadn't exactly been living in grinding poverty, but there had always been constraints on things I could or could not do. No more. I was drowning in possibilities, standing in a field in which I could go any direction for miles.

It never occurred to me to look at how big the jackpot was. I buy tickets every week, $20 a pop, been doing this for years, and I long stopped paying attention to what the big prize was. I bought tickets when the jackpot was low, and bought tickets when the jackpot was high. Even when it was low, it would be life-changing money, so I did it anyway. I always knew that I could win; you don't buy lottery tickets expecting to lose. I just mechanically did it, week after week, concurrent with buying White Claw for $1.99 at the Circle K.

I went to my phone and typed in *pwwrbaal* and Google figured it out:

$586 million

I ran to the cupboard, took out one of those plastic souvenir baseball cups I got at the minor league baseball stadium, opened the refrigerator, held the cup under the box of Franzia White Zinfandel, and drained the contents into the cup. I swallowed about half of the pink liquid and thought about what to do next. Nobody ever plans for this, after all—you'd have to be a serious optimist to have a plan for winning the lottery before you win the lottery, outside of the mental masturbation you do about all the shit you're going to buy. Then reality takes over. You have things to think about.

Like: The obvious thing to do is to take the cash value, not the annuity value, which is a terrible deal, and only for people who aren't responsible enough to manage their finances. Besides: I might not live that long. Taking the cash was the smart thing to do, and would result in about a $250 million lump-sum payment after taxes. I'm a finance professor, so I can do this math quickly.

But wait—I didn't buy the ticket in South Carolina. I bought it in New York City last week, when I was there for a security analyst conference. I bought it at a bodega on 39th and Lexington Avenue, one that mostly sold Gatorade, Pringles, and packets of nuts, across the street from a restaurant called House of Lasagna and a sad Indian restaurant. The bodega had a sign that said someone else had bought a $10,000 ticket earlier in the year. Well, now they just sold the winning ticket for the whole damn thing. I had read somewhere that the lottery authorities drive to the establishment that sold the ticket and confiscate the video footage first thing in the morning. I hoped they were doing that right now.

That meant I would have to go back to New York to cash in the ticket. Where in New York? The city? Albany? I googled it: *How To Redeem Your Prize.*

Syracuse. I could go to Syracuse. I took another long slug from the baseball cup full of wine to calm my nerves. I was feeling better.

You always read these stories about how people win the lottery and they wait a full year to cash in the ticket, to line up lawyers and financial advisors and all that stuff. That wasn't going to be necessary—I already had a brokerage account at Merrill Lynch, a smart accountant, and the sophistication to handle a lot of money—not a problem. I figured the longer I waited to cash in this ticket, the more likely I would be to lose it. Speaking of which, maybe I had better sign the back of this thing before I forget.

Looking for a pen. No pen. I don't have a pen anywhere in the house. I will do it later.

I figured the first thing I would do when I got the money would be to buy a high-rise condo South of Fifth in Miami beach, in one of those decadent luxury buildings. I'd get a 4,000 square foot, $10 million place overlooking the ocean, eat at Prime 112 and Joe's Stone Crab, and probably pay for some companionship when the need arose. I could get a whole array of TV screens playing adult movies like Mickey Rourke in *9½ Weeks*. Fucking amazing. My next-door neighbors would probably be some Venezuelan expats who smuggled money out of the country before the currency collapse. I could invite them over for parties along with a couple dozen models and crypto millionaires. And buying real estate isn't consumption, it's an investment. I could probably sell it for $15–20 million ten years from now. So, it wouldn't even count as spending money.

But that still left $240 million. Well, first of all, I was flying private from now on—the average flight on a private jet costs about $20,000, so I could do that fifty times a year without breaking a sweat. I could hire a personal chef and a personal trainer and finally stop eating all that garbage fast food. Before long, I'd be posting shirtless selfies on Instagram, flanked by bikini models. I could take six-figure vacations, the kind where you won't see cans of Bud Light perched around the pool. The longer I thought about it, the more I began to think that I could not possibly spend all this money in a lifetime. So why not invest it, and make even more? I traded stocks as a hobby, so now instead of trading 500 shares of a stock, I could trade 50,000 shares, and have it make a difference. I could make eight percent returns on a bad year, which would give me another $20 million. I could try my hand at trading commodities, something I've always wanted to do. I'd spent the last year looking at charts of corn and soybeans, seeing opportunities, and not having the money to take advantage of them.

All the permutations of having $250 million crashed over my mind in waves, and it was too much to handle. I went back to the fridge for another baseball cup full of pink wine, sat down, and stared out the window over the $300 stained couch I had bought on Craigslist from a divorcing couple, and my brown carpet. You did hear these stories about how people won the lottery and then lost it all, like that dumbass from West Virginia with the giant hat who was broke within a few years. That wasn't going to be me—I was too smart for that. I'd be the first person to turn $250 million into a billion. I'd invest in private equity, venture capital, and hedge funds. I'd build a diversified portfolio of alternative investments. I'd start my own family office, and hire some people to look after my money.

But first, I'd better make sure I put this ticket in a safe place. I thought about putting it in a folder somewhere, or in my safe, but I figured I'd just leave it in my wallet—at least I'd know where it was.

I felt the heat of the wallet against my ass. There was $250 million in there.

I got my laptop and went to the American Airlines website to search for plane tickets to New York. The flights leaving tomorrow were expensive—about $1,600 for first class. Well, I guessed that didn't matter, and clicked the button without hesitation. I'd only flown first class once in my life—I got randomly upgraded one time flying back from Los Angeles. I was seated next to a well-endowed, impeccably dressed young woman who drank white wine and read romance novels on her Kindle. I was too intimidated to talk. But it really made me want to fly first class again in the future: operant conditioning. I then booked the most expensive hotel in Syracuse, which, shockingly, was a Marriott. There were no high-roller suites available. The best I could do was three nights in a king room for $200 a night. I couldn't spend more if I tried. I got more pink wine.

By this point the room was spinning a bit, so I decided to lie down in bed. I took the wallet out of my jeans and set it on the dresser. Must not forget that in the morning—it was going to be a big day. I peered up from the bed periodically to check that it was still there.

I tried and tried to sleep. Unable. I caught patches of sleep, here and there, but I was awake most of the night, and sobering up small. By the time the sun began to rise, I had crippling anxiety. Winning money solves some problems but creates even more. One more drink to take the edge off, and then go to the airport.

———————

I arrived at the airport exactly two hours before my flight. Usually, I cut it closer than that, but not this time. When I got to the TSA screening, I suddenly thought about how I would have to take my wallet out of my pocket. One of these fucking goons could steal the ticket. I watched it rumble slowly through the X-Ray thing, and hurried through the body scanner, so I could see the bin travel out the other side. I recombobulated and put the wallet back in my pocket. It then occurred to me that I should keep the wallet in my *front* pocket, in case someone tried to pick my pocket. But then I remembered that I was wearing my favorite pair of navy-blue slacks (I dressed up a bit for the occasion), which had a button on the back pocket. I quickly buttoned it, and felt the wallet hot against my ass.

After leaving security, I had to drain the lizard, and headed over to the men's room. I stood and emptied the contents of my bladder, the urine clear and copious. I thought that I could get a urinal installed in my new place in Miami. Maybe right next to the bed, so I didn't have to go to the bathroom in the middle of the night. Except that would be a little weird when I had women over. The stuff you think about when you win the lottery. I tucked in my shirt, buttoned my pants, and thoroughly washed my hands before heading off to the gate.

I sat down to wait for my flight—a full hour until boarding. Wilson Phillips was playing over the loudspeaker. I was thinking about how Carnie Wilson was not so bad-looking by today's standards, and slid my hand to my back pocket to check if the wallet was still there. I felt nothing.

No wallet.

I leapt to my feet, feeling my ass and looking at the floor around me. I looked under the row of chairs. I looked in my bag, to see if I had put it in there.

No wallet.

This can't be happening. I felt both pockets, all four pockets—the wallet was gone.

"Fuck! Motherfucker!" Everyone in the gate area was staring at me.

A young girl in a tank top and short shorts touched me on the shoulder. "Sir, is everything okay?"

"I can't find my wallet!" I said, practically screaming.

"Sir," she said, "it's right here," and I felt her tugging on my pants. "What?"

I reached back, a little higher this time, and felt it. My back pocket had flipped over the top of my pants, and the wallet was flapping in the breeze.

"*Thank you,*" I told her. "You are a lifesaver." I figured I should probably flip her $10,000. I undid my pants, in public, shoved the pocket back in, and sat back down in my seat. That was close. *I need a drink.*

I boarded the plane without incident, sat down in my seat, waved over the flight attendant, and ordered a double vodka on the rocks.

"It's a bit early for that," she said, "but okay."

It was 9:30 a.m. Maybe a touch soon to start drinking in public, but this was a special day. *Check the wallet.* I slid my hand down my side and felt the corner of the wallet against my fingertips. This time it was there. Good. The attendant brought two airplane bottles of Smirnoff and a plastic cup full of ice to my seat. I chugged one of the airplane bottles, feeling the burning liquid in my throat, and poured the other over the ice, sipping it slowly. *Check the wallet.*

Once airborne, I ordered two more vodkas. The flight attendant eyed me skeptically. Better slow down. *Check the wallet.* I poured them both over the ice, and drank them leisurely, looking out the window. Nothing to see but clouds. My seat neighbor this time was a hipster in his early thirties with geometric tattoos on his arms. He had taken off his shoes and crossed his legs, displaying a foot proudly in my face. Any other time I would have been annoyed, but not today. *Check the wallet.* I took another drink.

I ordered two more vodkas. The flight attendant, a stout woman in her late fifties, looked at me with an expression that conveyed nothing but disapproval. "Is everything all right, sir?"

"Everything's fine." Except for the quarter of a billion dollars on my ass.

"I'll give you one more, and that's it."

My nerves had been calmed a bit. On any given day I needed about six drinks just to feel normal, so this about got me there. *Check the wallet.* Then the captain said we'd be landing in twenty minutes, and that flight attendants should prepare the cabin for arrival. I finished off the vodka and deposited the empty cup and bottle into a thick plastic bag carried by the flight attendant. *Check the wallet.*

The airplane landed with a thud, and taxied to the gate. While getting off the plane, I almost forgot my carry-on bag, and had to run back for it. I checked my wallet five more times on the way to the taxi stand.

Fifteen hours from now, I would be stupendously rich.

———————

The one added bonus of winning the Powerball is that I wouldn't have to share it with my ex-wife. Signed the divorce papers six months ago. Done and done.

We met in grad school at the University of Florida, both of us pursuing PhDs in finance. She wasn't my type—I'm not into blondes—but we were doing a group project as partners and she kept giving me shit about my haircut, calling me a dork and a stiff. Which was funny—*she* was the one who was a stiff, wearing suits to class all the time. I thought the whole act was cute, and we started dating shortly thereafter. It actually took a while to consummate the relationship, but when we did, she was an absolute freak, talking dirty and generally behaving like a porn star, constantly sticking out her tongue and squeaking like a mouse. We became more and more sexually adventurous, but she drew the line at threesomes—no third parties allowed. I didn't press the issue.

The problems began soon after we married at the county courthouse. She didn't have much of a sense of humor about my drinking, my gambling, or anything else. I always wanted to go out, she always wanted to stay home. I wanted to take vacations;

she said she had to catch up on her research. Not long after we were married, the sex kitten routine stopped as well. She started to hide my bottles of vodka, even when I tried to explain to her that my drinking was having no impact on my life or my career—I was next in line to be department chair, and had my eye on being dean of the business school someday. She was just a giant fucking buzzkill. And she was on my ass constantly.

She was also jealous. If my gaze fell on any woman, no matter how unattractive, she would scold me in public. The final straw was at the university Christmas party when I was having a private conversation with a female professor of anthropology with a black cocktail dress and septum ring—my wife came up, grabbed me by the jacket, and dragged me away, the anthropology professor covering her mouth with her hand and giggling. That resulted in a screaming match when we got home, and ended with throwing shit all over the house. It was at about this point that I was contacted by one of my exes over Facebook, looking for financial advice. It was totally innocent (though at one point in the conversation she had called me "sweetie"), but that effectively ended the marriage. We split everything down the middle, and since there were no kids and we didn't yet own a house, the divorce was relatively straightforward. I actually came out the better of it, because she had a small amount of inherited money from her parents.

I didn't have any lingering resentment at her; I just refused to be controlled. I'd get on the dating apps, but I was having fun doing my own thing, and I wasn't especially lonely. I was accountable to no one, I could drink as much as I want, I could leave pizza boxes on the floor, and I could abuse myself on the couch in the middle of the day if I felt like it. Up until that moment, I had never had a belief in karma. Think of what could have been possible, what we could have done together. It's actually pretty goddamn tragic when you think about it.

———

I am the kind of guy who knows how to have fun in a hotel room. One word: minibar. But not this time—gotta keep it together. Tomorrow morning, I would be headed to the New York state lottery office to claim the prize. It was right up the street from the hotel.

But there was so much *time.* It was 6 p.m., and I had a good five hours to kill before I went to sleep. There was an uninspiring hotel restaurant, where I got a cold club sandwich and fries in solitude, along with three IPAs, while looking up Miami Beach real estate on my phone. I had also noticed a bar across the street as I drove in—Finnegan's. It looked like a legitimate Irish pub, the kind of place where I could grab some Jack and Cokes and run my mouth for a little while, marked with a green sign and gold lettering. I finished up the beer and paid the bill, leaving a one hundred percent tip, which was arguably too small. Checked the wallet. Then I headed across the street to Finnegan's.

The pub looked like what Disney might have imagined as an Irish bar for Epcot Center. This might have been a mistake—I was expecting some business travelers or tourists, but instead it was a crowd of locals: mostly burly-looking men with checkered shirts and trucker hats. I sat down at the bar, checked my wallet, and ordered a Jack and Coke. The bartender looked like a true alcoholic. She was in her late twenties, but with stringy hair, and bloated, splotchy skin. Still, she looked promiscuous, and like she might be fun to roll around with for an hour. She didn't smile as she fetched my drink. I deleted it and promptly ordered another.

The bar was quiet. I decided to liven things up with a pick-up line.

"You must be a carpenter, because you make my banana stand," I said, grinning.

The guy nearest to me with a trucker hat turned and said, "What the fuck was that? You can't talk to her like that."

"Maybe I just don't like your fucking hat," I said.

"What's that accent?" he said. "You from the South? You some kind of hillbilly?"

"Leave him alone, he's just messing around," the bartender interjected. Then she said, "*Are* you from the South?"

"I'm from South Carolina. Did you know that the toothbrush was invented in South Carolina?"

"No," she said, doubtfully.

"Because if it was invented anywhere else, it would be called the teethbrush!"

Trucker Hat laughed. I drain the second Jack and Coke, and the alcoholic bartender got me another.

"What you are doing up here?" Trucker Hat asked.

"Well, I heard that Syracuse is the most depressing place in the world, so I figured I'd see for myself."

"It *is* pretty fucking depressing," said the bartender. "Did you know that Syracuse gets fewer days of sunlight than anywhere else in the country?"

"I did know that. I'm a professor, I know everything."

"You don't look like a professor," Trucker Hat said.

"What do I look like?" I asked.

Trucker Hat thought about it. "You look like someone out of that movie *Office Space*. Been working on your TPS reports?"

This was a surprisingly good characterization. I wore business casual clothes pretty much all the time. Checked my wallet. Ordered another drink. Bartender brought it to me. "Someone is pretty thirsty tonight."

"In more ways than one."

"You do realize that hitting on a bartender almost never works, right? We get hit on by assholes all the time."

"So you're saying there's a chance?" Checked my wallet.

"No, I'm saying you're an asshole. You're drunk," she said, and walked off.

"Why don't you come feel my shirt?" I asked. "It's made of boyfriend material."

"I don't know what your deal is, man," said Trucker Hat's friend.

"I'll tell you my deal," I said, pounding my fist on the bar. "I won the fucking Powerball."

"You're pulling my leg," said Trucker Hat, nursing his beer.

"I'm not shitting you," I said, and took out my hot wallet and set it on the bar. "In this wallet is the winning ticket for the Powerball for $586 million. I'm going to cash it in tomorrow. Right up the street, at the New York state lottery office. That's why I'm here."

The two truckers stared at me for a moment.

"So why don't we just beat your ass and take the ticket?"

"Because my whole body is a weapon. I'll flip you like a cheese omelet."

"You're so full of shit," Trucker Hat said.

I ordered another drink, the wallet sitting on the bar. "There it is, come and take it."

The two truckers stared at me.

"I don't feel like sitting in jail tonight," said Trucker Hat. "I just got out two weeks ago."

"What for?" I asked.

"Beating the shit out of a professor."

I stood up, and stumbled a bit. "Well, I've enjoyed y'all's company, but I have to get a good night's rest. Tomorrow's a big day. I bid you *adieu*."

The whole bar stared at me as I staggered out the door into the cool air.

———

I woke up face down on the floor of the hotel room, massively hung over, sun streaming through the window. The bed was still made, completely undisturbed.

I lifted my head, and spied a puddle in the closet. *Peed in the closet. Again.*

My first thought was the lottery ticket. I couldn't wait to cash in this—*my wallet*.

I was still wearing my pants from the night before. I checked my back pocket.

No wallet.

I had left it on the bar.

In a panic, I bolted out the door of my hotel room, down the stairs, through the lobby, and across the street—in my bare feet.

I ran up to the door and pounded on it. No answer. The sign read: HOURS: 4 P.M.–2 A.M.

I pounded on the door of the bar until my fists began to bleed. *This can't be happening.*

Why does this shit always happen to me? A word ricocheted around my mind: *failure*. Everything I touched was a failure. My marriage was a failure, my career was a failure, my life was a failure. Shit rained down on me all the time.

I stood on the sidewalk, utterly defeated.

I headed back to the hotel to get a drink.

GLOWING

———————————

LOGAN smiled awkwardly.

There were only so many economics books she could read during her summer break. She went to the library a few times, but it was mostly filled with children's books—the economics books were among the dusty tomes in reserves and were woefully out of date. She would have reached out to an ex-boyfriend, except she had never had a boyfriend. She had, in fact, never been kissed. A boy had once told her that she had a "rocking body" hidden underneath the giant, goofy T-shirts she always wore.

She thought about this as she leafed through the *Playboy* magazine she had purloined from her late father's collection. Her body was not too different from the women in the magazine, she thought, though she was not as tan. But as a result of her books and her T-shirts and awkward smile, she had remained entirely asexual. A fat boy had tried to hold her hand in sixth grade, unsuccessfully.

Logan switched from economics textbooks to romance novels she had borrowed from the library. They brought about a profound sadness in her for her celibacy, but she read them all the same. One night, after her mother retired to the bedroom subsequent to her nightly ritual of Jay Leno and wine from the gallon jug, she decided to go for a walk—at midnight, out in the dark. She was wearing her trademark extra-large T-shirt, and shorts, and wandered out into the crisp night air—typical for Provo in July. She looked at the houses, surprised at how many of them still had their lights on. They must have been watching Jay Leno too.

A house just up the street was set back from the road, light on in the living room. With trepidation, Logan traversed the front yard, stood on her tiptoes among the hedges, and looked in the window, peering between half-open vertical blinds. A middle-aged man with dark, curly hair, was reclining on a sofa, his feet on a hassock. He was holding his penis. Madonna's "Vogue" video was playing. In the background was a small dining-room table and a grandfather clock.

Logan's heart raced. She recognized the man as the friendly character who offered to shovel their driveway in the winter. She stepped back from the window and paused, before jogging home, six houses to the south, where she gently opened the door to the porch and crept inside, tiptoeing across the carpet and into her bedroom, where she sat on the edge of the bed, not seeing the floor under her feet. Thoughts swirled inside her head. Did anyone see her cross the yard? Probably not—it was well past midnight. She listened outside the house for sirens. There were none.

She found the experience *thrilling*. Doing something that was forbidden, the fear of getting caught, the surprise at what she had found. She knew instantly she would do it again at the first opportunity.

———————

Throughout most of her life, Logan had been told that her smile was lopsided and strange. What she knew, and others didn't, was that when she smiled, she wasn't smiling.

Logan entered the kitchen, grabbed the remote, and turned the TV down a couple of notches, and sat at the table with her mother. Her mother took a long draw from a brown cigarette, and tapped the ashes into an already-full ashtray.

Logan smiled awkwardly at the worn kitchen table. She wanted to ask her mother to come to her graduation, but she already knew what the answer would be. She also knew that it would be better not to ask that question until the date drew near—still, she had to have the answer. And even though she knew the answer, she also knew that hearing it would be devastating.

"No," her mother said.

"I didn't even ask you yet."

"I knew what you were going to ask me. No."

"Why?"

"I'm busy," her mother said, letting out a puff of smoke.

Logan was incredulous. "You spend ten hours a day smoking at this table. You're not busy."

"You have no idea what I do for you. What I did for you kids, after your father passed."

"I think I get to ask for one thing," Logan said. "I have never asked for anything else, and I will never ask for anything again. Please come to my graduation."

"No."

"I don't understand," Logan said, on the verge of tears.

"I don't need to give you an explanation. I don't want to do it, and I'm not going to do something I don't want to do."

"I'm sorry I asked," Logan said, crying now.

"You should be. And you'll get over it."

No explanation was offered. Her mother said "no" to anything and everything as a matter of reflex. Sometimes she would say "yes" later, but not often. If you asked her to do something, to go one inch out of her way, to deviate from her daily routine for even a second, the answer was always "no." It wasn't as if she had anything else planned, aside from sitting at the table and smoking her brown cigarettes, watching *Night Court* reruns on TV, and chatting on the white rotary-dial phone with her sisters, which was where she would be when Logan crossed the stage to receive her diploma.

Logan was studying for a PhD in economics at the University of Utah, concentrating in econometrics. Numbers had always fascinated her—she took calculus her sophomore year in high school and did independent studies in discrete math and linear algebra. She earned a perfect score on the math SATs. She was the school's valedictorian, effortlessly, the progeny of smart parents, who, along with her siblings, never amounted to much. Her older sister Hannah attended gifted-and-talented programs as a teenager and now made quilts. She was perhaps the best quilt-maker in the country; she'd won a passel of awards. Logan was surprised to learn there were awards for making quilts. Her father, who passed away in 1988, was the king of living room *Jeopardy*, knowing all about Italian operas and French royalty and such, and drove a forklift for work. She came from a family of virtually limitless potential who consistently underperformed in all facets of life. Logan would change that, she thought—one day she would be an economist at the Federal Reserve, maybe even becoming a Fed Governor, one of seven powerful people conducting monetary policy.

But there was an inertia associated with being a member of the lower classes. There were no concrete examples of success, the path not taken—nobody had gone before you, so it was impossible to know what it was like. Logan had carefully chosen her classes and activities without the help of her parents or sister. She was an enigma to her high school guidance counselor. It was not easy, coming from Provo. She was in the tiny Gentile minority in a predominantly Mormon city, which meant less than it did in the 1890s, but prejudices persisted. Her family, atheists, had an every-man-for-himself worldview. While Mormons were busy tithing and going on missions and manicuring their lawns, her family hoarded whatever money they could gather, in a bank account that was yielding six percent interest. Everything in the house was old and brown. Only recently they disposed of the old wooden cabinet television, replacing it with a slightly less ancient tube TV. They moved to Provo nine years ago from Los Angeles, after the real estate boom in the 1980s. A middle-class existence was what they yearned for, but found difficult to attain.

Logan knew full well a private sector economist could make well into high six figures, or even more. She wanted prestige, to be universally recognized as *smart*, since her family was so indifferent to that reality. She won so many awards and scholarships that college was practically free. To pay her way through graduate school, she worked as a TA. She had very little in common with the hundreds of students in the Economics 101 class that she taught, most of them massively hung over from partying, with little interest in the Solow growth model. She marked down their grades remorselessly. Her graduate advisor had led a small economic consulting firm, then retired to teach. She admired him, though his forecasting ability was unimpressive. She learned that was true of most economists— most of them were terrible forecasters, so focused instead on econometrics, which measured the *here* and *now* of the data.

Summers were the toughest, when she returned to her 1,600-square-foot family home back in Provo, with the awful TV and the shag carpets, the cigarette smoke and the loud talking. The house, built in the early 1960s, was small and simple—her bedroom had just enough room for a double bed and a small pathway around it, any leftover space taken up by a large collection of books. She had saved most of her textbooks from college, especially the math ones, which she consulted frequently. Most of her childhood books were gone. She thought of her mother as an *anti-hoarder*—she threw everything in the trash once it had outlived its usefulness, which included most of Logan's books once she started grad school. Logan was crestfallen that her entire childhood collection of *Choose Your Own Adventure* books had been discarded, along with many other belongings. The stuffed animals were spared, thankfully—even her mother must have known they held sentimental value. Logan had no intention of ever reading the books again, but they were a part of her vanished childhood— and, who knows, they might have been worth something someday. Without a trace of nostalgia, her mother threw out any items left unattended. Logan's mother owned nothing but her smoking table, a few garments, and two pair of shoes. When she learned that her books were gone, Logan smiled awkwardly.

Her summer consisted of reading books in her tiny room, surrounded by wood-grain-paneled walls. There were friends from high school who had stayed in Provo—many, in fact, but by this point Logan had little in common with them. There was the intelligence differential, but that had always been there. They were working low-end jobs, drinking and fucking. There was also a social stigma attached to never leaving your hometown, especially when your hometown was underperforming. Utah had a gravitational pull. Part of it was because of the Mormons— they stuck with their own—and part of it was the geography— you are surrounded in all directions by mountains, a provisional barrier against the rest of the world. It occurred to Logan that she had only been outside the state of Utah three times in her life. The last time was a conference she went to six months ago in the Cayman Islands, attended by some of the top economists in the world. Her graduate advisor went, and she tagged along, experiencing luxury beyond her wildest imagination. The shower in her hotel room was made of glass, and she spent forty-five minutes in it at a time, sitting on the floor until her fingers wrinkled. She wanted a glass shower when she grew up, which would be vastly better than the tub in her house, with the flower-shaped non-skid peeling off the fiberglass.

When Logan was in her teens, she took trips to the grocery store and loaded up with Kraft macaroni and cheese, which is what she ate for lunch and dinner. If she had a few extra dollars, she would buy a package of hot dogs to mix in with it. There was no dinner time in her house—everyone ate when they wanted. Her sister subsisted entirely on potato chips and rice. Logan was more or less emancipated as a teenager: She bought a car for $500 with the money that she made waiting tables, and drove herself to club meetings and soccer practices. Her parents did not attend her high school graduation, her middle school graduation, or any other graduation; they did not attend sporting events or any other activity. In the brief time that her sister, the quilt-maker, went to UNLV, her parents put a UNLV sticker on their car. Oddly, her parents bragged to everyone they knew about her sister's award-winning quilts, yet completely ignored Logan's academic accomplishments.

———————

The next few days, Logan obsessed about her crime. She would get in her car and drive slowly past the house with the window she had looked in, thinking maybe its resident would be outside, working in the yard for some reason. He never was. Some days, his car was parked in the driveway; other days, it wasn't. She thought about it some more—what made it so dangerous was what she had seen. If she had looked in the front window and seen nothing, and got caught, nothing would have come of it.

She wondered if someone had placed a call to the police, and they had ignored it, or they drove by, looking for her, after she had returned to her home. She was easy to spot—blonde hair not quite long enough to pull back in a ponytail, oversized T-shirt, basketball shorts, Asics running shoes. She wondered if she would be placed in a police lineup with other five-foot-three blonde girls, and the man with the penis would have to pick her out of the lineup. It was dark, after all, and there was the glare on the window from the television—there was no way he'd be able to make a positive identification. Or maybe one of the other neighbors saw her walking by, thought it was unusual, and made a call. It was voyeurism, though she didn't derive any sexual pleasure from it—it was perhaps the first foolish risk she had taken in her entire life. She wore her seat belt, paid her taxes, and kept her hands and arms inside the car. She did what she was told, until now.

A few nights later, Logan got the courage to do it again—tiptoeing across the carpet, out the porch door, taking care to close it quietly. This time she wore a black T-shirt and black shorts, hoping to blend in with the darkness. She went through backyards, to avoid the main road, where the odd car would still rumble through in the middle of the night. Some of the backyards had fences, but not all, so it was still relatively easy to navigate. She came across an above-ground pool, and thought it might be fun to take off her clothes and skinny-dip in the pool in the dark. But she kept moving, looking for a house with lights on, bypassing the penis house—she already knew what went on there. She wanted to know what people did in the middle of the night, besides masturbating to Madonna videos.

She came across a small gray ranch house with all the lights on. This time, she was more careful—she approached the home on her hands and knees, crawling through the grass, feeling the moisture in her fingers. As she reached the exterior, she could hear voices—loud voices. She slowly stood up and peeked through the window.

She saw a married couple, arguing. It was serious. The man yelled, "You fucking bitch," and the woman threw a picture frame at him. In the background, she could see a small boy, around three, in tears, who had wandered out of his bedroom, awakened by the noise. At that point the man reached back to strike the woman, but stopped short—the woman covered her face in fear, then glared at him. The man disappeared, and a series of loud crashes ensued, as he took all the dishes out of the cabinets and smashed them against the floor. The woman cried hysterically. It was 1:30 in the morning.

Logan momentarily forgot herself, thinking that she was inside the house, a participant in this argument. She was three feet away from the woman, at most, but the woman was too distraught to pay any attention to her. Logan crouched down and slowly backed away from the window. She could still hear the husband breaking things, the woman screaming, and the little boy crying. She didn't know this couple—they were about thirty houses up the street—but she thought they were probably Mormon, and they would probably be back in temple on Sunday, happily united, if only for a few hours. She thought of the secrets we all have; the things we do in the privacy of our homes, when we think no one is watching.

Logan returned home somewhat carelessly, prancing through backyards, not being too careful to not be seen. She was getting bolder—she was learning that people were mostly preoccupied with their own problems, not looking out the window. Besides, she was wearing black. It occurred to her that if she was caught, she might be mistaken for a burglar, and wondered what her alibi should be if she was nabbed in someone's backyard in the middle of the night. Just going for a walk—wearing all black and going through people's backyards. An absurd excuse, but she had no plans on getting caught. She got back to her house, without taking too much care with the door, letting it thump a little, and went to her room.

Her mother opened the door.

"Were you outside?"

Logan had rehearsed the answer. "Yes, I went for a walk."

"At two in the morning?"

"Couldn't sleep."

Her mother frowned. "There's a bunch of weirdos out at this time of night. You had better be careful. I don't think you should be going for walks at two in the morning."

"Mom, I'm twenty-three years old."

"Living in my house."

"Fine." Logan sighed.

"Why are you wearing all black?" Her mother asked. "I've never seen you wear all black."

"It's what I sleep in nowadays."

Logan's mother looked at her, utterly frustrated. "Good night. Don't wake me up." She closed the door.

Logan wasn't thinking about her mother. She was wondering if she should call in a domestic violence report to the police about the arguing couple. Bad idea—the only way she could have had known was by peeping in their window. Maybe she could do it anonymously. Maybe she could write a letter to the police station. Of course, her fingerprints would be on it. She decided it was foolish. She wasn't a caped crusader. She was a criminal herself now, after all, looking for cheap thrills.

———————————

As the summer drew to a close, Logan began taking more and more voyeuristic risks. She didn't bother to slink through the grass, and she didn't even go through backyards. She walked along the street, and if a car came, she acted casually, as if it were completely normal for a twenty-three-year-old blonde girl to be walking around at two in the morning. Over the preceding weeks, she had watched an obese woman trying on bras in her bedroom, two elderly couples playing bridge, a housewife working on a giant jigsaw puzzle, and dozens of people watching late-night TV. She had a hobby. Different from making model airplanes, but a hobby nonetheless. She was interested in the lives of others. Her own life consisted of reading books and breathing secondhand smoke. The lives of others were uniquely uninteresting as well, but they were *different*. Nobody in her house stayed up after midnight.

On the final night before she was scheduled to move back to campus, she thought about the above-ground pool she had passed weeks ago, thinking she might go for a swim. This time, she did—she took off her T-shirt, shorts, and underwear at the edge of the pool, put her hands on the edge, and lowered herself carefully into the water so as not to make a splash. By this point in the summer, the weather had cooled off a bit, and the water was exceedingly cold, but invigorating. It occurred to her that she had never swam naked. She thought she would like to make a lot of money someday and have her own pool, surrounded by landscaping, so she could swim naked all the time in privacy. She stayed in the pool a good thirty minutes, sinking down so that the water was at her lips, making motorboat sounds. After a time, she climbed out, and suddenly remembered she should have brought a towel. She dried herself off with her clothes, and then decided not to put them back on—she carried them with her for a spell and stashed them beside a tree.

There was a house that she had always skipped on her nightly runs because the lights were always off. Tonight, they were on. Fully nude, Logan slid up to the side of the house and peeked in the living room window. There was a thick woman in her fifties, doing a crossword puzzle with a pencil. Likely she was suffering from a bout of insomnia, and was trying to relax so she could return to sleep. Logan focused on her for a moment, thinking she had seen her before. She recognized her as one of the fourth-grade teachers from her old school—not her teacher, but the one for the other section. Logan thought it best not to get spotted by someone she knew, and quickly stepped away from the window and back towards the street.

At that moment, the headlights of a car came around the bend. She stepped behind a tree, half-expecting the car to stop and for someone to get out and accost her. This was the most thrilled she had been in the last two months, the idea that someone might see her, catch a glimpse of her in the nude. But the car kept going.

She felt herself drawn to the house of the masturbator for a second time—she jogged through the darkness, feeling the cool air surround her naked body. When she got to the house, she stood on her tiptoes as before, expecting to see the man masturbating again. The light was on, but the TV was off, and nobody was there. She waited a while, to see if he would come out. The bushes scratched the tops of her bare legs.

She headed up the road a bit, trying to find a more suitable target. There was a house she had bypassed several times before, as the windows were too high and the lights were always off. This time they were on, and so were the outside lights, illuminating the entire front yard. Logan dismissed her concerns and strode up to the house, grasped the windowsill, and heaved herself up, her breasts resting on the window.

Inside was a young girl of three with an enormous collection of Barbie dolls arranged in front of her. Some of them were sitting at a table, drinking tea, some of them were in a Barbie house, and others littered the floor in a variety of contortions. There were no adults present, and the TV was off. Abruptly, the girl looked out the window and made eye contact with Logan.

Their gazes locked for what seemed an eternity—but could not have been longer than a few seconds. Logan fully expected the child to cry out for her parents, but instead she took one of the Barbie dolls and held it up for Logan to see. The doll was wearing a business suit—much like an economist, Logan thought. Logan smiled awkwardly.

Suddenly, she heard a car screech to a halt behind her. On the side of the car was emblazoned PROVO POLICE. She turned to face the car. The driver flashed a spotlight on her—her body glowing in the light, hair and nipples for all to see, blue eyes flashing wildly. A policeman sprang from the car and yelled, "Stop!"

She froze. And then she ran.

Logan ran as fast as she could, sprinting so hard she couldn't feel her legs, leading the cops on a chase through two dozen front yards. Logan had the advantage, completely unencumbered, while the cops were weighed down by guns, and handcuffs, and batons. She leaped over bushes and fences, the cops falling behind. She knew she would be caught—she was headed straight for home, and they would find her there. She ran there anyway.

She ran to escape, she ran to freedom, to a world that made sense. She knew that when she was caught, she would be sentenced to a lifetime of mediocrity.

Things would be different, and the same.

IN SEARCH OF TRUTH

T HE third time I ran away was in November 1996, when my boyfriend took me on a midnight drive to Las Vegas on I-15. I dangled my feet out the passenger window of his decrepit Ford Taurus, feeling the night breeze between my toes. We ate hamburgers and drank Cokes from roadside stands, letting the wrappers flutter around the passenger seat of the car. We had very little money, so we stayed in a motel far off the strip, alternating between swimming in the chronically underfilled pool and making love, which we did at least three times a day for five days, until the police found us. Someone had called in a missing persons' report, and we had been spotted eating in a local diner. *Boy, nineteen, six feet one inch tall, brown curly hair. Girl, fifteen, five feet four inches tall, long, straight blonde hair, wearing a tank top.* I saw the photographs of us in the police station; we looked like felons. They held me at the station until my mom made the drive from Los Angeles, which was most of the day on Sunday. Once in the car, she punched me in the mouth. My lip bled all over my shirt.

Sex at fifteen was not the issue. The issue was truancy, bailing out of school, leaving her in the lurch. She did not want me to become *uneducated*, like the rest of her family, like her brother delivering pizzas, with an eighth-grade education. I didn't think delivering pizzas was a terrible outcome; there's honor in that—people are hungry, you bring them food. And even though sex at fifteen was not the issue, at least ethically speaking, she did not like it that I was an immoral, pleasure-seeking person. She was the ascetic offspring of flinty New Englanders. My father's side was a bunch of dissolute bastards, gambling, drinking, and hosing prostitutes. The two sides could not be reconciled. Whether she was capable of admitting it or not, my mother married my father precisely because he was who he was—she needed excitement in her life. And my father needed stability. This persisted until the day that a male/female pair of cocaine dealers showed up at the house while my father was at work, threatening to blackmail him at his office for his extracurricular activities. What my mom didn't know at the time was that my dad had already paid them off twice. That was the end, and that was how we ended up in Los Angeles, in the sprawl of El Segundo, not far away from the power plant. A different school district from Manhattan Beach, to say the least.

I have had sex with eight boys, which I suppose makes me promiscuous. In the library, I once read that girls whose fathers abandon them turn out to be oversexed, and girls whose fathers committed suicide were frigid. I don't know who comes up with this stuff, but it was true in my case. I hadn't heard from my father since 1990, when I was nine years old, and he unexpectedly showed up in El Segundo with a giant, stuffed teddy bear. My mother chased him off the front porch and into his BMW, and that was the end of that. He sent money—he was always good at making it—but I imagined him being pursued on a merry chase by avaricious cocaine dealers. My mother never made an attempt to conceal his drug use. She used it as a weapon. *Your father, the drug addict.* That lesson I took to heart. I have never tried drugs, even though there was ample opportunity. I mean, it was El Segundo.

I was reinstalled in school after my escape to Vegas. Things were different. The students treated me with deference—and so did the teachers. It was a very *adult* thing to do, for a fifteen-year-old. It was not the sort of thing that good girls do, run away to Vegas and get fucked for five days. I sat in class with the knowledge that I had experienced things that nobody else had. I did feel like an adult, and I didn't feel much like sitting in class, learning about the Treaty of Westphalia. I had escaped this prison once; I could do it again. Nothing could contain me. My boyfriend went back to working in a convenience store—there were no consequences for him. My mother agreed to not press charges on the condition that he left me alone going forward. I was forbidden from calling him, or even leaving messages on his answering machine. I had no problems defying my mother when I would be the one to bear the consequences; the last thing I wanted was to be responsible for sending him to jail. Besides, he was not the answer, though I didn't know what the answer was. I just knew it wasn't *here*.

Unbeknown to me, my mother was looking for solutions. She was watching me carefully, and she knew what I knew—that I would escape again. There were no practical repercussions for my journey, no juvenile detention or anything like that—we hadn't stolen anything—but she was looking for ways that I could be reformed that didn't involve the criminal justice system. She happened across an advertisement in the free weekly paper for something called ISOT. It read: REFORM SCHOOL FOR GIRLS, and then in smaller letters: *Located in the scenic high desert of Northern California.* The fine print said that girls aged thirteen to seventeen would be admitted, applications were reviewed semiannually, in January and July, and that girls would be cared for and educated until they graduated at eighteen. The tuition was very affordable, at $3,000 per year. In the high desert of Modoc County, the girls would be free from outside influences. The closest city was Klamath Falls, Oregon—hours away. There was no trouble to get into.

One morning, I found myself at the Greyhound station carrying a hard-sided suitcase with about two weeks of clothes, an alarm clock, some snacks, and a handful of comic books inside—stuff to read on the ten-hour drive north. My mother stood with me until the bus came, figuring there was a nonzero probability I'd run away again. The contraceptives had been left behind. I boarded the bus in the darkness and took a seat in the back, next to the bathroom. There were four people on the entire bus, exclusive of the driver. I had brought the comic books, but the sheer inertia of everything kept me from fishing them out of my belongings to read.

Modoc County, California, is in the upper-right-hand corner of the state of California. There is not much there but ranchers and the forest service. The biggest town, Alturas, has a population of a few thousand, at most. I was headed to Canby, about eighteen miles up the road from Alturas, which had a population of about fifty, not counting the reform school. I looked it up. The weather would be hot and dry in the summer and cold and dry in the winter. There would be snow. Mountain passes would be closed. I would be completely isolated from the outside world—the marketing materials from the school said that there were no televisions or even radios on the property. I didn't know who these people were, and I found it unusual that my mom would send her daughter away to a bunch of weirdos on the basis of a classified ad in the paper. I thought that she must really be sick of my shit, and truly desperate for help, and that particular thought weighed on me with the mass of a thousand sad days. It really had come to this. I didn't hate my mother, and I wasn't abused. I simply could not remain within the walls of our tiny apartment, with the water damage on the ceiling and the soiled kitchen tiles. There was so much to do, so many things to experience.

Ten hours later, I was deposited at the bus stop in Alturas, in the dust and the wind. I half-expected to be stranded there, learning that this whole thing was an elaborate ruse to abandon teenage daughters at bus stops in the desert. Instead, I was met by two young men wearing checkered shirts who took my bags and loaded me and my belongings into the back of a rusted white passenger van. They were nice enough, *How was your trip?* and such, and their affability immediately put me at ease. The drive was not long. I looked out the window and saw actual tumbleweeds, blowing parallel to the road, keeping up with the van. When we arrived at the compound in Canby, they heaved my bag out of the back of the van, took it to some unknown location, and handed me three long black skirts and told me to wash up before dinner. The compound was comprised of one large structure and several smaller outbuildings, with an extensive garden in the middle. Apart from the garden, there was dust. I would learn later that they searched my possessions for drugs or other contraband. There were none.

Almost immediately, the indoctrination started. ISOT was supposedly a charitable organization designed to educate and rehabilitate troubled girls. Parents, after exhausting all other possibilities, would send them to the high desert and the sagebrush to be reformed. The pamphlets sent in advance of my journey indicated that I would continue my studies and finish with a G.E.D., but in the first few hours after my arrival I saw nothing resembling educational material. No textbooks, no classrooms, no nothing. There was no education other than an indoctrination manual; how to speak to elders, how to bow, how to curtsy, how to grow cucumbers, how to clean a kitchen, and how to perform first aid, since a doctor only came to the compound once a month.

Magazines, television, and computers were forbidden. Almost immediately, I lost track of the days and the date. I had traveled to the ISOTs on a Tuesday—this must be Thursday, right? *It's been two days, or has it been three?* In the morning, I cleaned the bathrooms, in the afternoons, I worked in the kitchen. It was all new to me, and I enjoyed it. I liked the sensation of feeling the vegetables in my hands, slicing them perfectly, placing them into pots with care. My mother never taught me how to cook, or clean, or do anything—she made my bed in the morning and vacuumed the apartment on the weekend. A spoiled only child is a bit of a cliché, but all my friends in school who had siblings had to help out around the house. *Maybe there was a relationship between my upbringing and my rebelliousness.* The things I thought about as I swept the floor of the girls' barracks.

The adults were called elders. Elder this, Elder that, Elder so-and-so. I lost track after a while. Elder Joseph took an interest in me, teaching me how to wash and cut vegetables, holding my hands in his. He had a beard, and a kindly expression. I thought that he had a good voice for radio, and that in some alternate universe he would be a big-name radio show host, during the Morning Zoo on Q105 or something like that. But he didn't have the disposition for it. He seemed to be more like a priest in seminary. And he didn't talk enough to be a radio host. His favorite phrase was "Very good," referring to my cooking or cleaning abilities. He seemed to stare at my hair. He sometimes followed me around the compound, not speaking, and then abruptly turning around and going the other direction.

It wasn't until the fourth day that I learned that ISOT stood for *In Search Of Truth.* The leader, who we all called "Father," was a trim man in his forties who wore priest's clothes save for the clerical collar. We never heard him speak. He would approach us silently, observe what we were doing, nod his head, and walk away. The elders deferred to him. He had the largest room on the compound, at least twice the size of our apartment in Los Angeles, with its own private office space. I never saw the inside of it. I gathered that one didn't want to be transported to Father's office for some transgression, however minor. As an authority figure, he was menacing—and this in a community where no one ever raised their voice. It was almost as if there was an inverse correlation between the volume of their speech and the authority they wielded. I watched the other girls when softly reprimanded by the elders—they quickly bowed their heads and averted their gaze.

There were about fifteen girls on the property, ranging in age from thirteen to seventeen. The girls didn't talk to each other, not even in the bathroom, if you can believe that. They were not friends, not even allies. They each had a haunted look to them that I knew I didn't have, and I wondered if I would get it. *Something* had happened that was responsible for their submissiveness. When the elders would approach a group of girls, the tension rose—when they left, it would fall. You could tell from their body language, bowing, shifting their weight, letting their hair fall in their eyes. If the object of this place was to teach obedience, that was certainly happening. For my part, I was unnaturally happy cooking and cleaning. My father once said that I needed structure in my life, and I had to admit that he was right. For the first time in my life, I got up at the same time every day, and went to bed at the same time every night. My entire day was planned out, which I found to be an existentially freeing experience. I rather liked the ISOTs. I liked this place. The other commercial enterprise in town was a small hotel, which they affectionately referred to as the Canby Hilton. They served cheeseburgers there, and the cheeseburgers were allegedly amazing. The best-behaved girl for any given month would be taken to the Canby Hilton for a cheeseburger. I hoped that one day it would be me.

Skylar slept in the bunk beneath me, a girl of fourteen who only whispered on the rare occasions she ever communicated at all. She had wild black hair which seemed to grow even more wild when she was frightened. Of all the girls at the ISOT compound, she seemed to be the saddest. She never spoke to me. Another girl told me that Skylar's parents had been killed in a car crash, and the executors of the estate, not in possession of the will or the resources to care for her, left her to the ISOTs. She had been here a year. I gathered she was not too smart— even after being here a full year, she was struggling with some of the basic tasks. If her fate was to live in the compound until she was eighteen, she was not resigned to it. She was the only girl who did anything approaching insubordination to the elders; occasionally, she would stand legs apart, arms akimbo, eyes full of fury, hair flying everywhere—and one of the elders would grasp her arm and lead her into Father's office. She'd be gone for a few hours, and then would mysteriously rejoin us preparing for dinner, her face stained with tears. I was a model citizen compared to some of these girls, and whatever went on in the inner reaches of the elders' quarters, I wanted no part of. Skylar wasn't the only one; this was a semi-routine occurrence.

The elders all ate together in a separate dining room. The girls ate together at two folding tables pushed together in the meeting room, chaperoned by one elder. Nothing was said at these meals, except for some light reprimands: *Don't chew with your mouth open—Pick up your napkin—Wipe your face.* The mood was lighter when Elder Joseph was the chaperone. He'd playfully quiz us on current events: "You see that ballgame last night?" When of course we hadn't, because there were no TVs. One time he asked Skylar: "What's with the sourpuss?" which got her to smile a little bit. He laughed and told us that we were good girls. If I ever were to confide in any of the elders, I would do it with Elder Joseph. He wasn't a religious zealot—you could see him pledging a fraternity in a former life, shotgunning beers. In a community where everyone took themselves *very* seriously, Elder Joseph was refreshingly self-deprecating. There were seven elders, one for each day of the week. We had Elder Joseph on Saturday, naturally. Tuesdays, with the entirely humorless Elder Martin, were the worst, eating in abject silence.

I was transported to the ISOTs in August. It was now

October, and the weather was cooling significantly. In my suitcase, I had brought a variety of clothes for all climates. After I arrived and the elders took my bag, I never saw my clothes again. I alternated between the three black skirts that I was given on my first day. For the first few weeks, I wore T-shirts with the skirts, but then switched to blouses after a shipment of women's clothes came in, mostly blouses. I didn't have to worry about what to wear, and I occupied the same five acres of earth day after day, never leaving the compound. But I was a little put out that I still hadn't yet gone to the Canby Hilton to get a cheeseburger; June had won two months in a row. I had a difficult time figuring out what June was doing to merit a trip to the Canby Hilton. She was constantly shirking her duties, but the elders seemed to favor her.

By this point, I had received a handful of letters from my mother, easily recognizable by the large, loopy handwriting. She wrote that she had been taking yoga classes, and she had a new boyfriend, named Thor of all things. The letters were unwelcome. It was clear that my mother was happier without me. She asked how my classes were going; evidently, she had no knowledge of what went on at the compound. She did not ask when I was coming home. After the fifth letter, I resolved not to read any more. Truthfully, I had no idea when I would be leaving the compound. Measured strictly by obedience, I was the best of all the girls, and by this point ready to return to polite society. Skylar was probably worse off than when she came in. She had several run-ins with the elders, even Elder Joseph, who would never reprimand her, instead wagging his finger at her and smiling. Shortly afterwards, one of the other elders would take her by the arm and haul her off to Father's office.

The night that I got the fifth letter from my mom, which included a photograph of her and Thor in a casino on the Nevada side of Lake Tahoe, smiling and holding martini glasses, I woke up in the middle of the night, and looked over the side of the bed.

Skylar was missing. I began to panic. My first assumption was that she ran away, or that she was hiding somewhere, and then I began to worry about whatever consequences might come her way. I laid awake, counting the holes in the panels of the drop ceiling above me, when the door opened. Two elders—one of them Elder Joseph—returned her to her bunk and left the room. I could hear her sobbing. Skylar and I weren't friends—none of the girls made friends—and I had detected some resentment from her that I was so well-treated. The sobbing stopped and I looked down again and saw her lying face down, her wild black hair spread all over the pillow.

From that point forward, I worked twice as hard as my chores. The elders told me *good girl* on multiple occasions, but after the Skylar incident I was not as receptive to their praise, not looking up and smiling as I had in the past. I wondered about that haunted look that all the girls had, their indifference to me, their complete disengagement with the world around them. I looked at Skylar—not a mark on her. June, the happy warrior, spent little time washing vegetables, instead sitting at a wooden desk penciling detailed drawings of beaches. The elders left her alone. Skylar, by this point, had nearly stopped eating; June had second helpings of everything. I began to think of returning home, but by this point my mother had probably eloped with Thor and had a Viking wedding. My father's whereabouts were unknown. I wasn't entirely confident that the ISOTs would even let me go when I turned eighteen. I thought about plotting my escape, but even if I could get out of the compound, there was nothing but desert for miles. I didn't sleep as soundly as before; I laid awake, listening for the door opening, to hear if any other girls were hauled off in the middle of the night. It happened several times more with Skylar, twice in succession. Every night it was the same, lying face down under a pile of black curly hair. I heard the elders come in the bunkroom and take her away, returning her after an hour. They took June a few times as well, but June, when returned to her bunk, would lay on her back, smiling.

It was a few weeks more before I started getting unwanted attention from the elders. Elder Martin, who I disliked personally, came up behind me while I was sweeping the barracks, grabbing the broom from behind. He held me to his chest. I felt what seemed to be a roll of quarters on my backside. I immediately knew what that was—and froze. "There's no hurry," he said, "you can take as long as you want." He was smelling my hair. I was in the middle of resisting and cooperating, playing dead, hoping that he would detumesce and go away. Eventually, he did. It was at that point that I began to think about the height of the fence. It was about ten feet, but did not have barbed wire. The gate was locked with a large bicycle chain.

I had not yet written a letter to my mother. In any event, the letters had stopped coming about a month ago, concurrent with a change in the weather. I regretted that I hadn't saved the envelope with the return address. It occurred to me that there was little chance that the ISOTs would allow a letter from a girl to leave the compound without being inspected. I didn't have to get home; I just had to get to a mailbox. I didn't remember seeing one in Canby, but there certainly was one eighteen miles away in Alturas. Of course, in Alturas, I could knock on someone's door and ask for help, and the letter would be superfluous. Running away came naturally to me, after all.

One night, when the elders returned Skylar to her bed, I got up the courage to ask where she had been.

"Shut up," she said.

"Where do they take you at night?"

"It's called 'reconciliation,'" she said. "You have to leave."

"Leave?"

"Before they do it to you."

"Do what?"

"They're *rapists*," she said. "They'll do it to you next. I heard them talking about it."

But the reason I'm here is because I ran away.

"This place is a fucking *cult*," she said, letting the word hang in the air.

I thought about Skylar and the men, their pubic hair, their groans of pleasure, the smell of their semen, them taking turns, and I immediately began getting ready to escape. A skirt was impractical for running away, but all my other clothes had long since been confiscated. I crept out of bed, put on my black shoes, opened the door, and looked across the compound. I would be illuminated by floodlights, but the compound seemed to be deserted. I ran to the edge and scaled the fence, landing on the other side with a thud in the dirt.

I started jogging up the road, on the way to Alturas. I jogged for a few miles, until I remembered that mountain lions attack joggers. It was so cold, and within minutes of leaving the compound it began to snow. I walked, hoping to see a car drive by so I could wave it down, but the chances of that were negligible, especially at this time of year, in the middle of the night. In my haste, I had forgotten to bring water. Home was very far away, and for all I knew, it no longer existed.

I walked in complete darkness, crunching the dirt with my feet, knowing that either the ISOTs would find me or I would freeze to death in the desert. The sun began to rise and I was utterly alone.

NIGHT MOVES

———————

O H good, the UPS guy came.
  I heaved the box onto my chest, balancing it there
while opening the front door with my left hand, squeezing
in through the opening so as not to let the cats out, closing
the door behind me with my backside. I called out to the
cats—"Zeus! Rosebud!"—and the two fuzzballs appeared,
momentarily satisfying my cat-escape neurosis. I lugged the
box into my studio, gently setting it down on the carpet. I
fished my house keys out of my pocket and cut straight down
the middle of the masking tape. I opened the box, finding
a Styrofoam top, which I removed, revealing a set of new
twelve-inch studio monitors.

I had been wanting these for a while. My last monitors,
smaller and older, began to develop a farting noise in the woofer.
I wasn't nostalgic about them; they were fully depreciated. I
unceremoniously removed them from the stands, carried them
outside (watching for the cats again), and brought them out to
the oversized green plastic bin, unsuitable for recycling as they
were made of wood. They would decompose in some landfill
somewhere. I went back inside, pushing Rosebud and Zeus

away from the front door with my foot, and set about putting together my new sound system.

The new monitors had cost $1,600. They weren't cheap, but money wasn't a concern, and I couldn't have farting speakers for music production. I had it good, I thought—somewhere out there was a fourteen-year-old producing trance music in his tiny bedroom on a ten-year-old laptop on a cracked version of Ableton. I had invested, probably, about $100,000 in my studio, mostly on modular synths that I rarely used. Most of my production was done with software synths and plug-ins that I downloaded from the web. But the racks of modular synths surrounded my desk, with an array of flashing lights that I found pleasing, like sitting in the cockpit of a fighter jet. In the center of the studio was an 88-key keyboard, exorbitant because I only needed a keyboard one-third the size.

I'm rich. My father was the CEO of a publicly traded plastics and chemical manufacturer in Chicago. He retired five years ago, and was promptly diagnosed with stage four pancreatic cancer. He died within three weeks. I loved my father. I knew what people whispered about me, that I would one day be a trust-fund baby, but that was not to be. I inherited $30 million, no strings attached, and no trust fund. My mother got the rest, well into nine figures. Chicago had a good music scene, but Miami was better, and I made the move five years ago without much deliberation. I took $4 million and paid cash for a 3,500-square-foot house in the Morningside neighborhood of the city, a place full of bankers and bourgeoisie, with a few celebrities thrown in. I didn't invest the money. I made a little over a million off the interest alone, which was more than enough for my purposes. I didn't have expensive habits, like drugs—I got sober at age twenty-one after bouncing out of college because of a cocaine addiction. I even gave up porn six months ago because it was interfering with my music, and I didn't want to get any more malware on my production computer than was necessary.

My days consist of producing music and little else. Mostly downtempo, melodic, chugging progressive house at 121 or 122 beats per minute. My DJ name was Night Moves. My real name was Davenport. Hence the DJ name. Most people don't really have a sense of how time-consuming and difficult it is to create music, especially in the beginning. It's mostly a process of trial-and-error and watching YouTube videos on how to do shit. There are some people who will spend two solid months trying to engineer the perfect kick. Not me; I'm not a perfectionist. I'm not like BT who has to build every hat and clap from scratch. I'll just use a sample and tweak it.

As I was finishing setting up the new monitors, plugging in the last of the cables, the doorbell rang.

I opened the door a crack. It was my neighbors, Paige and Randy. Randy was one of the bourgeoisie bankers in the neighborhood, a wealth manager, who pitched me on his services when I first moved in next door. I didn't give off any vibes, so he dropped it. Originally from Charlotte, he was one of the squarest people I knew, his wardrobe a steady diet of striped pastel polo shirts and pleated khakis. He had met Paige, improbably, at a bar in Charlotte; improbably, because they had nothing in common—Randy seemed the type of guy who might have grown up in a dry county in the Virginia panhandle; local boy done good, he made his way to the big city. Paige, flat-chested, could have been a goth girl in high school—as an adult, she wore mostly black, and had such exceptionally curly brown hair in ringlets that it was too perfect to be naturally occurring. Paige never shut the fuck up. I liked her, but she'd drop by during the day when I was busy producing and stand at my front door yapping about some baby shower she went to. Early on, she took an interest in my tattoos. She was shocked when I told her that my last tattoo I left completely up to the discretion of the tattoo artist. "That's a lot of trust!" she said, which is something someone without tattoos would say. They had a five-year-old son, Julian, who was very loud, and roughhoused with the other young boys in the neighborhood. I was glad that I never saw much of him.

"What are you doing three Saturdays from now?" Paige asked, grinning.

"Sounds like you have something planned for me."

"The community association wants to have a block party," she said, "and we want you to be the DJ!"

"You know what kind of music I play, right?"

Paige half-smirked. "Now that you mention it, not really."

"It's very underground," I said. "I don't want to be in a position where I'm playing music and people aren't digging it."

"They'll dig it," Randy said.

"Will *you* dig it? What's your favorite band?"

"The Allman Brothers!" he said.

"You wouldn't dig it. Look, I just don't want the responsibility. I've played bad parties before. It's not fun. People have strong feelings about music."

"Can we listen to your music? Maybe we can come to one of your gigs," Paige said, shaking her ass a little, showing me what she might do at a club.

I tried to picture Randy with his pleated khakis at one of my gigs. Paige might have been able to pull it off, a cool-looking mom. "Sure, I'll let you know when I'm playing next. Right now, I have nothing set in stone."

Paige frowned. "Nothing soon?"

"I'm actually a little uncomfortable in front of a crowd."

Randy slapped me on the shoulder with the force normally reserved for a fraternity brother. "I find that hard to believe. You look the part."

I wanted to say, *So do you*, but suppressed it.

"So you'll do it?" asked Paige, making a cute face.

She was persuasive. "Perhaps. Let me think about it."

"Good!" Paige said, hopping a little. She and Randy headed back across the street to their house.

"Don't you want to listen to my music first?" I called.

Paige blew a kiss at me.

———————

I've been doing this for five years and I still don't have a solution for basslines. I have huge kicks, I have hats, I have claps, I have ride cymbals, I have great tambourines, I have synths with a couple of presets that I like, but it seems as though I have to engineer a new bassline on every single track. I've been doing it in Massive, but I know that isn't the solution. It's fucking arduous. I spend hours listening to tracks with great basslines—Tim Green is the best—and I still can't get it. No matter how many YouTube videos I watch, I can't seem to figure it out. Fourteen hours a day, me against the computer.

I don't mind living alone. It's a popular misconception that DJs get laid all the time. Maybe some do. It never happens to me. I am painfully shy, which is another way of saying that I don't really give off any vibes. I'm not *emotionally available*, and that's perfectly fine. I've had four tracks crack the top 10 in "Progressive House" on Beatport. One of them got to number three. That track was featured by Above and Beyond on their *Group Therapy* podcast, my biggest break yet. I'd sent tracks to Anjunadeep, but they'd been on a hipster organic kick lately. This is all a long-winded way of saying that I was not very interested in a relationship at that moment. It would have pulled me away from my music.

I was still struggling with this bassline, which currently sounded like a spoon in a garbage disposal, when the doorbell rang. The cats scattered.

It was Paige.

"Can I come in?" she asked.

It occurred to me that, in the time that I'd been neighbors with Paige and Randy, neither had set foot in my house. I let her in. It was the neighborly thing to do.

Paige was wearing a skirt. A black skirt, but in the style of a tennis skirt.

"You're wearing a skirt," I observed.

"So?"

"I've never seen you wear a skirt."

"Well, it's hot."

I paused. "I suppose you're here to listen to my music?"

"That's correct."

"You didn't look for it online?"

"I don't know your DJ name! Is it under Davenport?"

"No. My DJ name is Night Moves."

Paige brushed my shoulder with the back of her hand. "Ooooh," she said. "*Night Moves*. Very sexy."

"Do I look sexy?" I asked, without thinking. "On second thought, don't answer that."

Paige smiled.

"Okay, come into my studio and sit down. I have an extra chair over there. Pull it up."

"Wow, what is all this stuff?" she said, looking at my racks of modular synths flashing like a mainframe in the basement of the NSA. "What's this on your monitor?" she asked, inspecting the screen, full of complicated diagrams and colors.

"That's a track I'm working on. Let me pull up one of my old ones. One of the old hits." I clicked the mouse. "This one's called Gemini," I said, and pressed play.

"It doesn't sound like much," she said. "Just beats."

"All dance music is like that—there's a one-minute intro with just beats so that the DJ can beat-match. Give it a minute."

She waited. "Oh, I *like* this," she purred.

"Yeah, that's a good bassline. One of the few good ones that I've ever done."

"It's amazing. You did this?"

"It's what I spend all my time doing in this house. Turning knobs on a screen. Exciting stuff."

Paige stood up and danced around the studio. Her skirt was bouncing, and I caught a glimpse of her thighs.

"I think this would be perfect for the block party!"

"I'm glad you think so, but not everyone in this neighborhood is so open-minded."

"Well, *fuck* them," she proclaimed, the first time I'd heard her swear.

"Indeed."

"So you'll do it?"

"I can. I have all the gear—I used to do mobile DJing years ago. All I need is a power source."

"We'll find one. Do you have any gigs in town anytime soon? You *promised*."

"I'm pretty sure I didn't promise anything," I said. "But, actually, I do now. Except it's the week after the block party. I got asked to play at Trade."

"Where's Trade?" she asked.

"It's on Washington. Are you sure you want to do this? I don't even go on until 1:30 a.m. Are you going to drag Randy to this thing?"

Paige laughed. "No, I'll go alone. I'll get a hall pass. Isn't that what guys say?"

I wanted to discourage this. I didn't see how Randy would allow his wife to go down to Washington with all the riffraff in the middle of the night, and I didn't want to be responsible for keeping her company. It was work. My solution to these situations is to push the problem off into the future, hoping it will go away.

"We'll talk about it later," I said.

"Can I get your cell number? Pretty please? I should have it if we're going to plan for the block party."

I grabbed a business card off my desk and handed it to her. "Here you go."

"Cool card! I'll be in touch." She turned and walked toward the door, the skirt bouncing.

"Here, let me get it. The cats." On cue, Zeus ambled towards the door.

"I won't let him out. Ciao!"

"Yeah."

———————

I finally finished the track I was working on. Andromeda. Naming tracks was actually the hardest part of making a track; usually I just picked something related to astronomy. It fit pretty well with progressive music. I had finally tamed the savage bassline after four days of effort. I had also fiddled with the arpeggiator to make a shimmering trance breakdown over the top. I was looking forward to test-driving it at Trade in ten days.

Test-driving tracks at a club is fun. There's a whole subculture of music geeks and bedroom DJs who like to stand around with their phones in a club and Shazam all the tracks. You'll see them standing there, the app screens lighting up the whole fucking room. You'll play an unreleased track and Shazam chokes on it, and then they're posting video clips online trying to get people to ID it. I have a small following of fans in Miami, and they all show up when I play out. Typically, male nerds in their early thirties wearing Anjuna T-shirts. That is the main reason I never get laid at DJ gigs. If I played hipster house, like Justin Martin a few weeks back, I'd have a bunch of bimbos in the DJ booth, blasted on e-bombs. They're fun as long as you keep giving them drugs. That has never been my scene, at least not since I got sober. I don't have good memories of those days. Besides, very few DJs actually play wasted—there are too many knobs and buttons, the whole thing is a high-wire act. DJs manage to trainwreck mixes even when they're stone cold sober.

I hit compile on the track and headed off to the kitchen to eat some eggs. I'd been doing the keto thing recently, along with intermittent fasting, and it was a good way to keep the weight off if you were basically sedentary. You didn't see too many jacked DJs in the progressive world. Cristoph was one of them, and I suppose you could count Bossi from Cosmic Gate. I met him backstage at Nikki Beach in 2013; the guy was a unit. But people spend eighteen hours a day in front of a computer, and zero hours a day working out. Dance music does not have a culture of physical fitness.

My phone buzzed. It was Paige texting me.

Did you see the weather report this Saturday?

No?

Rain all day. No block party. :(

That's a bummer.

I know! What are we going to do?

At least now I don't have to get all sweaty hauling gear down the block.

Funny. Why don't you come over for dinner?

Can I get back to you?

Dave. I know for a fact you don't have anything going on Saturday night.

> Only if you're serving gnocchi.

> R U serious?

> I'm dead serious. It's my favorite food.

> Ok. We can have gnocchi.

> Hooray.

> I guess the way to a man's heart is through his stomach...

I paused.

Paige's displays of affection were unwelcome, and I felt as if by going to dinner I would be a slow-motion human highlight reel of bad decisions. I hadn't asked if Randy would be there; my assumption was that he would be. I was not the most socially astute person in the world, but it was becoming clear that Paige had taken an interest in me. The last thing I wanted was drama, especially with my neighbors across the street. I was absolutely allergic to drama. I sat there and produced music in peace in a drama-free existence. Also, though Randy was a hick, I liked him. He blended the amiability of a Southerner with the business sense of a New Yorker. He didn't have a mean bone in his body. The closest I wanted to get to a woman was to walk down Lincoln Road and make eyes at all the Argentine girls hanging out in front of the steak restaurants. Miami, in spite of all the beautiful women, was a notoriously difficult place to form a relationship. A lot of them were gold diggers, and all of them were obsessed with status. I didn't have a Lamborghini SUV. I had a 2013 BMW X5, only because I thought I might need it to haul around equipment. At age twenty-nine, I was one of the most eligible and profoundly boring bachelors in history. My mother had been on my case for me to find a girl. There was a much better chance of that in Chicago, with the husky blonde girls that used to hang around Spybar. Hearty Midwestern stock and all that.

I supposed some good might come out of the dinner. As much as I hated it, it was smart to be social. I'd get the neighborhood gossip, which I was mostly not privy to. I was interested in what Paige did with her time. Julian was in kindergarten now, which I was sure was a relief, because the kid was louder than an Iron Maiden concert. I wasn't aware of her having any hobbies. She was a mom. Apart from the skirt-wearing incident last week, she wore mom jeans and mom shirts and mom shoes. I had to concede that she was attractive on a second look. She had great hair and not an ounce of fat on her. I could spy a treadmill through Paige's living room window, although I'd never seen it in action. She must have used it when I wasn't looking. The natural gravitational pull of middle age would have begun to diminish her figure by now. I was partial to flat-chested women anyway.

I took Paige to be in her late thirties. The math checked out. Like a lot of successful white couples, Paige and Randy didn't even consider kids until their early thirties. Julian was five. Paige had mentioned in passing a year ago that her pregnancy had been difficult, and that she and Randy would stop at one. I, too, am an only child, and I, too, had been an insufferable prick at age five. My dislike for Julian had grown over the years. He was a screamer, and I would hear him outside, through the window, when I was trying to tweak some oscillator into position. Temper tantrums were frequent, to the point that I was wondering if he would ever grow out of them. I used to think that temper tantrums were the product of bad parenting, but Paige and Randy couldn't have been better parents. Julian got his mom's dark complexion, and fit in well with the kids of South American descent in the neighborhood. Truthfully, he'd be passable as my son.

———————

When faced with the prospect of going to Paige and Randy's for dinner, I was engulfed with existential dread. I was thinking of ways to get out of it, texting her, *Cough, cough, came down with something, regrets,* but that would be too transparent. Paige was a one-woman press gang, and the sheer proximity of my house to hers ensured that canceling our plans would make any future meetings especially awkward.

Fuck. I don't have a bottle of wine.

With fifteen minutes to go, there was no time to hop in the car and buy one. Maybe I could give them a red Gatorade and play it for laughs. I'm an ape.

I walked across the street, my heart pounding in my chest.

I rang the doorbell. Paige answered.

"Here." I handed her the red Gatorade.

"You shouldn't have!"

"Sorry, forgot the wine."

"You don't drink anyway, right?" she said, walking inside, looking over her shoulder.

"I don't... think I ever told you that," I said, following her into the kitchen.

"I know *ev-ery-thing!*" she said, sounding a bit like Isla Fisher in *Wedding Crashers*.

I glanced around. "So where's Randy?"

"He had to go on a trip. He won't be here." She looked me straight in the eyes.

"And Julian?"

"Play date."

"So it's just the two of us."

"That's right."

I didn't smell any food. There was no dinner cooking.

"It's a trap!" I joked, channeling Admiral Ackbar.

"You better believe it, buddy. Can I get you something? Aside from the Gatorade?"

"I'll take the Gatorade. It's cold." She handed it back to me.

"So what do you do in that house all day, Mr. Davenport?" She smiled at me playfully.

"You saw what I do. I make bleeps and bloops."

"Nothing else? No girlfriend?"

"Haven't had a girlfriend in a few years."

"Don't you get lonely?" she asked, practically cooing at me.

"I'm an introvert. Human interaction stresses me out."

Paige blushed. "Is *this* stressing you out?" She took two steps towards me.

"Candidly, it is."

She put her hand on my chest. "Why don't we see if we can do something about that stress?" And she kissed me.

I had rehearsed this moment a thousand times, and in each of those rehearsals, I gently pushed her away, *no, no, what about Randy*, and took my leave and went home. That was not what happened now. I kissed her like a wolf, grabbing her shoulders and pulling her towards me, ravenously seizing her chest and her ass. We kissed for what felt like ten minutes, and I sprung an erection harder than a one-meter bar of tungsten.

"Why don't we see if we can have some fun?" she said, and knelt down on the tiles in front of me. She unbuckled my belt, opened my black jeans, pulled down my boxer briefs, and I sprung free, bouncing absurdly in front of her face.

She grabbed it by the base. *Wow*, she exclaimed.

At that point all the hydraulics of my reproductive system irrationally broke free and—how high it went—splattering on the tiles around her. She stuck her tongue out, like a girl trying to catch snowflakes.

"Uh, sorry."

She erupted in gales of laughter, leaning backwards. "That was *awesome*. You must have really wanted me!"

As much as I hated to admit it, yes.

"I swear to God that's never happened to me before," I said.

She hugged me, my honker still hanging lasciviously. "Maybe we can try again some other time?"

"Are you sure that's a good idea?"

"Oh *come on*," she pleaded, "we can do this anytime we want. You're alone over there, I'm alone over here."

I could see the future, and it was closing rapidly around me. "Maybe." I started putting myself back together.

"When am I going to see you again?" she asked, kissing me on the cheek.

"I'm not sure."

"I'll text you."

"Okay—and hey—I never got my gnocchi."

———————

I hadn't heard from Paige since the inchoate blowjob incident. Given her level of motivation, I expected to hear from her the next day, even an hour later. The phone was silent. But *miamimom1978* followed me on Instagram. I looked at her page—it was mostly pictures of Julian. There was an old one of her in a halter top, from three years ago—I must have spent fifteen minutes staring at it.

For someone who valued a drama-free existence, my life was suddenly full of drama. I half expected Randy to show up at my front door with a baseball bat, but he was too mild-mannered for that. I knew this would end in tears. Affairs always do: tears, divorces, alimony, and child support. I was the *other man*, when really I had been shanghaied into this whole situation. I had dutifully resisted up until the point at which I hadn't. I replayed the events of the last month in my mind, and I couldn't see how it might have ended with any other outcome. The whole thing had been inevitable.

The longer it went before I heard from Paige, the more I began to believe that she regretted the incident and went back to the Dyson vacuum cleaner, being the *miamimom* that seemed to be her identity. It was unbearable sitting in my house at my computer, 200 feet away from her sitting in her house watching *Days of Our Lives*, or whatever she did with her free time. There were moments I felt like walking across the street and banging on the door, looking for some hardcore pound-fucking. But time changes everything. Until it doesn't. *I'm sure this will go away if I ignore it long enough,* said nobody ever.

I had spent most of the last few days submitting "Andromeda" to record labels. I've been signed to three labels so far, and I usually stick with my knitting, but this track I blasted to a wider distribution. I was hoping it would get signed by Replug—it had one of those long-building Cid Inc breakdowns. There was, of course, my upcoming gig at Trade. I was actually looking forward to it—it would get my mind off the whole Paige situation. I randomly got an email from an agent in Los Angeles who wanted to take me on as a client. This would be the gateway to playing at all the big festivals, like Ultra and EDC. I'm a better producer than performer, but the big festival gigs would at least get me cash flow positive, so that I'm not chewing into my inheritance. I agreed to meet him before my set at Trade, in the green room, where we would hammer out details. It had the potential to be my big break.

In the old days of DJing, you used to have to cart around crates of vinyl with you to gigs. After that, you were bringing books of CDs. Now, all your music is on a USB drive that you stick into the CD player. Preparation consists of loading a bunch of tracks onto the USB, which is actually more time consuming than you might think. It takes a long time to put 256 gigabytes onto a USB drive—the computer is slow. Usually, when I was performing, I kept a lid on the energy, saving the big tunes for festivals. But this time, I thought I would slay it, and play the biggest monsters in my collection, the real dancefloor killers. Why not? My life was about to be over, anyway. The news of the affair would get out and my name would be mud.

I got to Trade around 11 p.m., after having a late dinner at one of the Argentine steak places with the cute Argentine girls. I walked upstairs and introduced myself to the bartender. Usually they knew me—this time they had someone new. The manager took me to the green room, a tiny space with a refrigerator and a small sound system where I could hear the warmup DJ's set. I never have alcohol in my rider, but there is always vodka in the fridge. A pair of hangers-on were in the green room with me, and I offered them all the vodka out of my rider. They were thrilled.

I was habitually early, but the agent had told me that he'd meet me at Trade at 11:30 p.m. and it was past that now. I'm not good at waiting, and I had a knot in my stomach. I thought about Paige, and I wondered if under different circumstances a relationship with her would have actually worked. But she was too energetic, too earnest, and she would never leave me alone to produce music. Then I thought back to the way her body had felt in my arms. I still hadn't seen her with her clothes off, but it felt as if I had. I sensed that this would continue until I finally did. What happened last week couldn't have been the first and last time. But it had to be.

By midnight, there was no agent, and the hangers-on had stumbled out into the club. Typical for nightlife people— always late. Early in my career, I showed up to a gig and nobody bothered to tell me that the club was closed. This guy would probably end up being a no-show and then I would get an email from him a week later as if nothing had happened. I wasn't really in the right headspace to be playing. I was stressed about the agent, and stressed about Paige. But one of the reasons I had been looking forward to this gig was the prospect of getting out of my head and going to space for four hours, then collapsing into bed and sleeping until noon.

By 1:20 a.m., there was still no sign of the agent, and the manager collected me and led me through the crowd to the DJ booth. This was the worst part of the night—people recognized me and I was pawed and manhandled on the way to the booth. I high-fived about six different people, all fans. I got in the booth and the opening DJ, a guy named Slytherin, had serviceably warmed up the room with some funky stuff I hadn't heard before. The BPMs were at 123, giving me enough room to take it up a little. I looked into the crowd—everyone was having a great time—smiles all around.

I mixed in with my new track "Andromeda," which was sure to stump the Shazam guys. The crowd was digging it. It was a great first track. During the breakdown, I looked up, expecting to see hands in the air. Instead, I saw Paige and Randy. We made eye contact. They both waved—Paige was jumping up and down and grinning broadly. I smiled back. Randy was wearing a black T-shirt, looking like a guy who was wearing a black T-shirt because his wife told him he would look cool if he wore a black T-shirt. They kept jumping up and down and waving—they were so glad to see me. The moment I saw them, I felt a pang of dread, *I'm doomed,* but they were being such happy goofballs that eventually I was relieved that they were there. Paige must have kept her secret.

As I applied the reverb and the white noise during the breakdown, bringing the club to a massive crescendo, the lights flashing and the CO_2 cannons going off, I considered the path of least resistance. I considered the consequences of resisting and not resisting. I didn't know the path forward, but I knew that my life was immeasurably better than it was a month ago, fuller and more meaningful, because somebody loved me.

DR. BURNS

————————

As I hobble towards my office, my lower back seizing up from leaning over my tenth patient of the day, the receptionist stands up and calls out to me: "Dr. Burns, you have someone to see you in the waiting room."

"Who is it?"

"It's a Jason Phelan?" She gives me a shoulder shrug. I purse my lips and shake my head. I have no idea who he is.

I open the door to the waiting room. Seated at the far end is a young man in what appears to be an expensive suit, like nothing you'd see in this part of the country, typing away on his phone, perhaps sending an email. He looks up at me. "Dr. Burns?"

"That's right."

He walks briskly across the room, his hand extended. "Pleasure to meet you. I just want fifteen minutes of your time."

"I see. Are you the guy who's been calling every week for the last three months, trying to set up an appointment?"

He smiles and stands up straighter. "Yes sir, that's me."

The transition manager.

I have to respect the hustle. As a dentist, I deal with aggressive salesmen all the time, usually equipment vendors trying to put me further into debt, selling expensive X-Ray machines and other accoutrements that are entirely unnecessary. Most of them wear gray or burgundy shirts, the kind that come in plastic boxes with matching ties. Jason is different—he could have walked off the set of *Billions* and into my office. I am not an expert on ties, but whatever he is wearing doesn't come from the Midwest, definitely not from the cornfields of western Ohio. He would look more at home on Park and 54th in Manhattan. I imagine that he just stepped off the plane in Columbus from LaGuardia, Louis Vuitton bags in tow, checking his Rolex to make sure he got to his destination on time.

"I can meet with you for fifteen minutes. Let's go to the conference room." I open the door to the office and Jason follows. I can't see him behind me, but I imagine that he is getting a good look at all of the operatories and the hygienists, and they are looking back at him. The only people who wear suits in this part of the state are the car salesmen, and they're not suits like *this*.

The conference room isn't a conference room in the corporate sense—it's a small, round table in what had been a storage room when I took over the practice thirty years ago. My employees and I mostly use it to eat lunch, and for the occasional performance review. We take a seat at either end.

Jason unbuttons his jacket and leans forward in his chair. "Dr. Burns—how is it going?" with the implication that it might not be going so well.

"Fine," I say.

Jason begins to sigh, but suppresses it. "I'll get right to the point. Every doc is one day faced with the decision as to when to sell his practice and retire. You have a great practice here—I can tell by looking at it—and you may not want to retire, but you might want to know that practices like yours are selling at extremely high valuations right now."

"Why is that?"

"Low interest rates, for one, but also the presence of several large corporate buyers who are willing to pay increased multiples of cash flow."

"Private equity?"

"Smart man."

"So?"

"I'll put it in terms you can understand—you probably have a rough estimate of what your practice is worth, but at this moment in time, it is likely worth a million dollars more."

"And?"

"And if you were thinking about retiring, right now the timing would be very good. You don't have to retire at the moment—you can stay on for a period of time—three years, perhaps, and slowly transition into retirement as we bring a new dentist into the practice."

I fold my hands in front of me and lean forward, which communicates that I mean business. "Mr. Phelan, I'm sixty-five years old. I could do this for another fifteen years."

"Do you like what you do?"

"Of course."

"How's your back holding up?"

I frown. This guy is good—he saw me limping into the conference room. I might have touched my back with my right hand.

"Dr. Burns, dentistry is a physically demanding profession. It's hard on your back, it's hard on your eyes, it's hard on your hands, you're dealing with insurance companies and Medicaid and deadbeat patients, and you're surrounded by a bunch of crazy women and drama all the time. The same cavities, the same root canals, the same aligners, there are no more problems left to solve. Are you married?"

"I am. Nineteen years."

"Is she working out there?"

I smile, but say nothing.

"Of course. I talk to dentists every day—this is what I do. None of them want to quit. Being a dentist is part of who you are as a person. It's your identity. You've been a pillar of this community for thirty years. You've put your kids through school and you're involved in a number of charitable organizations. People have a great deal of respect for you. But it's better to jump than to be pushed. Wouldn't it be nice to go out on top, instead of some ballplayer that stays way past his prime, watching his numbers fall off over time, and eventually being designated for assignment?"

"Is that all?"

"There's more, but we can stop there."

I draw in a breath. "Mr. Phelan, I appreciate what you're trying to do here, but I just have no interest at the moment. I'm fine. The practice is fine. Everybody's happy here. I have a lot of money—it's not about the money."

Jason has an answer for everything. "For sure, at the moment, everything *is* fine. The patient rolls are stable or even growing, you have five operatories that are running eight hours a day, but I can tell you that the time to sell is often when things are the best. If the practice starts to decline—for whatever reason—it will be much more difficult to sell."

"I'm fine."

Jason, completely unfazed, takes a business card out of his jacket pocket and hands it to me. The business card looks like something out of *American Psycho*. "No problem at all, Dr. Burns. When you are ready to make the transition, let me know, and I'll be here. You can email me or call, and we can meet someplace other than your practice, so your staff doesn't get freaked out by a guy in a suit walking in here again."

"Thank you," I say, at a loss for words. This guy is as slick as it gets, and he's persuasive enough that if I spent any more time in the conference room with him, I'd agree to sell the practice, my car, my house, and my wife. I want to get the hell out of this meeting as quickly as possible.

We make our way out of the conference room, the hygienists all turning to stare at Jason and his expensive suit. We shake hands again, and he looks me in the eye and says, "Dr. Burns, if you ever need anything—*anything*—give me a call." And he and his Ferragamo loafers turn and exit the building, walking out to his car. I watch through the window as he lowers himself into a brand-new Audi Q5. I take the business card and put it in the side pocket of my wallet, next to my insurance card.

———————

Somewhat shaken by the experience, I go to the bathroom, stand at the sink, and take a small plastic bag from my right front pocket. Vicodin. I throw one in my mouth, grab a handful of water with my right hand, and wash it down. In twenty minutes, I should feel normal again.

I replay the conversation in my head. How did he know that my wife is a hygienist? Foolishly, I had told him that we had been married for nineteen years. I've had the practice for over thirty. He must have surmised that I had married one of my own hygienists—a terrible cliché. It was true. I left my wife of nine years for Spring, with her dark hair and skinny ass and exotic good looks. Spring had a lilt in her voice—she came from the southern part of Ohio, near Kentucky and West Virginia. I could hear her with the patients, saying *mmm-hmmm* as she had them rinse out their mouths with water. We'd both be leaning over a patient, and the smell of her hair and her perfume would be too much for me. She was twenty years my junior. I took her to the Hampton Inn weekly and hung myself in her, fully intending to get her pregnant, which I thought would be a straightforward but messy way out of my current marriage. Mother Nature eventually obliged. My first wife, not skilled with the legal system, went away for not much money, but we didn't have many assets at the time anyway. It was a bit of a scandal in town. But that was almost twenty years ago, and the community had grown accustomed to seeing Spring and me together. Now forty-five, Spring has complete control over hiring hygienists into the practice—only the ugly ones. She knows my type, so she hires the five-foot-one wombats with rusty-red Scotch-Irish hair, bad attitudes, usually smokers. It is a pointless prophylactic measure. At sixty-five, my days of carousing are long over, and it would at least be good to have some nice scenery in the office, but Spring isn't taking any chances.

This fucking guy—Jason—was right about everything. He *saw* me, I thought, as I take another Vicodin. My back is a wreck, and has been for about four years—that's when I started taking painkillers to get through the day. I am not an idiot. I know I am addicted to them. They used to be easy to get, but ordering truckloads of Vicodin to a dentist's office had the potential to raise some eyebrows at the DEA, and I started ordering them off the dark web. They came in FedEx boxes, 1,000 pills at a time. Spring co-signed this—she knew that it was impossible for me to work without them. Most of the stash I keep at home, in the bathroom, in the cabinet under the sink, but I have a subset of the pills in my office at work; about 200 of them. On a typical day, I take four. On a day like today, with Jason parachuting in, when I can barely stand after my last patient, I will take six. Over time, I know the job will kill me.

So why send Jason Phelan packing? I know that my life is unsustainable, and some guy comes along and offers to take me out of it and pay me a few million dollars in the process, and I tell him to pound sand? Pure ego. I know plenty of dentists who keep going well into their eighties, like Rosenblum up the street. The guy looks like Brian Boitano. In addition to the back, I have a litany of health concerns—cholesterol, high blood pressure, a few colonoscopy scares, and even a bout with skin cancer. Why not take a few million dollars and spend the rest of my days drinking out of a pineapple?

———

On Tuesdays, Spring and I order Chinese food, and have it delivered to the house. I always get the General Tso's chicken and wonder why they put that piece of undercooked broccoli in there. Is it meant to be eaten, or is it a garnish? I eat it, crunching it slowly, thinking that it might do me some good.

Spring eats the same food that I do—Chinese food, pizza, and other garbage—and never puts on a pound. She has metabolism that movie stars would kill for. Additionally, five years ago, she set about trying to reverse the aging process, getting botox and fillers. She also got minor breast implants—good ones, not the ones that look like lacrosse balls—which have served to make the age difference between us seem even larger. It's a good thing we don't hire male hygienists—they'd be chasing her around the office.

Spring dips into her sesame chicken. "Who was that Gordon Gekko guy?"

I smirk. "He's a practice broker. I hear from these guys about two or three times a year."

"He doesn't *look* like a practice broker," Spring says. "He looks like—"

"I know what he looks like. He looks like a Wall Street banker."

"What is he doing here?"

"My assumption is that he lives here. He had Ohio plates on his car. Could have been a rental, though, but I doubt it."

"What did he have to say?"

"Just that I could get a lot of money for my practice."

"We *know* that."

"But we might be able to get even more than that."

Spring stops eating. "Are you *considering* it? Are you going to sell what it took you over thirty years to build? All that hard work?"

"Spring, I'm a mess. I'm held together with duct tape. My back is fucking killing me. I can't see. I sleep with rolled-up socks in my hands at night. If we could sell the practice for four million, we'd have twelve million saved up. We could do anything we wanted."

Spring taps her chopsticks against the side of her plate. "But what am *I* supposed to do? You may be ready to retire, but I'm not."

"You could always keep working there."

"For someone *else*? Not a chance."

I pound the table with my fist, not hard, but enough to make the plates rattle. "Springtime. I'm addicted to painkillers. I'd like to not be addicted to painkillers. I'd like to stop bending over all day. You know, sometimes I think things happen for a reason. Maybe Gordon Gekko showed up in my office earlier this afternoon for some divine purpose. Maybe God puts people in your life for a reason at exactly the right time. It's too good to be a coincidence."

Spring glares at me for a minute, then begins to clear up the dishes. Silent treatment time.

I'd get out of jail tomorrow, at work. Tomorrow, I will see more patients. A thirty-eight-year-old man whose bruxism is so severe that soon he will need a mouthful of crowns. Four fillings, two on one patient. Two well-behaved children, for a change. A woman in her forties who cries at the sound of the drill.

It's been said that dentists are susceptible to investment scams because of the emotional distress of causing pain to people on a daily basis. We also become addicted to substances, get divorced, and commit suicide at rates far higher than the general population. A dentist spends his entire career in a small, windowless room, leaning over a disgusting mouth, with patients who would rather face a firing squad than visit their friendly, helpful ivory carpenter, surrounded by a group of pre-menopausal angry women. But it is lucrative. Even an average dentist can end his career in the low eight figures. Some do much better than that. The dentists never sold out to corporate like the physicians did to hospital groups years ago. Nowadays, a medical doctor is a working stiff, a nine-to-five worker with a brown-bag lunch. Dentists retained their autonomy, and their upside potential. But it is a very tough living.

Spring has been a hygienist since she was twenty-four years old. She knows nothing else. She raised our son well. He's skating through Ohio State with a GPA in the twos, and has designs on selling audio equipment for a large distributor in Indiana. A longhair, he plays guitar in his spare time. She raised him to be self-sufficient, having been self-sufficient herself. Our wedding was poorly attended, after the scandalous series of events that led to my divorce, but people have forgotten all that by now. My first wife remarried quickly, to a gym teacher named Jim, and the word is that he is also having straycations, though it never gets back to her. Some people just ask for it, I guess.

———————

I have a reasonably long drive to work, but I like it. When I bought my current practice I was under a restrictive covenant from my previous employer, and I had to work twenty miles away. At thirty-five minutes, the commute was just the right length—long enough for me to think about shit, but not so long that my back would start to hurt. Spring drives separately—I get the office started early in the morning and she cleans up at night.

It has been three days since my conversation with Jason. Since then, I have been obsessing over the idea of selling my practice and retiring. I haven't slept much. The trouble is, I don't have any plans for retirement—up until Jason walked into my office, I hadn't thought about it at all. What would I do? I can't play golf. I am worried about the prospect of scads of unstructured free time, sitting at home like other Boomers with the cable news turned up to eleven. I don't want to be like that. When people retire, they need a *purpose*, whether it's rescuing cats or playing pickleball—not sitting at the bar at the country club at 11 a.m.

It is 9:00 in the morning—early. What the hell—I decide to call Jason. While keeping one hand on the wheel, I fish my wallet out of my back pocket and remove his business card, retrieve my phone from the cupholder, and type in the digits, swerving all the while, three times driving over the rumble strip on the side of the road. Jason picks up on the first ring.

"Hello?"

"This is Dr. Burns."

"Dr. Burns! To what do I owe the pleasure?"

"I was thinking about our conversation the other day and… well, I don't really have an agenda. I just want to think out loud on this."

"Let's do it. What's holding you up?"

"My wife, mostly—she's forty-five and doesn't want to give up working. She likes things as they are."

"Dr. Burns, in all my years of doing this, I can tell you that that friends or family rarely have your best financial interests in mind. They may want the best for you, but financial decisions aren't driven by emotion. I buy and sell dental practices. You know how in real estate the real estate agents will say that this is either a buyer's or seller's market for houses? This is a seller's market for dental practices. And that might not always be the case."

"I get it. Like I said before, it's not really about the money."

"What is it, then?"

"Honestly, I don't know."

"Dr. Burns, I can't make these decisions for you. One of the hardest things to do is to walk away from your life's work. I can tell that you're still mentally sharp—sharp as ever. But I can also tell that your body is failing you. You've still got some time left. Remember, I'm a *transition* expert; I'm not just a broker. We will bring in a younger dentist to work with you for a few years. He can phase in, and you can phase out. It's not like one day you will be sitting in a nursing home. You can continue to work, and pass on your knowledge to someone else. You can slowly introduce your patients to the new dentist, and they'll get used to the idea of working with him. Do whatever you want with the money. Go to Vegas and stick it in the high-limit slots. You wouldn't be calling me if *every cell in your body* wasn't telling you to walk away."

"What about my wife?"

"I wish I had advice for you, Dr. Burns—I'm certainly no expert on relationships. Surely your wife must know that this is inevitable. Keep bringing it up—she'll adjust to the idea. Maybe we can give her a managerial role in the new practice. Think of all the things you can do together—there will be lots of time for it."

"Okay."

"Dr. Burns?"

"Yes."

"Are you all right?"

"Yes." *But I'm not.*

"I'm here for you, sir. And if you decide not to do the deal, or if you want to put it off for five years, that's fine too—but in five years, it might be a buyer's market.

"Thank you," I say, and hang up.

I sit silently in my car, once again turning my attention to the road ahead. Jason stands to make a lot of money on this transaction—he'll earn a broker's fee of about $150,000. But it doesn't sound like he needs the money. Possibly he is my friend, or possibly he is very good at his job, and just that cynical. At the moment, he is my angel.

———————

I arrive to find the office in crisis.

Spring greets me at the receptionist's desk. "Josie quit," she says. "Why?"

"Because I wouldn't let her take a four-day weekend. She's always taking time off. So she called me a fucking bitch and started throwing shit all over the place and left."

"Did any patients see it?"

"Just one—he said it would be best if he came back another time."

This will be a six-Vicodin day. I already woke up with my hands frozen in the shape of claws from my carpal tunnel syndrome. I spent ten minutes at home running them under hot water to get them back to normal. My back is killing me, and I haven't even seen a patient yet. I think today may be an ideal day to have a conversation with Spring. And if she doesn't like it, she is going to get the cramdown—I can't live like this anymore.

I spend the day nearly in tears, as my back, hands, and eyes conspire against me, causing me as much pain and discomfort as possible. A six-Vicodin day turns out to be an eight-Vicodin day. At the end of it, I am no longer in pain, but I am high as shit.

Spring is still cleaning up the Josie mess. I exit quickly amid the chaos, haul my ass in the 4Runner and start the drive home. I know I will be calling Jason as soon as I hit the highway. I still haven't saved his number in my phone, but find it quickly in the recent calls and hit the button, swerving madly from the Vicodin.

Jason answers on the first ring again. "Dr. Burns—I thought I might hear from you."

"You were right," I say. "I'm ready."

"Did you get everything worked out on the home front?"

"Yes," I say, which wasn't entirely true.

"You sound like you are in a hurry. I have to warn you, this process could take some time. We'll do some due diligence on your financials, the buyer will have to line up financing, and so on. These transactions can be complex and will take some patience."

"Fine."

"Dr. Burns, I will need to speak with your accountant at some point, and your attorney."

"That's not a problem. My attorney is a cousin of mine."

"That actually *is* a problem—my experience in hundreds of transactions has shown that when either party has a family member as legal counsel, there is a high probability of the transaction not being completed."

"Are you saying I should get a different attorney?"

"I'm suggesting that, yes."

"Fine. What else?"

"As it turns out, I have a buyer who is a perfect candidate for your practice. I can probably get you a letter of intent within the next few days. Then we can get the process rolling."

The relief I feel begins in my heart and expands throughout my chest and my limbs. *It is finally happening.* The pain in my back starts to fade. One thing I knew when I was younger, and had since forgotten, is that when you take action on a problem, you instantly feel better. I had not been allowing myself to believe the full extent of my misery in this profession. Now that I have *made a decision*, and am *taking action*, and the path forward has revealed itself, I am experiencing genuine happiness for the first time in years.

"Jason, you are a lifesaver."

"That's appreciated, but we are at the beginning of a very long and circuitous path. I just want to manage your expectations. There are a number of factors that can scuttle a deal, including the relationship between you and the buyer. After I draft the letter of intent, we will arrange a meeting. I probably don't need to remind you of this, but I need you to be on your best behavior."

"Understood," I say, with the knowledge that many dentists are social misfits and impossible to deal with.

"I'll be in touch in the next few days," Jason says.

So this is it. Thirty-five years in dentistry, and this is how it ends. No more pain and suffering. And, since my practice is debt-free aside from some small equipment loans, the proceeds of the sale will all come to me. Four million dollars hitting the bank on the closing. Spring and I could have fun with that. We could remodel the house. We could buy a new house. We could travel. We could donate to charity. This seems immeasurably better than being hunched over in a chair every day, in excruciating pain.

Not being physically infirm, Spring doesn't mind working. She likes it quite a bit. I don't think she will be persuaded to stay on and work for Dr. Monkeynuts or whoever takes over the practice. I don't worry about that much, but I worry about Spring with a bunch of free time on her hands. She'll be mowing the lawn three times before noon. She is absolutely incapable of sitting still. Me, I could lay around and watch Ohio State football on Saturdays. She always has to be doing shit. Forty extra hours in the week are going to be unkind to her. Plainly, she is going to have to get another job. But there isn't a dentist in a hundred-mile radius that she would work for. I take a Vicodin.

Spring arrives home about an hour later. I break the news to her.

"You *what?*"

"I did."

"I thought we were a *team*. I thought we were supposed to make these decisions *together*."

"I'm an old man. I'm in pain every day. My balls are low. I can't do this anymore. I had to make a decision fast."

Spring reflects. "How much does Gordon Gekko think he can get for your practice?"

"Four million."

"We could have a lot of fun with four million."

"Right?"

And so we spend the rest of the night dreaming like lottery winners, about condos and boats and RVs. Spring will find something to do, maybe involving cats.

I get out of bed the next morning like I am shot out of a cannon. I am ready to go fix some fucking teeth. I take three Vicodin right off the bat, mostly for fun, because my back isn't hurting too badly. The effects of the carpal tunnel wear off after about ten minutes.

Yesterday I received a shipment of Vicodin before Spring got home. I signed for the FedEx package and the delivery dude didn't suspect a thing. Inside were five 200-count plastic bags of Vicodin. I take one with me on the way out the door, to replenish my supply at work, placing it on the passenger seat beside me. Spring stays home with a whole new attitude, celebrating our freedom and our newfound wealth. I have no idea what she'll do all day, but this will be a pretty good test run for her retirement.

I have another long day of teeth ahead of me, but the knowledge that there is closure to this makes it much easier to bear. I turn on the classic rock station, 97.1, and rev the engine. The speed limit is forty-five through here, but there are never any cops on this road.

Until now.

It takes me a good thirty seconds to notice the flashing lights behind me. I pull off onto the shoulder, watching the policeman approach the car in the side-view mirror. I don't often get pulled over, but when I do I like to have the license, registration, and insurance ready. I fish it all out of the glove compartment, and wait.

"Good morning, sir," he says, leaning into my window. "Can I see your license and registration?"

"Here you go, officer," I say, smiling.

He stands up and looks at it, then leans in again. "Do you know how fast you were going?"

"I might have been going sixty-five?"

"You were going sixty-seven in a forty-five—" He stops, his eyes fixed on something in the car. Then he says, "What is that on the passenger seat?"

I had forgotten all about it. The bottom drops out of my heart and through my ass.

"That's Vicodin, sir."

"Do you have a prescription for that?"

"No, sir."

"Please step out of the car."

What happens next is a series of memories that blur together—I am handcuffed, and forced into the back of a police cruiser, brought to a dingy police station, booked and charged with possession of a controlled substance with intent to distribute, fingerprinted, photographed, and placed in a cell with two drunks. Spring posts bail. Within twenty-four hours, news of my arrest spreads through the entire community. I temporarily close my practice.

Charged with a felony. I speak with my cousin, the attorney, and he says that he'll probably get it pled down to a misdemeanor possession charge, given that I have no previous criminal record, and there wasn't really any evidence that I had any plans to sell the stuff. If it ends up in drug court, I'll probably get out of it without jail time, and will have to attend a drug treatment program. I have already disposed of the rest of the Vicodin, and quit cold turkey. I am detoxing horribly, sweating, shaking, adding to my worries about the arrest. But my biggest concern of all is the sale of the practice. I call Jason.

"Dr. Burns, how are you?"

"Have you heard the news?"

"No, what happened?"

I tell him.

"Well," he says, "I was hoping it wouldn't burn you—but it burned you."

"What do we do?"

"The deal is off."

"Off?"

"The letter of intent states that one of the buyer's contingencies is adverse material effect on the practice during the due diligence phase, prior to sale."

"So it's totally off?"

"I can still sell your practice—at a greatly reduced price. In a week or two you won't have half the patients that you have now. They'll go to other docs. That means the practice is worth less. Potentially far less. If it was worth four million before, I'd estimate that it's worth less than a million now."

"Less than a million?"

"That's right. This is what we call a distressed sale."

"Is that my only option?"

"Well," Jason says, "you could continue to work, and maybe in about five or ten years people will have forgotten all about this, and you will have built your patient base up again. That's assuming you can keep your license, pending a favorable disposition of your criminal case."

"Are you suggesting I work until I'm *seventy-five*?"

"Unfortunately, those are your options. Sorry to be the bearer of bad news, Dr. Burns. You kind of painted yourself into a corner here. I'm sorry this happened. I really feel for you."

It is not a difficult decision. I will sell the practice, get what I can for it. For the first time since dental school, my future is wide open. Yes, I will be the disgraced former dentist of Western Ohio. But I still have $8 million. And I still have a hot wife. And I will be free of the painkillers at last. God did for me what I couldn't do for myself.

I began to laugh. I laughed some more. I laughed hysterically, until I could hear Spring's footsteps coming down the stairs to see what the hell was going on.

And then I began to cry.

INSIDER

————————

J ACOB ALAN GREENE placed a trade for 500 of the 15 strike put options in Key Bank on June 12, 2022. He had heard from a loan officer that the bank was about to make a "major announcement," and that it was likely to be "catastrophic." Two days later, on June 14, Key Bank announced a pronounced increase in loan losses and an impairment to capital. The stock declined thirty-four percent. The value of Jacob Alan Greene's put options increased in value by $324,525. Jacob quickly sold the put options and pocketed the profit. What Jacob didn't know was that options in Key Bank were relatively thinly traded, and the market maker who executed the trade would find the trade to be highly suspicious and report it to the SEC. On October 24, 2023, the FBI staged a pre-dawn raid of Jacob Alan Greene's home, arresting him and taking him into federal custody. Jacob was charged with one count of insider trading, to which he quickly pled guilty, and was sentenced to three years in prison with a penalty of $100,000 and a disgorgement of profits. He was scheduled to report to the Halverson Federal Correctional Institute in West Virginia on March 6, 2023, where he would serve his sentence.

Jacob had been married to Alyssa Vartenigian for eight years, and had two daughters, who inherited their mother's Armenian complexion. Alyssa worked in the grants office of the local university. They were not hurting for money, but Jacob had seen the trade as a way out of their middle-class existence. They had a pre-owned BMW and a 77-inch TV. Alyssa had little knowledge of Jacob's day-trading habit, and she had no reason to suspect he was trafficking in insider information. Jacob was about as far from privileged information as you could get as the second-in-command at a local online marketing firm. The tipper was a college buddy—Jacob had connected with him to talk about the reunion and asked him how work was going, when his friend let slip about the announcement. During the trial, the prosecution noted the alacrity with which Jacob acted on the information, and the contents of his search history following the trading, with such terms as "can you go to jail for insider trading" and "federal defense attorneys near me." It was revealed that Jacob had a previous shoplifting conviction from when he was 16, which had been sealed.

Ray, a neighbor from two streets over and the proprietor of a tiny accounting firm, was best friends with Jacob. They had moved into the neighborhood at the same time, around ten years ago. At the time, Ray was married to Olivia, and the four of them had double dated at Jacob's house, where they would play board games and drink cheap wine while Jacob's kids played in the living room. Ray's marriage deteriorated when he discovered flirty text messages on Olivia's phone with a co-worker. He interrogated her about it, and she disclosed that she was in love with the co-worker, though had not yet consummated the relationship. They had an amicable divorce, and Olivia moved to Pennsylvania with her paramour, leaving Ray alone in the house. After the divorce, Ray and Jacob grew closer, and Ray spent as much time or more at Jacob's house than before the divorce. Ray enjoyed spending time with Jacob and Alyssa; it eased his sadness. Alone in his house, he was capable of little more than watching Yankees games or having the occasional cigar on his back porch.

Ray learned of Jacob's arrest through Alyssa—she called him frantically when the FBI agents showed up at 5:30 a.m. Ray thought it best not to drive to their house, and sprinted two blocks to find at least a dozen federal law enforcement officers wearing their trademark blue-and-yellow windbreakers. Alyssa, still in her pink pajamas, ran to him with her daughters and embraced him. Things were happening fast. FBI agents were streaming out of the house, carrying boxes of books, files, and computers. Eventually, Jacob emerged in handcuffs, an FBI agent leading him by his right elbow. His daughters shrieked. None of them had any idea what he was being charged with; Ray hoped it was nothing too salacious.

"I got it under control!" Ray yelled out to Jacob. "We'll get you an attorney!" Ray had no idea about any of these things— he wouldn't know the first place to start looking for an attorney. He knew that Alyssa would be leaning on him heavily for help, and that they would have to figure this out together.

––––––––––

Two nights before Jacob was scheduled to report to prison, Jacob, Alyssa, and Ray went out to dinner at a middlebrow local Italian restaurant. Jacob barely had the $100,000 he needed to enter a guilty plea, let alone the $2 million he would need to mount a defense. Jacob was silent as he approached the hostess stand. He held up three fingers, and the three of them were led swiftly to a table. It was a Monday night.

They had all dressed up without discussing it. It was a special occasion, of sorts. Alyssa looked wildly out of place here, with a slimming, sequined black dress. Jacob wore a tie, his last opportunity to do so for a long time. Ray had put on weight and didn't own a jacket that fit properly, but he wore his nicest shirt, one that he got tailored on a trip to New York, the sleeves shortened.

The three of them sat down and looked at each other.

"You ready?" asked Ray.

"As ready as I'm going to be," said Jacob. "I've been doing a lot of reading online on what to expect in prison. I don't think it's going to be so bad."

"Can we send you anything?"

"Letters. Write letters."

Alyssa interjected. "He's going to be *fine*. Three years will go by in a flash."

"And that's when it really gets hard," said Jacob. "I'll be a convicted felon."

"Bullshit," said Alyssa. "There are a lot of things that you can do with a felony conviction. You just have to get creative." The busboy stopped by the table and filled their glasses with water.

"Anyway, can we please not talk about prison?" said Jacob, taking a drink. "I've been thinking about it for six months, I don't want to have to think about it tonight."

Ray paused. "How about them Yankees?"

"Yeah, they look terrible this year."

"I'm actually hoping they lose a hundred games so we can get rid of Cashman."

Alyssa looked at Ray. "Ray, want to take the girls to a game this year?"

"Actually," said Jacob, "that's really what I want to talk to you about. Ray, I need you to listen carefully."

Ray's eyes widened. "Sure, hit me."

"I want you to take care of my girls while I'm gone. All three of them."

Alyssa started: "Jacob—"

"I want you to check in on them every day. In person. See if Alyssa needs anything. I need you to support them financially, if necessary."

"Jacob! We have enough—"

"We're broke. You make $50,000 a year and the mortgage is going to eat two-thirds of that."

"Well, Ray can't—"

"I can," said Ray. "I will do my best."

"Ray, you don't have to," said Alyssa.

"I am politely telling you to shut up," said Ray.

"The last thing I need to worry about while I'm in prison is that my family is cared for," said Jacob. "I'm going to get out and my daughters will be three years older. I will have missed three years of their lives. And Alyssa is going to have the weight of the world on her shoulders. I'd be surprised if she's even around in three years."

"Jacob—"

"We have it all under control." Ray reached out and touched Jacob's shoulder. "*Trust me.* You don't have to worry about a thing."

It was obvious that Jacob was holding back tears. "Thank you," he said.

"Besides," Ray said, "I heard it's beautiful in West Virginia this time of year."

Jacob pulled himself together and laughed. "Well, I'm not going to see much of it."

"I bet you're going to lose some weight."

"Fuck," Jacob said, "I've already lost thirty pounds since this all started."

"No person should have to go through what you've gone through," said Alyssa. "You're a good person."

"If you can't do the time, don't do the crime, right? I made a mistake. Though the punishment does seem disproportionate."

"I've read a lot of stuff that says that insider trading should be legal. That it shouldn't even be a crime," Ray said.

"Trust me, I've read a lot about it," said Jacob. "It's about the misappropriation of information. It's a crime."

"You got more time than Martha Stewart," said Alyssa.

"Big difference. Martha Stewart went to jail for lying to investigators, not insider trading."

Alyssa continued, "Well, if Martha Stewart can make it through this, so can you. She's had a pretty great life. You're forty-one years old. Lots of time left to do great things. Nobody will remember this in twenty years."

"I can't even think about where I'm going to be in twenty years. I can't think past two days from now."

"I heard if you just act crazy then everyone else will leave you alone," said Ray, grinning.

"I've heard everything. And yes, I've heard the dropping the soap jokes. I don't think this is going to be like Shawshank. It's probably just going to be really fucking boring. Just take care of my girls, will you?"

"I got this. And so do you."

———

On the cold winter morning of Wednesday, March 6, Alyssa drove Jacob to the prison in West Virginia. She would later tell Ray that it was the scariest place she'd ever been, and that when she and Jacob made eye contact for the last time, he did not look scared.

Alyssa managed to get the entire week off of work to deal with her husband's imprisonment. The university was very sympathetic, and in any case she had banked a month each of vacation time and sick time. Alyssa had been hiring babysitters to fill in during the entire legal process. They, too, were sympathetic, and worked for little or no money. It was understood that Ray, while supportive, was not in possession of the parenting skills to look after the girls for even a couple of hours. His own marriage had been childless—he simply had no experience with it.

Alyssa returned from West Virginia late that evening, paid the babysitter half of what she was entitled, put the girls to bed, and settled into the quiet house. She observed the family photos on the mantle, with Jacob and Alyssa and the two girls skiing, fishing, and camping. They were all smiling—their happiest moments. There would be no such moments for the next three years. And even when Jacob returned, it would be different—he would be a changed man, exorcised of his innocence. She got up, poured herself a glass of wine, and returned to the couch. She turned on the TV, and lingered on *My 600-Lb Life*. She thought that she should have some perspective—these people had real problems.

She had been home a grand total of three hours and was already lonely. She could almost feel Jacob's presence next to her on the couch. He'd be sitting cross-legged, his laptop on his knees, researching baseball statistics or sending emails, balancing a plastic cup of flavored water on the cushion. Jacob and Alyssa never spoke much in the evenings, but at eleven, when it was time for bed, Alyssa would brush her teeth, and Jacob would arrange the weighted blanket on the bed. There hadn't been much in the way of sex for the last few years, but every night they would cuddle. Alyssa would feel Jacob's breath against her ear, and after a few minutes he would be snoring softly, twitching. He always fell asleep first. It was his rhythmic deep breaths that eventually put her to sleep.

Alyssa's phone buzzed.

Ray.

> How'd it go?

Ray had always been a night owl, catching the late edition of *SportsCenter* on ESPN. Jacob would wake up in the morning to find texts from Ray.

> Awful. He's at the worst place in the world.

> He'll be fine.

> He's in there with a bunch of criminals

Criminals aren't necessarily bad people

> No?

No. They're just people who broke the law. It doesn't make them bad people.

Jacob's not a bad person.

Alyssa thought about this. What if all those men in the prison were just like Jacob—good people that simply made a mistake?

> I'm glad you texted.

Get some sleep tonight.

> Jacob won't be sleeping.

He would want you to. Now go the fuck to sleep.

:)

Alyssa downed the rest of the wine and headed upstairs to the bedroom, changed into her pajamas, and slid under the covers. They hadn't replaced the mattress since they got married, and it had a large depression in the middle like a crater that the two of them would slide into in the middle of the night, where they would sleep piled on top of each other. A solitary car drove by, and the headlights shone through the window. It was a bright night—a waning gibbous moon. After an hour of tossing and turning, Alyssa got up, went to the bathroom, opened the drawer, and took out a bottle of melatonin. Jacob needed it to get to sleep; Alyssa swore she would never use it. She placed two tablets on her tongue, got in bed, and let them dissolve. She suddenly realized that Jacob wouldn't have his melatonin in prison—he wouldn't sleep for days.

She tried to cry, but couldn't. There had been a lot of crying in the last year—her tears had run dry. Her sobs turned into a soft moan. Face down in the pillow, she breathed her own breath until complete emotional exhaustion took her away to sleep.

———————

Ray decided to drive to Yankee Stadium. He could have taken New Jersey Transit, but would have had to switch to the subway, scratch his way over to the East Side, and take the 4 train up to the Bronx, all with two kids in tow. It was easier to just take the car. It was a Saturday afternoon game, one o'clock start. Between traffic on the bridge, and parking, Ray thought it best if they left Alyssa's house at 10 a.m. If things went smoothly, they might even get a taste of batting practice.

Ray pulled into Alyssa's driveway at 9:45. He honked the horn. He saw Alyssa in the living room window, giving him the *what the fuck?* hand gesture and pointing at her watch. Ray was early—he was early for everything. Ray showed up to his wedding five hours early, sitting on the steps of the church for hours before anyone showed up.

Ray unbuckled his seat belt, opened the door, and walked up to the front door of the house, figuring he would help Alyssa and the girls get organized. As he was about to reach for the doorknob, the door abruptly opened, revealing Alyssa in Jacob's enormous Yankees jacket.

"I like the team spirit," he said.

Alyssa regarded him. "You're wearing short sleeves? Aren't you going to be cold?"

"Eh. It'll be in the sixties."

The two girls swarmed out of the house and jumped in the back of Ray's car, each carrying a naked Barbie doll. Ray knew the game would be wasted on them, but he also knew that they were capable of sitting still for a few hours. As much as Ray wanted to get Alyssa out of the house, he also wanted to watch the game—an early season matchup with the Red Sox. Ray hoped the girls would stay put for the duration of the game. They had their dolls; Alyssa would probably get bored first. Ray's plan was to keep feeding her beer.

Ray pulled out of their neighborhood and navigated towards the highway.

"You hear from Jacob?" he asked.

"You know, you ask me that every time we talk, and you also know I would tell you the moment I heard from him."

"So did you hear from him?"

"I got a letter yesterday." She reached into her purse and pulled out a small slip of paper.

> Alyssa, just wanted to let you know that I'm fine. I'm not being mistreated, and I haven't made enemies with the guards or the prisoners. They have me working in the library. Just like *Shawshank*. I'll try to write to you next week. *Jacob*.

"See," Ray said, "he still has his sense of humor! It's still in there, somewhere."

"He wrote five sentences," Alyssa said. "Five. What the hell is he so busy doing?"

"Maybe he's not quite sure what he's allowed to write in letters yet. You know the guards have to be reading them. Maybe he's just feeling it out."

"He seems to be having fun."

"I doubt that. When can you visit him?"

"June. Still two months away."

"Well, let me know if you need a ride to West Virginia."

"*Girls!* Caroline! Thea! Keep it down back there," yelled Alyssa. They were prattling away with their toys and had gotten carried away. "No, I think I can manage. Although—he might want to see you, too. But I don't know if it's just family that's allowed. I'll get back to you."

"No problemo, señorita. You get that a lot? People thinking you're Spanish?"

"Not really. People know Kim Kardashian, so they know what Armenians look like now."

"Well, you're better-looking than Kim Kardashian. She has an enormous ass."

"Are we really having a conversation about my ass?"

Ray laughed along with Alyssa. "When you put it that way..."

"Hey ding-dong," Alyssa said, "you're going to miss the exit."

"Oh shit. Thanks."

Ray found his way to the Yankee Stadium parking lot through a circuitous series of off-ramps, rolled up to the booth, paid $25 for parking, and promptly found a spot in section F4. He got out of the car, and took a picture of the F4 sign, as well as the cars on either side of him. Alyssa watched in amazement.

"Are you always this anal-retentive?"

"I have a black SUV. Look around. There's about three thousand black SUVs in this parking lot."

"No judgment here, keep doing what you're doing."

Ray looked at the tickets. Section 430, row 32. Nosebleed seats in the third deck in left field. They almost ran out of numbers. They went to the outfield gate and through the metal detectors, which Ray set off with his business card holder. It was 12:10 p.m. They bought hot dogs and sodas and Cracker Jack and candy and took their seats up in the sky. Between the tickets and the food, Ray was already into this for $400. But there was nothing else he would have rather spent his money on.

"Gerrit Cole is pitching today," Ray said.

"So that's why you wanted to come to this game?"

"No, it just worked out that way. But we are in for a treat."

"Are we going to talk, or are you just going to have your nose in the game the whole time?"

"You sound like my ex-wife. Few women can truly appreciate a man's passion for Major League Baseball."

Alyssa rolled her eyes. "What do you think Jacob would be doing if he were here?"

"He'd probably be three beers deep before the national anthem and hatching a plot to assassinate Cashman."

Alyssa laughed. "I hope he gets to watch baseball in prison."

Ray paused, and sighed. "Me too." Then he added, whispering, "How are the girls holding up?"

"The day he left for prison was terrible. So much crying. They seem to have fallen into a routine, though. I don't want to say they've *forgotten* about him, but they've stopped asking when he's coming home every fifteen minutes."

Ray looked at Alyssa, with her black ponytail sticking out the back of her Yankees hat. "It's going to be okay."

"Sometimes I think you're just telling yourself that."

"I am. Say it enough times, and it's true."

———

Ray picked up Alyssa at 4 a.m. to make the drive to see Jacob at Halverson. Visiting time was 10 a.m. This was Ray's first time in West Virginia. Once he experienced the geography, he understood its essence. People would live in their hollow and just never leave, or go to the next hollow over. He had also heard that flat land was valuable in West Virginia—houses on level ground would trade at a premium. The highway was covered in dense fog, which began to lift as the morning progressed. Ray fiddled with the defroster in his Toyota Camry, unable to find a balance between clearing the windshield and heating up the car to uncomfortable levels.

Alyssa half-expected to see Jason gaunt, emaciated, and clearly showing signs of abuse. She had been getting letters from him over the last two months—a handful—each one about five or six sentences, not giving a lot of detail on what he was up to. He never mentioned his daughters in the letters, not once. Ray assured her that this was probably a result of some dynamic at the prison where prisoners were careful not to reveal anything about family members in case of, you know. Just to be safe. In one letter, Jacob mentioned that he could really go for a Diet Coke. There were no aluminum cans allowed in the prison.

Ray and Alyssa hardly spoke in the car. It was understood that there was to be no talking while it was dark. Besides, they had been through it all before. The girls were asleep on the back seat. Alyssa would roust them when they got to the prison, but by this time Daddy seemed a distant memory to them. It had been three months. Eventually, Thea stirred.

"Mommy?"

Alyssa turned around. "Yes, dear?"

"Are we almost there?"

"We're almost there, honey.

The sun was up, and the kids were awake. It was time to talk.

"How have you been paying all these babysitters?" Ray asked.

"They don't even charge me anymore. They're like family."

"Yeah, but—how are you getting by?"

"We're managing."

"Are you in debt?"

"Ray."

"This is something Jacob explicitly asked me to do. How much debt do you have?"

"Forty thousand. All credit cards."

"So what was your plan, just keep racking up credit card debt until Jacob got out of prison?"

"Ray, I don't fucking—" Alyssa stopped herself, looked at the girls, lowered her voice, and continued. "I don't want to talk about it."

"I make two hundred grand a year and all I spend money on is pizza and beer. When we get home, I'm writing you a check, and I'm marching you down to the bank to deposit it."

"For Chrissakes, Ray."

"You know I'm right."

Alyssa looked out the window. Ray knew her well enough by now to know that this was the end of the conversation.

"It's about ten minutes up here on the left," Ray said.

They had been driving through a heavily wooded area when a clearing suddenly opened ahead of them, revealing a low-slung white building with machicolations for windows. There was a chain-link fence surrounding it—Ray noticed that it did not have barbed wire. Ray thought that even if you did escape, you could run miles in any direction before hitting anything resembling civilization. Ray pulled up to the front gate and stated his intentions. A humorless guard with a Federal Bureau of Prisons patch on his shoulder waved them through to the visitors' parking lot. Ray pulled the car around the side of the building, a few hundred yards away, and brought it to a stop in a parking spot marked VISITORS ONLY.

"Ten minutes early. Pretty good timing," Ray said.

Alyssa was silent.

"You ready?"

Alyssa said nothing.

They both sat in silence.

"Come on, you better get moving. Girls, you ready to see Daddy?"

"Daddy!"

"I can't do this," said Alyssa.

"Yes, you can. Get your ass out of the car."

Abruptly, Alyssa pulled the door handle, kicked the door

open, got out, and slammed it shut, shaking the whole car. She collected her children out of the back seat, and the three of them walked towards the entrance of the prison.

Ray futzed with his phone while they were inside. First, checking his bank account balances, making sure he had enough saved up to give $40,000 to Alyssa. Then, to Facebook, where he was served ads for T-shirts for fat guys. Then, to Instagram, scrolling through a series of models. Then, to Twitter, where people were arguing about transgender issues. Then, to The Weather Channel app, where he saw that the ride home would be hot and sunny. Then, to his email, which had been curiously silent over the weekend. Ray looked up at the clock on the dashboard of his car. Thirty minutes had passed. He decided to get out of the car and get some fresh air; he was wearing shorts and his legs were sticking to the seat.

Ray opened the door and stood up outside, stretching his arms above his head. Suddenly, he saw Alyssa and the girls leaving the prison, walking towards him. They were walking fast. Alyssa was dragging the girls by their arms.

She crashed into Ray, embracing him, squeezing the life out of him. Tears were streaming down her face.

"Take me home."

"What happened?"

"I can't do this for three years."

"What—"

"Get in in the car.

Ray slammed the car in reverse. "You want to tell me what happened?"

Alyssa was nearly hysterical. "He had no facial expressions. He didn't smile or laugh at all. He didn't even seem happy to see us. Just nothing."

"What did he say?"

"Just the same stuff he's been putting in his letters. Just nothing."

"How did he look?"

"Physically, fine. He looks the same. Maybe even in better

shape. But he's different. He'll never be the same again."

She added: "I don't want to come back."

Ray opted not to argue with Alyssa at this particular moment. He would strike when the iron was cold. He would wait a few weeks from now to bring it up again, after she calmed down. She would see that it was unrealistic to let Jacob mold away in prison for three years with no visitors. But not in this moment, with her still sobbing in the passenger seat.

———————

"Acey-deucey," said Ray.

Ray took his one and his two, and then sized up the board, trying to figure out what doubles he would take. He could take double sixes, but if he took double fives, he could hit two of Alyssa's pieces, leaving them stranded on the bar.

"You just rolled an acey-deucey, a double sixes, and another acey-deucey. What the hell am I supposed to do?" asked Alyssa.

"On the comeback trail. You can do it."

But it was not to be. Out of the five games of acey-deucey they played, Ray won all five. "I guess I'm not very good at this game," said Alyssa.

"I just got good rolls."

"You *always* get good rolls."

"I'm just a lucky guy."

"What makes you so lucky, Mr. Weathers?"

"I have you."

Alyssa looked at him, darkly.

"I mean, I have you, you have this house, we have each other—you know what I mean."

"I don't think we're very lucky, for reasons that should be obvious."

"It's all a matter of perspective. You have your house. You have your daughters. You have your job. You're playing backgammon at 11 p.m. on a Tuesday with your drunk divorced neighbor. That seems pretty lucky to me."

"You are such an annoying fucking optimist."

"It works for me. Maybe you should be a blonde. Kim Kardashian went blonde, you know. It looks great on her."

Alyssa picked up the doubling cube and threw it at him. It hit him squarely in his right eye.

"Fuck! You hit me in the eye! I'm calling the police. You can both be in jail."

"Such a baby. Let me look at that." Alyssa stood up, held Ray's head back, and examined his eye. "Looks fine to me. I'm going into the kitchen, you want anything to drink?"

"I'll have some of your wine."

"We're not out of Miller Lite."

"Never mind, I'll get it."

Ray followed Alyssa into her closed kitchen, an unwelcome feature of the 1960s-era home. It was small and cramped. Ray camped out against the kitchen counter and watched Alyssa fix him a drink.

"Yikes. I'm a little tipsy," she said.

"You're five-foot-four and weigh 115 pounds, and you had four glasses of wine. Do the math."

As Alyssa closed the refrigerator door, Ray figured it was as good a time as any. "When are you going to go back and see Jacob?"

"I don't—"

"Alyssa."

"Not here, not now, I don't want to think about it, I don't want to talk about it. I just want to be present, to be here, and enjoy this moment." She took two steps toward him and placed her head on his chest.

Ray froze, as if trying not to frighten off a feral cat. "Just give it time. Things will get back to normal."

"This *is* normal," Alyssa said, looking up at him. And looking up, she kissed him.

Ray kissed her back.

THE CRASH

———————————

THE National Mall, the Lincoln Memorial, and the Washington Monument. All were visible from the top of the Kimpton rooftop bar in Washington, D.C., on an unseasonably warm night in April, which had evolved into a sneak preview of May. Soon, the bugs would be out, and the dense summer air would descend upon the city. But not today. Today, the sky was filled with possibilities, in a universe of things that could go right. The stars were filled with money. For now, Andrew was holding a Maker's and Ginger, the condensation dripping off the glass, and experiencing an uncommon moment of peace. This was the beginning of the beginning; he could feel it. The Cialis was in his pocket, in a plastic bag.

Hector came up from behind and put his hand on Andrew's right shoulder. "We did it, buddy," he said, raising his glass to the sky. Hector was a less-ambitious employee of Andrew's at his real estate firm. He was five minutes late to everything, so unusually punctual in his tardiness that Andrew wondered if the time on his phone was simply incorrect.

Andrew turned to him and clinked his glass against Hector's. "Yes, we did."

"You ever think you would be doing $100 million deals at age thirty-four?" Hector asked, taking a sip.

Andrew grabbed Hector's nipple through his shirt, and twisted. "I always told you I was going to be a billionaire someday, dummy."

Hector swatted Andrew's hand away as if he were a team handball goalie. "Yes, you did—and you are well on your way."

"Honest opinion—do you think we paid too much?"

"Honest answer—absolutely not. It's a totally reasonable cap rate given the current environment. I know you're a value guy, but this is 2021—there are no deals to be had. If you want a good property, you have to pay up."

"Well," Andrew said, "it doesn't really matter what we paid for it, because we own it now."

"How does it feel to be a landlord to 350 people?"

"They're the unluckiest people in the world," Andrew said. "Those stimulus checks are free cash flow to Andrew."

"Any second thoughts?"

"The only way a $100 million apartment complex in Chevy Chase, Maryland, goes tits up is if the federal government suddenly stops spending money. And I don't see Rand Paul getting elected any time soon. The government doesn't have economic cycles. This is about as low-risk as a funeral plot. I do lose sleep, but not over this."

"I admire your conviction."

"Want to get out of here? Go celebrate?"

"We *are* celebrating," Hector said.

"You're such a tool. I'm going to the Mpire."

Hector took a long draw from his drink and declared: "Only degenerates go to strip clubs alone."

Andrew removed the plastic bag from his right front pocket, opened it, tossed the Cialis in his mouth, and washed it down with the balance of his Maker's and Ginger.

"I have not yet begun to defile myself. Besides, I'm like the mayor in that place. You should come along. I'll make sure they treat you like a king."

"You're a true gentleman. I just have a big day tomorrow, doing all the grunt work on this deal you put together, cleaning up the mess. I don't want to take an Uber home at four and pass out on my front steps in my own puke."

"More boobs for me." Andrew clanked his empty glass on the bar and headed downstairs to the sidewalk, thinking he should click his heels together like some 1930s movie star.

It was only a four-block walk to Mpire. Strip clubs had been decreasing in popularity for a decade, but in Washington, D.C., they were thriving thanks to lawmakers and their predilection for extramarital sex. Congressmen of all ages (and their aides) get lonely in their pieds-a-terre when away from their districts and their families. Drugs were also widely available. From the outside looking in, one would never know that D.C. was one of the biggest party towns in the country. Nobody was worried about getting caught or having their picture splashed in the paper—the strippers and hookers were a vault of secrets, because it was bad for business if they weren't. They might as well have had security clearances. Some of them were probably spies.

Andrew didn't see much wrong with his strip club habit. *Good, clean fun*, he thought. He wasn't one of these guys who would wiggle off their wedding ring and put it in their pocket before going inside. He wore it proudly. Besides, he was less likely to lose it if it was on his finger. It wasn't as if the strippers had an aversion to giving lap dances to married guys. Andrew didn't consider it cheating either—just a hobby. It didn't detract from his sex life with Oksana, he thought; if anything, it probably enhanced it. To him, the idea of having an actual affair, with the clandestine text messages and love notes and afternoon hotel rooms, was much worse than going to a strip club. That would be an emotional betrayal. He wasn't going to marry a stripper, but by now he regarded many of them as his friends.

Andrew approached the building, covered in pink and purple lights, paid the $20 cover, walked inside, and was immediately met with the sight of at least a dozen women in various stages of undress. Some on stage, some giving lap dances, and others hanging around, talking, and eyeballing the customers. It was an enormous playground for men. Andrew didn't immediately spy any politicians he recognized, though they were undoubtedly here. There were two DJs who worked at the strip club, with different tastes in music. Andrew knew instantly that DJ Depp was playing, given his affinity for 1980s hair metal. Poison, Mötley Crüe, and Whitesnake gave the club a trashy vibe; Andrew disapproved. It attracted all the riffraff and tourists. And on the club's aging sound system it sounded like a 17-car pileup. Andrew recognized the dancer on stage as Savannah, swinging around the pole wearing only platform heels. He had spent a night in a VIP room with her, months ago, but found her to be lacking energy, and not a very good conversationalist. Andrew felt a tap on the shoulder and turned to find his favorite dancer, Raven, standing behind him, smiling, wearing a black negligée.

"You were here just last week!" said Raven.

"Hey, Raven. Wanna go somewhere?"

"Jesus. You in a hurry? We have all night. This club is open until three."

"The whole point of this place is to dispense with the foreplay."

"You're lucky you're so good-looking or I would slap the shit out of you right now."

Andrew smiled.

"I'm picking up some vibes," Raven said. "Is this a special occasion?"

"I closed a big deal today," said Andrew proudly, as if he were telling his mother.

Raven hugged him—Andrew felt her tiny breasts against his chest. "That's *amazing*. I'm so proud of you."

"So are we going to do this? Enough chit-chat."

"So impatient. Okay, let's go." Raven took his hand and led him to the VIP area, which was guarded by a truly enormous bouncer, who must have subsisted on a diet of ribeye steak and creatine, wearing a black shirt and blue tie, with rings on both his index and pinky fingers. Andrew took out six $100 bills, handed them to him, and then deftly handed him a seventh, as sort of a tip in advance—and a bribe to keep him from checking on them, catching them *in flagrante delicto*. The bouncer held out a clipboard on which Andrew was expected to sign his name, an odd security measure—as was customary, he always signed it "Marty Lipschitz," with Raven hanging off his arm.

Raven led him down the hall and into the VIP room, which had a couch on one end and a large TV on the other, in case you wanted to watch ESPN while getting your dick sucked. He couldn't imagine what the carpet looked like in the daytime. She promptly jumped on his lap and bounced up and down.

"What are we going to do tonight, big boy? Cocaine?"

Andrew shook his head. "Not tonight, I have to get some sleep." He'd gotten only a few hours in the last three days.

"You mind if I do it?"

Andrew shook his head again.

Raven reached into her purse and withdrew a small plastic bag filled with white powder. She emptied the contents of it on her index finger, stuck it up her nose, and sniffed.

"You sure you don't want any—"

"Christ. Okay." He sniffed it off her finger and felt his senses awaken. The dark room suddenly became brighter—and Raven looked even hotter.

Raven felt him tumescing into a hard log against her leg. "You don't need much encouragement, honey." She promptly began to rub it through his slacks, watching for a change in his facial expression.

Andrew gently launched her off his lap, unzipped his pants,

and presented himself to her as she undressed, wanging it around. He had always wanted to ask this:

"Do you think it's big?"

"It's perfect!"

Andrew frowned.

"Same thing as usual, honey? Hands only?"

Andrew nodded. It was an inch away from her nose. Andrew's philosophy had always been that handjobs weren't cheating. For all his carousing, he had never had actual intercourse out of respect for Oksana. Or even oral sex. But he had had dozens, if not hundreds, of handjobs.

After it was finished, Raven wiped her hand on the carpet.

"I gotta go," said Andrew.

"The fuck? You have like twenty minutes left. Don't you want to sit here and chat with your baby?"

"Sorry Raven, I haven't slept in days, I gotta go home and get in bed. It was *great* to see you. We'll spend more time together next time. I promise." He gave her a quick hug, abandoning her in the VIP room with his discharge, and headed out the front door of the club into the crisp air.

Fuck, he thought to himself. *I shouldn't have done that cocaine. Now I'll never get to sleep.* Oksana had been on him about his meds, his lithium and his risperidone that he was supposed to take each evening. Andrew had been surreptitiously taking pills out of the bottles and flushing them down the toilet, in case she was counting. He knew what would happen if he took them— he would be a zombie. He *liked* the way he felt off the meds. He had just closed a $100 million deal. He could perform at a high level off the medication—he was a fucking superstar. He was the king of Washington, D.C. real estate. He knew that he was destined for success, that one day he would be a billionaire. None of this would happen if he took those pills.

If only I could get to sleep...

Andrew found his car, a Mercedes, in the parking garage,

and rolled it out the exit. At this time of night, there would be no traffic, and he would make it back to Alexandria in fifteen minutes. Oksana would be asleep—hopefully. If she wasn't, there would be a fight. *Why are you out so late? What the hell are you doing?* Andrew really didn't want to get into an argument at two in the morning, not today, not after he closed the biggest deal of his life. With any luck, she'd be in bed, snoring softly, and he'd sneak under the covers, lying still like a wooden plank, staring at the ceiling, his mind racing. At four in the morning he'd capitulate, give up on trying to sleep, head into his home office, get on the computer, and start doing work. At five, he'd get bored, start surfing porn, and would masturbate. Andrew would be in the shower at six when Oksana woke up. He hoped she wouldn't know that he'd been up all night, but she'd know.

Eight hours later, she knew.

"You're not taking your medication again," she said, in her thick Russian accent.

"Yes I am."

"Andrew, that's such *boolshit*. When you take your meds, you sleep eight hours a night. I know when you've been off your meds."

"I'm taking a shower," he said, waving her away.

"*You're fucking bipolar*, Andrew. Do you remember what happened in 2019? When you crashed and couldn't get off the couch for a month? When I found you googling ways to hang yourself?"

"It's not going to happen."

"It's absolutely going to happen."

"I have it under control."

"You have *no-thing* under control," she said, her English failing her a bit.

Andrew hopped out of the shower, sopping wet, and pointed

a finger at Oksana. "I closed a $100 million deal yesterday. I can't do that on the meds. I can't *think* on the meds. I can't get a hard-on on the meds. If I take the meds, I can't work. Let me put this in terms you can understand. No house. No vacations. No fancy clothes. No sex. It's over."

"And what happens if you kill yourself?"

"This conversation is over."

"Huh?"

"Over."

Oksana picked up Andrew's towel and threw it on the floor for effect, and left the bathroom.

Andrew wondered why Oksana couldn't just be happy for him, why everything had to be a fight. Perhaps it was because she refused to recognize his brilliance. Perhaps she was trying to bring him down. He had made more money by age thirty-four than most people make in a lifetime. He didn't much like the idea that he had a spouse who was trying to undermine him. On their first date, at the steakhouse in New York, he had held her hand and made her promise that they would be a team.

They met seven years ago at Marquee in New York when Andrew, then twenty-seven, was in his models-and-bottles phase, finishing up a short but profitable career on Wall Street. Oksana was just twenty, having come from Russia on a work visa, and was working as a bottle girl at the club. She wasn't looking for a husband, but stumbled into one in the form of Andrew. He had invited her to sit next to him on her couch, and spent the next three hours interrogating her on her life, where she was from, her family, her education. She couldn't tell how much of it he was getting over the loud music. He called her five days later and invited her to dinner at Del Frisco's, which served them more food than she had eaten in two weeks. Before long, she had moved into his apartment in Tribeca. At the time, she had about 80,000 followers on Instagram, and thought that Andrew might discourage her from posting her coquettish pictures, sometimes in lingerie. Andrew had actually bought 10,000 Instagram followers for himself and encouraged her to keep up her social media presence. Eventually, he helped take the pictures. Everyone knew that Andrew liked being associated with a Russian model. He convinced her to marry him, at city hall, with nobody in attendance, since his family disapproved of his Bond Girl girlfriend. Oksana converted her Instagram into a joint account, "okasanaandandrew," and the two of them traveled the world, posing for photographs, him in a suit, and her in a cocktail dress—in Tokyo, Dubai, and Milan. Oksana, with her cat eyes and angular face, could have graced the pages of *Vogue*—and Andrew went around telling anyone who would listen that he was going to be a billionaire. He found that Wall Street was the place to become a millionaire, not a billionaire, and switched to a career in real estate. In five years, he was already wildly successful, with an enormous portfolio consisting of both residential and commercial properties.

Andrew quickly dressed, yanking on his underwear and socks, and strode out into the living room to continue the argument.

"Hey."

"What?"

"I closed a huge deal last night. There was a party. This could be the beginning of something really big. Why is it that everyone thinks I'm a hero except for you?"

Oksana thought about this. "I know what you think. You think I married you for your money. But that's actually not true."

"No?"

"I married you because you light up the world. Because you're the sun, and when you shine on people, they feel your warmth. Everybody likes you. But you're sick."

"I'm not sick."

"You are, and I would rather have better Andrew than rich Andrew."

"You just want me to fail," Andrew said, taking steps toward her.

"That's not true at all."

"You know what kind of person roots for people to fail? A bad person. That's what you are."

"No," Oksana said, crying.

Andrew, smelling blood, stepped closer: "You're a fucking *awful* person. *And* you're ungrateful." Andrew looked at her— she was falling to pieces. "I'm going to work."

Andrew slammed the door to the garage behind him. *Fuck*, he thought. *Fuck*, because she couldn't see how great he was, how magnanimous, how generous, and *fuck*, because he loved her, and he knew he had hurt her like he never had before. *Fuck*, also, because the good feelings of closing the deal had all but evaporated—she had ruined it. She had ruined everything. So *fuck* her for that, as well.

As he pulled out onto the main road, thinking of all these fucks, another car struck the driver's side of his car at sixty miles per hour, crushing him, and killing him instantly.

———

Oksana had never been overly concerned about Andrew's carousing—when he was diagnosed as bipolar five years ago, she knew it was a symptom of his sickness, his mania, his hypersexuality. She knew if she could get him to take his meds, the wolfish behavior would stop, and he would be a *normal* husband—whatever that meant. But this was new—he had never been overtly *mean* to her. He'd hurt her in myriad ways, coming home with lipstick on his neck and glitter on his pants—she knew these things—but just a few minutes ago, he had tried to destroy her.

He will not succeed, she thought.

She started to pack. She fished her large pink suitcase out of storage, set it on the bed, and stuffed it with underwear, shirts, pants—all while crying, leaving stains of tears on her clothes.

He's the bad person, she thought. *Not me.* She had been there for him when he ended up in the psychiatric ward in 2016—which ended his Wall Street career. She visited him every day, and talked to the doctors about his diagnosis. He had been a model patient, they said, affable, charming, winning the doctors over with his big personality. They also told her that if Andrew failed to take his medication, he would one day think about suicide again—and possibly follow through with it. She had cared for him these last five years. She'd known instantly when he'd stopped taking his meds. He'd become moody, irritable. He'd disappear into his office for hours on end. He'd be out all night—sometimes not coming home at all. She knew he could crash at any moment. And she began to despise him for his disease, because they could never have a normal life.

Oksana was carrying her suitcase into the living room when the phone rang. She answered. It began: "This is the Alexandria Police Department..."

She dropped the suitcase.

———————

Oksana held the phone for a moment, thinking.

She tapped on the Instagram app and found her favorite picture of Andrew from her collection—a photo of him seated at Del Frisco's on their first date, wearing a suit, with his arm extended across the table, revealing his favorite Rolex. She wrote in the caption:

> I am sorry to report that my love, my companion, Andrew was struck by a drunk driver and killed this morning not far from our house. He did not suffer. He will be greatly missed by his family and friends. I will love you forever—Oksana

She posted it, and in a second it was received by her 200,000 followers.

The comments came pouring in—mostly variations of "I'm sorry for your loss." Some asked if it was a joke. Others asked her out on dates. Her phone wouldn't stop vibrating for fifteen minutes.

Abruptly, the phone rang, from a number she did not recognize.

"Hello?"

"This is Hector. Is it true?"

"Yes, it is true."

"When did you find out?"

"About a half an hour ago."

"And you put it on... *Instagram*? Didn't you want to tell Andrew's family first?"

Oksana stopped, and started to cry again. "I—I didn't think."

"Never mind. I was with him last night. Did he make it home okay?"

"Yes, I don't know what time he came home, but he came home last night."

"We're here for you if you need anything. We'll take care of you."

Oksana hung up. She felt a pit growing in her stomach, a sensation of dread spreading through her abdomen and into her crotch. She wasn't too sure that posting Andrew's death on Instagram was such a good idea. Nothing could be done about it now. She was imagining the angry phone calls she would get from her mother-in-law, who took a dim view of Oksana and her social media presence. She put the still-vibrating phone down on the counter, walked away, then walked back and shut it down.

In spite of being part of the New York club scene for a number of years, Oksana rarely drank. But she walked over to Andrew's liquor cabinet, took out his favorite scotch, the Laphroaig 10 year, and poured herself an exceptionally large glass, almost up to the rim. *This tastes like paint thinner*, she thought, wondering why Andrew had liked the stuff. But she resolved to drink the whole thing, as sort of a tribute.

Her head swirled with all the things she had to do. She would have to identify the body—later, she thought. There would be funeral arrangements. Andrew had said three years ago that he wanted a specific downtempo DJ set played at his memorial service. She was the beneficiary on all his accounts, she assumed. Andrew told her there was a life-insurance policy—she had no idea how big it was. She would have to take inventory of all his assets and debts. She would have to notify the family, though that was already done. She would have to file taxes—she had never met his accountant.

She took another drink.

Oksana went to Andrew's office and sat down in front of her computer. He kept a list of all his passwords underneath the keyboard. Always paranoid, he had a different, impossibly complex password for every website he visited. She decided to go to his brokerage account to see what was in there, logging into Merrill Lynch with the password "U7s*w^t%." The balance was just over $5 million, far less than she had anticipated. A bolt of anger passed through her as she wondered what he had spent the money on. She looked at the stocks in the portfolio—nearly all of them had six-figure losses. He wasn't a spendthrift, she thought, he was just a terrible investor. She was sure that Andrew's friends and colleagues perceived him as being much, much richer.

She logged into the Prudential website with the password "Y#d(w$m<." She quickly found the life insurance policy, which was worth $3 million—again, smaller than she had anticipated. Andrew had always had a saying for people like this: All hat and no cattle. It was true of him as well.

Her anger rising, she went to the browser history, and found a handful of links to PornHub. She watched the videos—mostly men sitting in cars flashing passersby, or flashing hotel maids. She wondered if the videos were authentic, but concluded they couldn't be, because the women seemed to be willing participants. A flashing fetish was inconsistent with the sex life they had; whatever extracurricular activities he might have had never interfered with his voracious sexual appetite. Given that there were only three or four links, Oksana concluded that he was probably using the private browser mode most of the time and must have forgotten once. There was no other explanation for the hours he spent locked in his office. She had never before checked his computer, out of respect for his privacy.

She went to the Google search history:

> Nationals tickets Sep 13
>
> What is a good gift to give your wife for 7th anniversary
>
> Hotel maid flashing cumshot
>
> Amazon
>
> Amaz
>
> Twi
>
> Mpire hours
>
> 2021 All-Star ballot
>
> Teen flashing

Oksana slowly, deliberately finished the rest of the glass of Laphroaig and walked away from the computer.

———

Andrew's mother called Oksana later that day. She didn't mention the Instagram post, or anything else Oksana had done or hadn't done. It was as if she had expected this outcome, given Andrew's penchant for fast living. She calmly and rationally offered to help plan the memorial service, and to travel down from Pennsylvania to help out around the house. Oksana accepted her offer willingly—she was feeling overwhelmed.

This was the beginning of months of work, trying to untangle Andrew's affairs.

Andrew had had a will written up shortly after they were married. Oksana had been present in the room with the attorney—she would receive substantially all of Andrew's assets, with none going to his parents. He had been an only child, so there were no nieces and nephews to worry about. He had set aside a small amount to his high school and college; for as much of a bastard as he had been, he had always recognized that the quality of his education contributed to his success in life.

Andrew had had a small black filing cabinet in his office. Oddly, he had thought to save every cable and utility bill they had ever received, along with all of his brokerage statements. Oksana opened the filing cabinet, finding it stuffed full of folders. She found the one labeled WILL, but saw another labeled OPEN IN CASE OF EMERGENCY. She took both folders from the filing cabinet and placed them on the desk. She looked at the will; it was as she had expected. She would receive the $5 million from his brokerage account, $3 million from his life insurance policy, and $2.5 million from the sale of the house. She wouldn't have to work, if she didn't want to.

In the other folder, there was a sealed envelope labeled OKSANA. She opened it; there was a letter inside.

Dear Oksana,

If you're reading this, it's because I have probably committed suicide. I know what people will say, that I was selfish, but they don't understand—it is because I was in so much pain, and I had to make it stop. I will love you forever.

Thank you for taking care of me for the last few years. I know it hasn't been easy; I know I haven't always been the best husband. I still remember the first time we met.

You were so beautiful, and I knew I had to have you. You're still beautiful, and I don't deserve you. You have been the kindest, most loving wife that I could ever ask for, and I haven't lived up to your expectations. I'm sorry. You're probably regretting you got mixed up with me in the first place. You should find someone else to marry, someone better than me. A high-school science teacher, or something. Someone boring. Someone who's not bipolar. But I was born like this, and I probably wasn't going to change. I loved you so much, and I will always love you.

By this point you have probably found the Merrill Lynch account and the insurance policy. There's more. Call Rosario Perfetto at Pictet at +41 234 238948 as soon as you finish reading this letter. I have $10 million in 1,000 CHF notes in a safe deposit box in Geneva. That is my gift to you—you will never have to work again. I have spent the last few years living close to death, knowing that it was always around the corner. I knew that someday it would come to this. I wanted to make sure that you were safe and secure for the rest of your life. It was the only way I knew how to repay you for taking care of me.

Life is short, Oksana—I want you to enjoy it without me.

Your love in eternity—

Andrew

It was noon. Oksana had to lie down.

She stripped down to her underwear and climbed into bed, topless, laying on top of the covers, caressing her skin with her fingers. She could feel Andrew's presence next to her. She wondered if he was looking down on her, at this very moment. He had kept so many secrets from her; she had kept nothing from him. *If only she hadn't confronted him, he might still be alive.* He might not have left the house at that very moment and been at that intersection at the precise time of the accident. He might have been there a minute later, and nothing would have happened.

She tried to cry, but couldn't.

200 HOURS

———————

MOZZARELLA sticks? No.
Chicken tenders? No.
Mini-tacos? Maybe.

The Applebee's was on an outparcel of a strip mall adjacent to a nondescript industrial park across the way from the Federal Home Loan Bank of Indianapolis. Michael never had a problem with middlebrow casual dining. Applebee's, in particular, because it was the cheapest of the category. Prior to the great inflation of 2021, you could be in and out for less than $16. Now, it was around $25. Still, it didn't make much sense for Michael to go through the effort of actually preparing a meal in his Extended Stay suite—the bigger concern was the extra calories. He could carpe per diem if he wanted to.

Some say that eating alone is a sign of social isolation. As an introvert, Michael didn't mind. He could always scare someone up from the bank to go out to lunch with, but there would be that interminable awkwardness as to who would pay the bill. As the consultant, it would be expected that Michael would pay, but at $80,000 a year he didn't have much wiggle room to be buying his clients lunch for the duration of his three-month stay.

This was simpler. But he would have to hit the gym in the hotel after work—after three months of burgers and mozzarella sticks, he would be fifteen pounds heavier by the end of his assignment.

"Can I get you something to drink?"

Michael raised his eyes to find a waitress in front of him, in her early twenties, with tanned skin, gold locks of curled hair and sea-green eyes. In the span of a microsecond, he glanced at her small, angular, almost adolescent breasts.

"I'll have an unsweet iced tea with some sweetener on the side."

"Splenda okay?"

"My favorite."

She regarded him suspiciously. "You must be from the South."

"I grew up outside of Atlanta. How did you know? Wait—the tea."

"Yeah. If you hadn't noticed," she said, sweeping her arm in a panorama, "this is Indianapolis, which is considered the *North*. We only have one kind of tea—unsweet."

Michael smiled. "Unsweet it is." The waitress departed, leaving Michael to his thoughts.

Michael spent a moment processing the interaction. The nameless waitress was unusually attractive, in a way that he was unaccustomed to seeing. The women in New Jersey were of Southern Italian descent, with their big hair and big jewelry and big mouths, and Michael thought that if he married one of them, he would be in a noisy marriage with yelling and throwing things and copious amounts of drama. He liked her sassiness, poking fun at him on their first interaction.

"Have you decided? Or do you need more time with the menu?"

Michael paused. "I'll get the garden salad."

"I didn't take you for a salad guy."

"I've eaten burgers three days in a row. I feel like I'm turning into a burger."

"It's your lunch." She turned and walked away, and Michael

craned his neck to watch her backside bouncing among the tables.

She's up on me, Michael thought. He didn't much like the idea of being outsmarted by someone about eight years his junior. She was so socially adept and precocious that Michael thought that she must have been one of the popular kids in school growing up. He imagined her at keg parties, *woo-hooing* and tossing her gold hair around. He imagined her being a platonic friend to boys. He also imagined her being sexually adventurous—she had that *vibe*. He couldn't let this one get away.

She reappeared. "How's the food?"

"Good—but the service is terrible," Michael said, smiling.

Zing. Waitress scrunched up her face and marched off.

Michael strategized how to get her phone number. Should he just ask for it outright? Should he write his own phone number on the receipt? He decided on the latter option—asking for it *out loud* just seemed too forward. But writing his number on the receipt had a much lower chance of success.

The waitress plopped the check down on the table. "So, clearly, you're not from Indiana. What are you doing here?"

Michael dreaded this question. "It's really boring."

"Tell me, it's probably not that boring."

"I'm an IT consultant, and I'm spending the next three months at the Federal Home Loan Bank."

"Doing what?"

"Database stuff."

She laughed. "You're right, that is *really* boring. Also, those guys come in here sometimes, and they're totally square." She brightened her tone, and said: "So I'll be seeing more of you?"

This was a good sign. "As long as you quit making fun of my salads."

"Deal."

Michael looked at the receipt. It read SERVER: CHLOE.

She had put a heart and a smiley face on it in pink ink, but that was pretty commonplace. He wrote on the receipt:

MICHAEL 201 525 0168 CALL ME

And left her a fifty percent tip.

———————

Michael was back in his cubicle at the bank, torturing the database until it confessed.

His phone buzzed.

> Hey it's Chloe

> Hey!

> Want to go out for coffee?

> Does a cat have an ass?

Michael was always proud of this line.

> Great I'll see you at
> Starbucks 2pm tomorrow.
> I'm off work.

Michael paused for a moment, vacillating on whether to "heart" or "thumbs up" her last communication. He settled on the "thumbs up"—a bit too early in the relationship for a Valentine. He would have difficulty concentrating on his database for the rest of the day.

He wondered what she would wear to Starbucks. It was summer, and hot, so maybe a T-shirt and shorts. But maybe she would dress up. Michael had no idea—he had only seen her in the Applebee's uniform. He was unquestionably physically attracted to her. That night, after she waited on him, he lay in bed, thinking about what it might be like to undress her from behind, looking at the tiny hairs on her tanned neck. Or watching her come out of his bathroom, hair wet, wearing only a towel. Or wearing an evening dress and drop earrings like that "jessieann_g" model he followed on Instagram, who lived in Dubai. He thought of these things over and over again, until he drifted off to sleep, underneath the whirring of the ceiling fan.

———————

She was wearing shorts and a T-shirt.

"How's the database?" she asked.

"It's my best friend, next to you. You want coffee?"

"It's ninety degrees."

"Iced coffee?"

"I don't. Starbucks can't throw you out for just sitting here."

"Okay. So I was—"

"How old are you?"

"Um, twenty-eight? How old are you?"

"I'm twenty-one. I'm going into my senior year at Butler."

"Age difference doesn't bother you?"

She laughed. "It's not like you're forty. You have all your hair. You dress very interestingly. You don't seem like a creep."

"Hey, I have to wear this for work."

"Blue shirt and khakis every day?"

"Sometimes I wear white shirts."

"Slow down! This is our first date."

"Boyfriend?" asked Michael, probing.

"Not at the moment. Girlfriend?"

"Her body is decomposing in the trunk of my car," said Michael, grinning.

"Do you love your parents?"

"They're divorced. Good father, crazy mother."

"Me too! My mother is a narcissist. She lies about everything. Are you rich?"

"Funny. I make eighty grand a year."

"Are your parents rich?"

"I had a boring, middle-class upbringing."

"Well, on eighty grand a year, you can afford to take me out to Elmo Steak House. Or we can just watch Netflix at my place."

Michael hardened his expression. "200 hours," he said.

"200 hours what?"

"200 hours until I watch Netflix at your place."

"I don't get it."

Michael began: "I grew up Episcopalian, which isn't even really a religion these days. Anyway, the priest had a more permissive attitude towards premarital sex—he told us that it was acceptable if the couple spent 200 hours together beforehand. In person, or on the phone."

"Are you religious or something?"

"Not especially—I haven't been to church in years—but I thought it was a good guideline, and I've done it ever since."

Chloe was incredulous. "So how many people have made it to 200 hours?"

"None."

Chloe burst out laughing. "So you're a *virgin*?"

"Shhhh. Yes, regrettably."

Chloe sat back in her chair. "Well, this sounds like a challenge. I will be the first person to make it to 200 hours with Michael—what's your last name?"

———————

r/relationships

chloegrace
I (21f) met this cute guy (28m) who says he won't sleep with me until we've spent 200 hours together.

I was waiting tables where I work and I met this guy who's visiting from out of town (cute, but kind of a dork). Had a coffee date and he's hilarious, and so endearing. I invited him over for some "Netflix and chill" and he told me that won't sleep with me until we've spent 200 hours together, either in person or on the phone. I guess a priest told him this was a good idea years ago. I'm basically going to have to spend 20 hours a week with him if we're going to do it before he leaves. He doesn't seem ultra-conservative. I just don't get it. Anyone hear of anything like this before?

sweetpotato
I just googled this, and the internet doesn't know anything about it. I bet he just made it up.

kyliebuzz
Well, look at it this way. He didn't say no.

sbarrrr
It's just delayed gratification. It will be that much better if you wait. I'd see where this goes.

———————

Downtown Indianapolis looked like the set of a Tom Hanks movie circa 1994, one involving burglars and a madcap chase. It wasn't unclean or dangerous, but most of the office workers had fled to the suburbs during the pandemic and had not yet returned, leaving behind the unemployed and the shiftless. Michael parked his car in one of those 24-hour parking lots for $12, and navigated his way over to the restaurant through the use of Google Maps— he was turned around and couldn't tell north-south from east-west.

By the time he had arrived, he was two minutes late. Chloe was standing in the entrance, wearing a purple, hip-hugging dress, with a string of faux pearls, teetering in high heels, which she was clearly unaccustomed to wearing. She smiled, evidently proud of getting all dolled up. Michael, for his part, had taken care to put on a blue blazer over his khakis.

Chloe leaned over and gave him a staccato kiss on the cheek. "That's legal, right?"

"In some jurisdictions," Michael said.

They were led to a luxurious booth made of red leather, surrounded on three sides by the Indy bourgeoise. Everything was made of wood. Chloe set her phone down on the white tablecloth.

"You've never been here before?" she asked.

"No, never."

"We're getting the shrimp cocktail," she said, firmly.

"Shrimp cocktail in Indiana? Sounds like a capital idea."

"Smartass. Wait and see."

The waiter arrived, wearing a steak-stained brown jacket. He looked as if he had taken the same shrimp cocktail order for the last forty years. They splurged, deciding to split a porterhouse, and got a side of asparagus as sort of a carbon credit.

Michael took a bite of the shrimp cocktail.

"What the fuck?" he said, choking. "Is this some kind of a prank?"

Chloe erupted in gales of laughter. "It's made of pure horseradish, dummy. Clears out your sinuses, doesn't it?"

"Holy shit. I can't breathe."

"You'll feel better in ten minutes. Have some water."

"I guess this is where you take all the tourists and out-of-towners."

"We may not have much in this cornfield, but we have Elmo's and shrimp cocktail."

"Better than tipping cows, I guess. I suppose you grew up with this stuff."

"Hey," she said, pointing a finger at him, "what's up with this 200 hours nonsense?"

Michael put down his glass of water, and regarded her without a hint of condescension. "Can I ask you a personal question?"

"Shoot."

"How many people have you slept with?"

Chloe leaned back, letting out a sigh. "That *is* a personal question. Okay. Five."

"And how was it?"

"Well, a few episodes of drunk sex in college at parties, so that wasn't great. I had a couple of boyfriends in high school, and once we did it they told all their friends, like I was some kind of conquest. So, also not great."

"Makes you feel bad, doesn't it?"

"Yeah, kinda."

"If you had waited 200 hours, it wouldn't have felt bad. After 200 hours, we are either going to love each other or we won't. We will know by then. And the decision will be obvious."

"Aren't you curious as to what it's like?"

"You're damn right I'm curious. I think about it constantly. I think about it with you. I sit around and think about all the nasty things we could do to each other." Michael caught himself, and said: "Sorry."

"No, go on, I love it."

"People have cause and effect reversed. They think that if they have sex with someone, they will feel love. But it is actually the other way around. You feel love first, and *then* you have sex with someone."

Chloe began a long, slow clap.

"Is that a sarcastic clap?" asked Michael.

"No," said Chloe, "I actually agree with you. I'll try it. Maybe I'll drop you like third period French right before we get to 200 hours. Then you'll be a *virgin* for three more years."

"Christ, keep it down."

Chloe giggled.

The old waiter brought the check. Michael pulled it across the table, and opened it.

"Are you going to tip him fifty percent?" Chloe asked.

"Of course not. He's a grumpy fuck."

"You only tip twenty-one-year-old girls fifty percent?"

"Yes," Michael said.

Chloe winked at him. "You're honest. You passed the first test."

———————

Michael opted to take Chloe out of town on a weekend trip to Eagle Creek Reservoir. He had googled it, and saw that it had trails, fishing, and other activities, though he didn't plan on doing any fishing or activities. They had a few more coffee dates, requiring Michael to sneak out of work, and three more dinner dates, including one at Applebee's, which Chloe said was on the house. He thought a little time outdoors would do them some good.

When he picked her up in front of her apartment near the university, she hopped in wearing short shorts and a halter top, with no bra.

"Now that's cheating," he said, looking her up and down.

"What are you, the Taliban? I bet you can't make it to 200 hours," she said, laughing.

"I'm an oak. Though I'm enjoying every minute of this."

They pulled into the parking lot of the reservoir, adjacent to the main building, which was from some 1970s architectural style Michael could not place. It was covered with tree detritus and needed a good power-washing. They set out on the first available trail, just to the east of the building, which looped around the southern part of the reservoir. Michael could hear the cicadas buzzing. *What summer sounds like*, he thought.

Chloe took his hand, but did not interlock their fingers.

"Forty-six hours and we haven't run out of things to talk about yet," she said.

"If you run out of things to talk about before 200 hours, it's a pretty good sign that the relationship is not going to work."

"What do you want out of life?" she asked, swinging their arms.

"A family."

"You don't seem like you're in a hurry."

"I'm not taking any shortcuts, if that's what you mean."

"So serious," she said, mocking him. "I want to work in marketing."

"Do you want kids?"

"I haven't decided. Is that okay?"

"That's okay."

"I thought you just said you wanted a family?"

"I want to be happy."

They walked a bit further, past two elderly couples, came upon a wooden bench next to the water, and sat down.

Chloe stared out across the water and said, "What did you think when you first saw me?"

"HOT."

"I liked your sense of humor."

"My cynicism has served me well."

"Why don't you move to Indy? There's nothing keeping you in New Jersey. I'm sure you could find something here. You're not even *from* New Jersey. Could you get a job at the bank?"

"No, it doesn't work like that. Trust me, I've been thinking about it."

"We could move in together. We could get a cat."

"Forty-six hours and you're already talking about moving in together. See how this works?"

"Forty-*seven* hours," she said, and kissed him with her open mouth. They kissed for many minutes, blissfully unaware of their public display of affection and the people who walked by staring at them.

Chloe jumped up and pounded her fists on an imaginary table. "*Grrrrrrr!* I can't *do* this!"

"Yeah, making out definitely makes it tougher."

"200 hours is an *arbitrary* number that some *ding-a-ling* priest made up to fuck with people."

"You gotta trust the process."

"Do you know anyone who has done this successfully?"

"Yes—the priest!"

"Forty-seven hours is good enough. We gave it a try. Let's go fuck."

"Let me ask you a question. How happy are you right now?"

"I'm horny. I could eat you alive."

"Yes, but I bet you're the happiest you've been in your entire life."

Chloe pouted.

"*Trust me*. It will get better, then it will get worse, and then it will get amazing."

"You're a bastard," she uttered, "but I love you."

———————

r/relationships

chloegrace

21f going out with 28m and not having sex.

About a month ago, I posted about this cute guy I met who had this rule about spending 200 hours together before having sex. So we're at hour 90 now, and I have to say, this has been a really good experience. We talk all the time, we're getting to know each other, and I told him the other day that I loved him. After I got over my initial desires, I really see the point of doing this, and it's got me thinking all kinds of crazy things. Like, maybe the sexual revolution wasn't a good thing. I don't know. But this is going great, and I can't wait to get to 200 hours—it's going to be spectacular.

kevin123

Glad that you're doing this. Maybe you'll start a new trend. Just don't build up expectations too much—it might be clumsy and awkward, and a disappointment.

alynaq

This guy is a total weirdo. Seriously. I don't see the point. Have fun, I guess.

83kristi

Are you sure he doesn't go to one of those Army of God megachurches out in Arkansas? You may like him, but this is not a normal guy.

————————

Chloe had developed a bad habit of playing with her phone while she was supposed to be working. She texted Michael throughout the day. Whenever she texted him, he responded within seconds—he was sitting at his desk, poking the database, and always had a moment to pick up the phone and text back. Chloe would sometimes steer the discussion towards sex, and Michael would steer it back, saying that they were just making it harder on themselves.

After the lunchtime rush, Chloe finished cleaning up after her last table, a mother and three children under the age of five. They had left a huge mess, with torn-up napkins and food smashed into the table—and left a $4 tip. Chloe wasn't living in poverty—she had her Applebee's job, along with some freelance photography occasionally, but she was doing less of that now that she was spending all her time with Michael. A $4 tip on a $45 bill was insulting.

She texted Michael:

> 123 hours!

She waited a minute, and there was no response.

> Hey love

Nothing. She tried once more, knowing that he couldn't resist responding to this:

> Netflix tonight? :)

Chloe's entire body tingled with fear. *Did he change his mind? Is he leaving me? Is this all for nothing?* She scrolled through their text messages from the morning—nothing out of the ordinary, just the kissy-poo sweet talk they had been engaging in for the last few weeks.

Maybe he had had to turn his phone off for some reason.

Maybe one of his old 200-hour girlfriends had contacted him, looking to complete the mission.

The restaurant was nearly empty. Chloe darted outside onto the sidewalk and pressed the button to call him, something she had never done in the work day.

Straight to voicemail.

It's nothing, it's nothing, it's nothing.

She called again. Straight to voicemail. She hung up and called a third time, and a fourth time, and a fifth time.

She called him fifteen times.

Chloe stomped back inside, shaking with anger and fear. *How could he do this?* She had been fooled, and she vowed to never let herself be duped again. She began to think of ways to get back at him, but couldn't come up with anything.

Her phone rang. It was Michael.

"Is everything okay?"

"Where *were* you?" asked Chloe, sniffling.

"I was in a meeting. I had to turn my phone off."

"You're *never* in a meeting."

"I know, but today I was. You sound worried. Everything's okay, I swear. I'm not going to leave you."

"I was so worried."

"Let me ask you a question. In seventy-seven hours I get to sleep with the most beautiful girl in the world. What possible motivation would I have to suddenly leave you, after we've been through all this?"

"*Seventy-two* hours. I almost had a heart attack. This counts for five hours. I am not yielding on this."

"Fine, it can be seventy-two hours. Chloe, I love you. I'm not going to abandon you. Now, do you want pizza or Chinese tonight?"

Through her emotions, Chloe managed to laugh. "Chinese. And you're buying. I've been getting terrible tips all day."

"I'll give you a tip. Have faith." Michael paused, and added: "Hang in there. We're almost done."

———————

"You wait until a week before you leave to break out the suit?" Chloe asked.

"It's cooler now. And it's not a great suit. In fact, it's a very cheap suit."

"Still, you look handsome."

"I look like I belong on the witness stand in a carjacking trial."

Chloe laughed. "Well, that too."

For their last official date, Michael and Chloe had chosen Mesh, which was number eight on TripAdvisor's top ten most romantic restaurants in Indianapolis. It was more casual than they had anticipated—Michael in his suit and Chloe in her black cocktail dress were out of place among the golf shirts and pleated pants. After dating Chloe for nearly three months, Michael had burned through quite a bit of the money he had hoped to save on this assignment. By this point, he had nearly finished his work on the database, and was spending his days joking around with some of the analysts and traders at the bank—he had made some friends and planned to keep in touch with them when he went back to New Jersey.

"I'm going to miss you," Chloe said.

"Easy, killer, I'm here until Sunday."

"We have twelve hours to go."

"So I can spend four hours with you on Tuesday, on Wednesday, on Friday, and you know what happens on Saturday."

"That's when you put the wand in the chamber of secrets."

Michael laughed.

"Personal question," said Chloe. "I don't know why I haven't asked you this before. Do you masturbate?"

Michael sighed. "I try not to, but I end up doing it about once every one to two weeks."

"Do you use porn?"

"I don't."

"So what do you think about?"

"I think about what you wore the day I took you to the reservoir."

"You are so incredibly full of shit."

"No, it's true," said Michael. "We had forty-six hours that day. I almost didn't make it. I almost gave up then and there. But I'm glad I didn't."

"So why didn't the other girls make it 200 hours?"

"It wasn't a moral failing on their part. I just think the relationships weren't meant to be, and we figured that out before we got to the end. So we went our separate ways, without all those icky feelings about having had sex and having racked up the body count."

Chloe's voice quivered slightly. "I'm sorry I had sex with those guys. I wish you were my first."

"We can just pretend," Michael said.

They both held back tears.

Their dinner arrived, transported by a tall, rugged young man of Southern European descent. His gaze lingered on Chloe a bit longer than necessary.

"Try not to stare," Michael said.

"Oh—I'm—okay," the waiter said, and hustled away, embarrassed.

Chloe cackled and clapped her hands. "That was *amazing*."

"I don't blame him. I'd stare, too. But he's better looking than me. I need a stick to fight off these swarthy foreigners. Maybe coming here was a mistake."

"I can't believe you're leaving on Sunday," Chloe said, somewhat wistfully.

"I won't be gone for long. Want to hear the good news?"

Chloe's eyebrows went up.

"I'm applying for jobs here. Interestingly, I'm starting to figure out that I was a bit underpaid and I can actually make more money here doing essentially the same thing."

"Oh my God! That's amazing! When would you move?"

"Potentially pretty soon, probably by the end of the year."

"We can move in together."

"Yes."

"We can—"

"Yes. But you need to graduate first."

"Okay."

"It's a brave new world."

———————

Chloe and Michael had long been discussing how they would celebrate the end of their 200 hours. Michael suggested a fancy dinner date, but Chloe said they had too many of those already; she just wanted to come over to his hotel room and do it. So on September 23, 2023, Chloe made the drive to North Indianapolis and wheeled her 2010 Prius into the parking lot of the Extended Stay hotel, parking under a tree. Michael was on the second floor, in room 213. She wore the same T-shirt that she had worn to Starbucks on their first coffee date. She knocked, and Michael answered, wearing a polo shirt and jeans. Chloe went inside—the first time she had been in his room. It was spartan, but comfortable, with a couch, TV, and desk in one room, and a king-size bed in the other. By this point, most of his belongings were packed.

They hugged, and Chloe unceremoniously began to undress. She wriggled out of her T-shirt, revealing a pink lace bra, then wriggled out of that, too. Michael stared for a moment, then reached out to touch them, then hugged her again. "You're shaking," she said, then looked at him. "Don't cry." She led him into the bedroom by his hand, and stretched out on the bed, her arms out, motioning towards him. He undressed quickly, and indulged her. They were naked, lying together on the bed. Michael tried to enter her, with some difficulty. "Not there. *There*," she said, and he was in. Michael's mouth made the shape of an O. He propped himself up on his trembling arms, and it was over as quickly as it began.

He rolled over, and they both stared at the whirring ceiling fan, knowing that this was forever.

HIT AND RUN

ROSS BEATTY forgot his car keys.

He got out of the car, trudged up the front steps, stuck his house key in the door, wiggled, and pushed the door open, feeling the warm, still air inside. He walked across the living room to the kitchen and found his car keys stranded on the counter along with yesterday's unopened mail and a new textbook that he was supposed to have reviewed three weeks ago. He went back out the front door, locked it, turned the doorknob three times, walked back to the car, got inside, and turned on the ignition. The windshield was iced over. Screw it, he would get it with the defrost.

He pulled out of the driveway onto Harland Road, drove past the reservoir and about two dozen houses, and got to Lambert Drive when he heard a loud *THUMP*.

Did I hit something? he thought.

He pulled the car over to the side of the road, put it in park, turned on his hazard lights, and pushed open the driver's side door, feeling a blast of cold air. The temperature was just above freezing. He walked out to the front of the car—there was no damage. He inspected the front quarter panels—no scratches or blood. He looked down the road behind him—no sticks or animals, or, God forbid, people lying on the side of the road. But he had heard a *THUMP*. It must have been something. Yet there was no evidence of a collision.

Unsettled, he got back into the car, and resumed his drive to school. He tuned the radio to 98.7, the New London classic rock station, and was slightly irritated to find that Foghat was still in heavy rotation—especially at seven in the morning.

He drove past Flyers Drive, Wayne Street, past the cemetery, and then down the hill past Harland Heights and Campion to the shortcut on Cuprak Road, when—*THUMP*. Startled, he put the car in park, turned on the hazard lights, got out, inspected the car, looked up and down the road, and, after a few minutes, was satisfied that—again—he had not hit anything or anyone. John Cougar Mellencamp was playing when he got back in the car, and by this time the windshield was mostly defrosted.

Ross resumed his journey on Cuprak Road, took a right onto Ox Hill Lane, and then a left onto Ox Hill Road, past Kelly Middle School, when—*THUMP*. He wondered if some early-bird middle-school student was roaming the grounds. He got out of the car, inspected the quarter panels, the grill, the entire exterior of the car. He looked at his watch—*dang it*—he would be late for homeroom again. Ross always left his house fifteen to twenty minutes early, knowing that he would have to stop to check if he had hit anyone a handful of times. On good days, he would only have to do it once or twice. On bad days, like today, three times, and on really bad days, it would take him 45 minutes to drive two miles. He scratched his way over to Mahan Drive and pulled into the faculty parking lot, thinking that if he really had hit anyone on the way to work, the police would be catching up to him right about now.

———

"We're going to be doing the epsilons and deltas again today, kids."

The class groaned.

AP Calculus wasn't an especially hard class to teach, and Ross found it enjoyable, teaching the best and the brightest math students in the state. The boys consistently underperformed the girls, though, and that was broadly true across the school. *A billion hours of pornography in their pockets*, Ross thought. The poor dears couldn't help themselves. The girls were alert and receptive, while the boys were zonked from being up until three in the morning, playing the ding-a-ling banjo. Ross's best student was Stephen, a junior with Michael Hutchence hair who had passed out of geometry his freshman year. He never took notes, but stared intently at Ross when he was deriving formulas on the board, just soaking it all in. He was constantly rotating through girlfriends and got in a spot of trouble for hacking into the school's phone system, leaving farts and burps on all the teachers' outgoing voicemail messages. Ross thought Stephen would one day either be a billionaire or in jail—nothing in between.

"Mr. Beatty, you seem unhappy," Stephen offered.

Ross was startled. "You mean, like, today, or in general?"

"I mean in general," Stephen said. "Like you have this existential dread."

Ross paused. *The kid sees me*, he thought. He always strove to be honest with his students. "Look, Stephen. It's the middle of winter. It's freezing out. We haven't seen the sun in two weeks. This routine—going to class everyday—is soul-crushing. But I can tell you that the unemployment rate for kids who know calculus is pretty much zero. So you all have a lot to look forward to."

Stephen was dissatisfied with this answer, but let it drop.

"Stephen," Ross continued, "where do you want to go to college?"

"The Naval Academy."

"You're not serious," Ross said, thinking that this authority-hating teenage rebel would last about six seconds in the military.

"Clearly, I have to get a haircut. But yeah. I want to be a nuclear engineer and go on submarines. Cruise around the world with nuclear warheads and Navy SEALs doing ultra-top-secret missions. Doesn't that sound cool?"

Ross nodded slowly. "I have to admit, it sounds a lot cooler than this."

————————————

Ross received a text.

Amy

> Has anyone told you that you're worthless today?

> Let me be the first

He was on his way to the principal's office when his phone buzzed. He had an open period at 2 p.m., and the principal's secretary had sent him an Outlook invitation three days ago. Bill Sherman was the new head of school—the previous principal, the beloved Scott Russo, had retired after thirty years. Sherman had liberal ideas about education—he worried about freshmen being thrust into the hard, unforgiving high-school environment, and created the freshman house, a self-contained building where they could be free from bullying and outside influences. Sherman had a short mop of curly hair and a broad mustache, and his face was fixed in an expression that fell just short of smug. Ross's anxiety ticked up when he got the email—getting called in the principal's office was even worse when you were a teacher than when you were a student. He figured that one of his students had ratted him out for saying something un-PC—he played back the tape in his head and couldn't remember anything untoward, but people took offense at anything nowadays. He had a handful of students who identified as nonbinary. Unable to keep track of all the different pronouns, he just referred to them by their first names. He wondered if that was what this was all about.

> Pick up some Tylenol on the way home, you pussy

> Or I'll tell everyone

Ross's school was different from most high schools, with a sprawling campus consisting of ten different buildings on as many acres. There was a track, football field, and two gyms. The arts program was enormous, relative to other schools in the area—music had one half of one building, and visual arts the other. The path to the administrative building was lined with cherry blossoms, which, at this point in the year, were devoid of leaves. Ross was cold-natured and typically didn't bother with a winter coat until it was well below freezing, but a stiff breeze was filling up his jacket, and causing him to shiver.

> Fuck you forever

> You fucking jerkoff

Ross entered the administrative building through the ground floor, walked up the creaky wooden steps to the second floor, where he was greeted by Shelley, the administrative assistant. She smiled at him. "Go right in!" she said. Ross opened the door to the office, which he had only been in once before, when he was hired eight years ago. He was greeted by an expansive bookshelf with volumes that ranged from the classics, to textbooks, to books on educational theory. He sat down in a chair across from the desk, his jacket still on.

"How are classes going?" Sherman asked, with his semi-smug expression, sitting at his desk.

"It's a struggle," Ross said. "The calculus class is fine. I worry about some of these other kids."

"I know. The demographics of this city have changed a lot in recent years."

Interesting, Ross thought. This was Sherman's way of saying that the town was struggling economically and a lot of minorities had moved in—something he would never say in public.

"Anyway, I wanted to meet with you personally to give you the good news. You've been named Teacher of the Year. Congratulations!"

Ross stared at him blankly.

"You've also been nominated for the statewide Teacher of the Year, and with the time you spend coaching tennis and the math team, and your community service, I think you have the best shot this school has had in years."

Ross kept staring.

Sherman looked at him with an expression like he was getting nowhere. "Ross, what do you think?"

"I mean, it's great, thanks," Ross said at last. "Obviously, that's not why I do it. But I appreciate the recognition." He felt his phone buzz in his jacket pocket. "Do I need to do anything? Is there a ceremony or something?"

"No ceremony. We'll call you back next week to give you the plaque and take some pictures. We'll put out a press release to the newspapers. And, of course, you will have the best parking spot in the faculty lot."

Ross felt his phone buzz again. "Great. Do you mind if I get back? I have to prep for my next class," he said.

"That's why you're teacher of the year!" Sherman said, looking a bit put out. Ross quickly exited, waved at Shelley, ran down the stairs, and checked his phone.

> Come home. I love you.

> No I don't.

———————

Ross found himself in Walgreens after school, looking for Tylenol. There was a bottle of Tylenol for $8.99 and a bottle of generic acetaminophen for $4.99. Ross settled on the latter, checked out with one of his former students at the cash register, who seemed not to recognize him, and got in his car for the drive home. Ross thought about the route—if he went down East Main St. to Harland Road, there would still be stragglers walking home from school, and he would have to get out of his car about six different times to check the tires. If he went home the way he came, up Mahan Drive, he would be driving by the middle school, which would be getting out at about this time. He opted for the more direct route. He drove as close as possible to the median, and away from the sidewalks. With all the willpower he could muster, he still had to stop twice on East Main, and twice more on Harland Road. Stopping four times—not bad considering he had left school a bit later than usual.

He rolled into the driveway, lifted his bag off the passenger seat, and trudged towards the front door, with hesitation. He never knew what to expect. He never knew if it was going to be a bad day, or a good day. Even the good days were bad.

He opened the door to find Amy standing in the kitchen, in a nightgown, holding a gin and tonic.

"About fucking time you got home."

"Sorry," Ross said, "I stopped at the drugstore." He handed her the plastic bag.

She looked in the bag. "I asked you for fucking Tylenol."

"It's the same thing—but cheaper."

She slammed the bottle on the kitchen counter. "You could fuck up a wet dream."

"How's the headache?" Ross offered.

"Worse from dealing with your bullshit."

"You've had this headache for weeks. Don't you think it's time to see a specialist?"

"I made an appointment today. I'm going to get a CT scan up in Hartford next week."

"I'll take you—"

"No you won't, you fucking loser. I'll drive myself."

Ross was more worried about her drunk driving than the CT scan, but let it go.

"There's a bill for the new roof on the counter," said Amy. "It's three months overdue. What are you going to do about it, dipshit?"

The house was forty years old, and their living room began taking on water during a storm last summer. They had a half dozen buckets positioned around the room. The only solution was to get a new roof, but they were broke and in debt from years of living together on one small income. Amy, with her alcoholism, was unemployable.

"Masters in applied math from MIT," continued Amy, "and you wanted to teach high school."

"We don't need to re-litigate this."

"You had offers from three different hedge funds. You could be a millionaire by now. But no. You wanted to *change the world*. How's that going?"

"Amy."

"Not only are you broke, but you have to stop ten times on the way to school like some kind of mental patient."

The house, barely 1,400 square feet, was too small for him to escape. He would be trapped with her tonight, like he was every night. Mercifully, they slept separately. Amy in the master bedroom, Ross on the couch. She would pass out in his recliner at about 8 p.m., and he would carry her off to bed, then spend the rest of the night watching MSNBC in the living room.

———

Black hair, pale skin, blue eyes, is what Ross thought when he first met Amy in a bar.

They were at The Black Rose. Amy walked right up to Ross, thrust her chest at him, and said, "Buy me a drink?" Though it was clear that she didn't need another drink. Twenty minutes later, she was grabbing his crotch, feeling him stiffen in her hand. Ten minutes after that, her tongue was in his ear. Ten minutes after that, they left the bar and got into a cab, gratuitously making out in the back seat. Twenty minutes after that, they were undressing in his tiny apartment. And thirty minutes after that, she was nude, kneeling on the floor, smiling, with her tongue out and eyes closed, saying, "Give it to me."

It was unlike any experience Ross had ever had.

Ross was originally from Lancaster, Pennsylvania, in Amish country, and grew up in a strict Methodist household. Strict, because his father was the pastor. Amy wasn't Ross's first sexual experience, but was by far the wildest. They had second and third and fourth dates, and he found her to be an excellent conversationalist. But she lied. She lied about how many men she had been with. She lied about how much money her parents had. She lied about her sister being divorced. She lied about big things and small things. The lies were revealed in dribs and drabs, and Ross felt like he was in a horror movie, walking slow-motion into a giant, spinning blade as the relationship progressed, but he could not break free of her. She had charmed him like a siren, and the sex was just too good. His parents disapproved; nonetheless, they got married. At the wedding, one of Amy's bridesmaids got drunk and went topless in the hotel pool, before getting fished out by a rent-a-cop on a Segway.

Eventually, he graduated from MIT with his degree in applied math, and Amy from UMass Boston with her masters in sociology. Ross was courted by a few quantitative hedge funds, the starting salary being $300,000. It would go up from there over time. Ross contemplated his future and decided that he didn't want his only contribution to the world to be making rich people even richer. Ross enjoyed his TA work at MIT—he knew he could teach—and he thought he could breathe some life into a failing high school in an underperforming area. He settled on Norwich, Connecticut, at the intersection of three rivers. Norwich was once a prosperous city, but decades of mismanagement had left it impoverished.

Amy was incredulous. She knew that a teacher and a sociologist together would be doomed to a lower-middle class existence—and she had no intention of ever working. Ross didn't have any money at the time of their marriage, but he wondered if she married him for his *potential*. Her drinking, which was unpredictable in good times, picked up speed shortly after their marriage. She went from binge-drinking to day-drinking to round-the-clock drinking in the span of five years. When they first met, Ross had noticed a mean streak in Amy—the drinking allowed it to flourish. They bought their house on Harland Road for $170,000 in 2018, a tiny two-bedroom affair with a finished basement. Acrimony quickly forced him out onto the couch at night, where he would lay awake and wonder if one of the cars barreling down Old Canterbury Turnpike would end up on his front lawn. There was little left over, living on his teacher's salary. He handed over $200 a month to invest in an index fund, satisfied that he was probably beating the returns of some of his potential employers.

Amy's bitterness was not solely directed at Ross. Ross learned later that she had been emotionally abused by her parents, and sexually abused by an uncle. In college, she had dreams of helping children who grew up under similar circumstances. Her alcoholism was partly hereditary, passed down from her father and grandfather, who both died of alcohol-related causes at sixty. Ross figured she would be dead by fifty at this rate—she was more or less drunk all the time. Amy once mentioned offhandedly that she had to drink a third of a bottle of gin just to feel normal in the morning. Ross thought about attending Al-Anon meetings, but Amy expected him home at 4 p.m., and he would quickly run out of excuses. Ross was trapped— his only outlet was school. Divorce was frowned upon in his Pennsylvania Dutch family.

He wouldn't tell Amy that he won Teacher of the Year.

———————

Ross was differentiating a complex polynomial on the board when he saw Stephen raise his hand out of the corner of his eye.

"Yes, Stephen?"

"Mr. Beatty—is everything okay?"

Damn this kid. "Stephen, everything's fine. Can we get back to—"

"You don't look fine. You look like you're carrying a burden."

Olivia raised her hand at the back. "Mr. Beatty, you don't seem yourself lately. I heard you won Teacher of the Year. Shouldn't you be—happy?"

Ross looked at the class and sighed. They had him dead to rights. "Let's just say my personal life is a bit chaotic right now."

"What's going on?" asked Stephen.

Ross made the *zip-it* hand motion.

Alex, a star cross-country runner, raised his hand. "Mr. Beatty, why did you become a teacher? I'm sure you could have done a lot of other things."

"I had some job offers, for sure. But this is what I wanted to do."

"Why?" asked Alex.

Ross looked at the class. "There are some things more important than making money."

The class erupted in laughter. "No, there aren't!"

Stephen added: "Mr. Beatty, you don't belong here. You're easily the best teacher in this school. By a lot. You could be a CEO or something."

Ross's phone buzzed in his pocket. "I don't regret my decision. I've been teaching here for five years. I've taught about a hundred and twenty students a year. That's six hundred people whose lives I've been able to touch since I've been here. That's a greater reward than any paycheck I might receive." His phone buzzed again.

For the first time in his teaching career, Ross reached into his pocket and checked his phone.

> Hey fuckstick

> I'm going in for my CT scan.
> Thought you'd like to know

Stephen tossed his Michael Hutchence hair out of his face. "Mr. Beatty, you deserve better."

———————

Ross posed for his Teacher of the Year photo with his fake smile. He hadn't posed for a picture with his real smile in years.

He tossed the plaque on the passenger seat, got in the car, checked his mirrors, and backed out slowly.

THUMP.

He put the car into park, turned on the hazards, disembarked, walked around to the back of the car, saw no victims and no damage. He took pains to get on his hands and knees and looked under the car, in case he had dragged a body underneath.

Ross looked around. Students everywhere. Some of them were staring at him. It was going to take him an hour to get home.

He got back in the car, put it in drive, and pulled forward slightly, when *THUMP*. He got out of the car again.

Ross did this eight times before even leaving the faculty parking lot.

As he headed up the hill, he wondered whether this affliction might disappear if he got into an actual collision someday. He had never been in an accident, ever, or even gotten a speeding ticket. He was an insurance company's dream. Ross was the driver going fifty-five on the highway in the right lane, with all the cars zooming past and honking. *Maybe it was good I never ended up on Wall Street*, he thought—he was not much of a risk-taker.

After fourteen stops, he pulled into his driveway at last, nearly an hour late. He thought about bringing the plaque inside, but leaned over and slid it under the passenger seat. He would smuggle it in some other time.

Ross wiggled the doorknob and pushed.

"How many times did you stop today, weirdo?" asked Amy, holding her drink.

"How was the hospital?"

"Well, those idiots didn't do anything about my headache. I don't know why people get freaked out by scans—I thought it was kind of fun."

"When do you get the results?"

"Next Tuesday."

"I can—"

"Shut the fuck up. We can't have the Teacher of the Year miss a day of school."

"How did you—"

"I saw it on the news. Congratulations, you're king of the dipshits."

"Thanks."

"Don't mention it. I know what keeps you going back there. It is all those high-school girls."

"Amy—"

"You get to see a bunch of hot, young ass every day. Maybe I should try this gig out. I can still catch a dick."

Ross sighed. "You want me to make dinner?"

"I ordered pizza fifteen minutes ago. With pineapple."

"I hate pineapple."

"I know."

Ross quickly went to the front door, opened it, and slammed it behind him. He went to the car, and retrieved the Teacher of the Year plaque from under the passenger seat. He went back inside, slamming the front door again, and went under the kitchen sink to find a hammer and nail. He found an open piece of real estate on the living room wall, pounded the nail home, and hung the plaque on it.

He pointed at Amy, and pointed at the plaque.

"Teacher of the Year."

———————

Ross would have walked to school if it wasn't so damn cold.

This time, he thought he'd try something different—he'd turn the radio to Q105, the pop station. Maybe that would distract him. And he rolled down the driver's side window; he was freezing, but he wasn't thinking about hitting people or squirrels.

THUMP.

"Son of a bitch!" Ross shouted. He leapt out of the car and started kicking the tires as hard as he could. "Fuck!" He had done this a million times before—he had heard these phantom *THUMPS* and had never found any trace of a collision. But he knew there would be that one time he would hit someone, and not notice, then get hauled down to the police station for a hit-and-run accident.

Ross arrived at school ten minutes prior to the start of the first period, when he was scheduled to teach a pre-algebra class. He had almost missed homeroom, arriving just in time to take attendance. He taught his pre-algebra class, two elementary mathematics classes, and his AP Calculus class, where the students eyed him suspiciously. Then he went to lunch. He got two sorry slices of pizza from the cafeteria, standing among students who were pushing and shoving in line, then headed off to the faculty lounge, a nondescript room adjacent to the cafeteria where Ross often ate in silence.

"Ross, how does it feel?"

Ross found himself face to face with Bill Sherman, who was not a management-by-wandering-around type. He wondered if he was here for some purpose, that he had engineered this meeting.

"Dr. Sherman! Good to see you," Ross said, vigorously shaking his hand.

"Take a seat," Sherman said, and sat ninety degrees from him at a round table.

Ross looked at him, eyebrows up.

"Ross, people tell me I'm a pretty perceptive guy—is everything okay?"

"My students asked me this just the other day."

"So?"

"I'll tell you what I told them. Things at home aren't that great."

"I suspected. As you know, the school has resources to—"

"I'm fine."

The smug expression disappeared from Bill Sherman's face. "You know what 'fine' stands for? Fucked-up, Insecure, Neurotic, and Emotional?"

"That's about right."

"Ross, these kids *love* you. It would be a shame if we lost you because of—something we could have potentially helped out with."

"Do I have a piece of paper stapled to my forehead that says I'm miserable or something?"

"Let's just say you don't have the best poker face."

Ross paused and considered whether to tell him about his alcoholic wife or his compulsion. In a split-second, he decided against it.

"Dr. Sherman, I really appreciate you looking out for me. It's nothing I can't handle. I've been handling it for years."

"You *are* Pennsylvania Dutch, aren't you? Not one to talk about his problems."

Ross chuckled. "No, I guess not."

Sherman began to stand up. "There is a saying I heard once. God's not going to give you anything you can't handle. But don't be a jackass. Get some help."

————————

Ross was teaching Algebra 2 and Trig when his phone rang.

Amy
(860) 887-7381

Amy *never* called—only texted. He suddenly remembered that she was getting the results of her CT scan today. He quickly excused himself, went out into the hall, and answered the phone.

What?

Slow down, I can't hear you

...

Brain cancer?

You what?

Inoperable?

Three months?

...

I'm coming home.

Ross re-entered the classroom, called the office to request a sub to cover the class, bid his students farewell, grabbed his bag, ran down the hall, thudded down the stairs, and sprinted out to the faculty parking lot. He jumped in the car, looped around the parking lot, and pulled out onto Mahan Street, and headed up the hill.

It suddenly occurred to Ross that hurrying wouldn't do him any good. Amy had called from the car on the way back from Hartford—she was probably on Route 2 somewhere, near Colchester. He could slow down and enjoy the ride. A light snow had fallen during the school day—he looked around to see it frosting the tree branches. The road was lightly dusted, with few tire tracks. Ross recalled that snow was in the forecast, about three to six inches—quite possibly enough for the kids to head to Suicide Hill with their sleds in the morning.

Ross hadn't taken the time to simply *look around* and see the natural beauty of his surroundings—Norwich was unquestionably gorgeous in October, but he rather liked the winter, too, even on the cold, gray days in between snowfalls. To think, all these kids with all their dreams, tucked away in the middle of the woods, the same woods where they would wield sticks and slash their way through imaginary monsters when they were in second grade. The woods where his own students would sneak off to display affection towards each other. The sound of football games in the fall, the whistles, the clashing of helmets, and the marching band.

The neighborhoods had been constructed and settled decades ago—Ross liked these houses because they were unpretentious. They were houses for factory workers and phone company workers and city government employees. None of them had more than three bedrooms. Many of them had wood-grain paneling. Outside of a few affluent doctors and lawyers, there was no wealth in Norwich to speak of. No Louis Vuitton bags, no Prada shoes, no Rolex watches. He remembered how he just *fit in* on his first job interview.

He passed the cemetery to the east. He had been in that cemetery a few times, and browsed all the headstones with the French names. Benoit, Dugas, Arsenault. This part of town was settled by French-Canadian textile mill workers in the late 1800s. There were no German names in town, but there were Polish names, Irish names, and a few Italian names. He taught their offspring. They were his children now.

He pulled into the driveway, got out of the car, walked up the front steps, and realized, as he wiggled and pushed open the front door, that he hadn't stopped once on the way home.

CREEP

———

"For the ten-day forecast, we're looking at the low nineties for tomorrow and Wednesday, and then you'll see those temperatures start to move up as that high pressure center moves in, with mid-nineties the rest of the week. No rain in the forecast, but there is a possibility of a pop-up shower in the afternoons, and perhaps even a thunderstorm. At the islands and beaches, it will be eighty-six on Tuesday and Wednesday, then will get towards ninety over the weekend.

"In other words, it's summer in Charleston, so stay inside in the air conditioning, and pour yourself a glass of iced tea, because it's going to get hotter as we get closer to the end of the month. Sharon—"

"Thanks, Jordan. And thanks for watching News 8 on Monday night, June 25. Stay cool, and we'll see you tomorrow."

Jordan relaxed, let the tension ease out of her shoulders and trapezius, visibly slumped forward, and allowed her posture to crumble. One year into this job and she was still thinking about her delivery. She had majored in meteorology at Clemson, had been hoping for a job as a meteorologist close to home, and eventually lucked into one when the previous occupant of her position, Laura, cited political differences with others at WNXT and moved to a station in Fayetteville, North Carolina. She didn't exactly have big shoes to fill.

Laura hadn't been well liked—the viewers found her delivery awkward, and she seemed to be—at times—not credible. Laura seemed happy in her new job up the road. Jordan followed her on Twitter and she was constantly tweeting out weather updates for central North Carolina, something she couldn't or wouldn't do when she was at WNXT. Jordan dug into her Twitter likes at one point, when she was scouting around for a job, and found that the vast majority of tweets she liked were those of Donald Trump, Dan Bongino, and Catturd. Jordan thought she would have a short career in news media with that type of hard-right ideology, though she seemed to be making it work in Fayetteville.

Before starting work at WNXT, Jordan bought fifteen dresses in solid colors, mostly red, yellow, and blue. Patterned clothes were strictly off-limits, appearing too busy for the camera and distracting the viewers. Her favorite was a solid yellow, gauzy dress that she had worn for today's show—perfect for the hot summer weather. Jordan found it impossible to get used to broadcasting in front of a green screen. She barely had enough time to get up to speed before she started broadcasting live.

She got to know the counties around Charleston: Colleton, Dorchester, Berkeley, and Georgetown to the north, as well as the surrounding towns, like Summerville, Mount Pleasant, Isle of Palms, and Folly Beach. Her job was fairly straightforward most of the time—until a hurricane hit. Then, she would be working round the clock, tracking the storm with spaghetti models and National Weather Service predictions. A competing TV station, WCBD, had a weather anchor, Michael Jewell, who had been broadcasting for over thirty years. He was the trusted source of information during a hurricane. Jordan meant to unseat him. Hurricane season had officially begun, though the storms that threatened South Carolina wouldn't arrive until September or October. Jordan wasn't wishing for a hurricane—a direct hit would have Charleston up to its eyeballs in water—but she was desperate for an opportunity to prove herself.

Jordan walked off set, gathered her things, put her laptop in her bag, and felt her phone buzz.

Damn it, she mouthed silently.

Sharon Gilchrist, the longtime anchor, was standing next to Jordan when she got the text. "What's wrong?" she asked.

"Nothing. Just another stalker."

"Let me see."

> Jordan, another great show. I love watching you every day. My name is James Hickey, and I'm a doctor at MUSC. I would love to get coffee sometime. Please let me know if you're up for it.

Sharon frowned. "This doesn't look like a stalker to me. This seems like a real person."

"Anyone who slides into my DMs is a creep."

"What kind of stuff do you usually get in your DMs?"

"'Nice tits,' 'Nice ass', the usual stuff."

"Well, this isn't that."

"No, it's not, but don't slide into my DMs."

"How else is he supposed to get a hold of you? Do you want him to show up at the station?"

"Of course not. He can write me a letter."

"Which means he would have to look up your address, which is even more creepy. There's absolutely no non-creepy way that he can reach out to you and ask for a date."

"I don't want to be asked on dates in my Twitter DMs. And it sucks that I have to have my DMs open, so people can give me news tips. I get hit on way more than I get tips."

"You just want to be asked on dates on Tinder? Clearly, that's less creepy."

"No."

"Look, he gave you his name, he told you where he works, so you can do your due diligence on him. I don't think this is creepy at all. You know, in the old days, we would call this having a *secret admirer*. You want him to stand outside your window with a boombox?"

"Embarrassing."

"This is why the human race will stop reproducing, and the insects will take over the earth," Sharon said, exhausted by the conversation. "I'm just saying—you get hit on by a lot of creeps, and there are a lot of creeps out there, but this isn't one."

"Are you saying I should go on a date with him?"

"Not necessarily. First of all, he's going to be a lot older than you. Second of all, doctors are weird. But you never know. You have to give him credit for shooting his shot. He knows what he wants and he's going for it. You can always block him."

"Maybe I will."

"Life is full of miracles," Sharon said, walking away. "If your eyes are open."

———————

Jordan returned to her King Street apartment in the stifling humidity just after 9 p.m. She set down her bag near the front door, and her cat, Marcus Brody, came waddling over to see her. Marcus was technically a *chonk*—he ate constantly, and Jordan would come home in the evenings to find his bowl completely empty. He kept the apartment free of palmetto bugs, picking up the insects in his mouth, crunching them, leaving roach parts all over the wooden floor. He would wake her up at 3:30 in the morning by licking her forehead and purring.

Jordan poured herself a glass of Yellowtail chardonnay, dropped two ice cubes in the glass, and sat down in front of her computer. First, she went to LinkedIn and entered "James Hickey" in the search bar. Hundreds of results returned. She narrowed her search parameters to MUSC and a profile appeared. She clicked on the picture—a man in his mid-to-late thirties with a striking resemblance to a young Matthew Modine. Unfortunately, Matthew Modine was not her type. She went through his CV. He was an osteopath, having graduated from the Philadelphia College of Osteopathic Medicine. Undergrad at Penn State and high school in Williamsport, Pennsylvania. It seemed as though he just parked the profile page—nothing in the way of cheesy skills or endorsements. As a gastroenterologist, Jordan imagined that James spent a lot of time doing colonoscopies. Her thoughts drifted for a moment, on how doctors could ever have normal sex lives if they saw thirteen buttholes a day. He also had a Facebook page—he was using the same profile picture for both social networks. It said he had 343 friends—not many at all. Maybe a brooding introvert.

She went to a handful of the spy sites and managed to sleuth his address without paying any money. He lived in the north part of Mount Pleasant. She knew the neighborhood—Brickyard Plantation—mostly new money that had come into the area from the northeast. She went back to his Twitter profile—just a rando, with thirty-four followers. He followed only five accounts, all meteorologists from local TV stations. Maybe his hobby was being a weather nerd. A brooding introvert Matthew Modine lookalike in a cookie-cutter development whose primary interest was weathermen and weatherwomen, and other people's buttholes. She would have felt more comfortable if he were a football fan and a face-painter.

Jordan set the computer to *sleep* and picked up Marcus Brody, who had been nibbling at her toes. He began purring instantly, vibrating against her chest.

———

Jordan arrived at WNXT the next morning, half-expecting to find a dozen roses.

Being a TV meteorologist is a value-destroying proposition. The average weatherman is paid about $90,000 a year. Fresh-faced Jordan had been hired at $65,000 a year out of college, with the expectation that she would be in a support role her first few years—but she had been thrust into the spotlight after Laura's disappearance. Jordan hoped that management would take this into account when she renegotiated her compensation in eighteen months. They were getting a stupendous deal.

WNXT wasn't located in Charleston proper—it was across the bridge in Mount Pleasant. Jordan did the reverse commute, avoiding traffic, usually around 10 a.m. She would arrive at the station and immediately dive into the weather models. This time of year, the weather was stable and predictable: hot as hell, with an afternoon thunderstorm. About once every two weeks, a low-pressure system would hover over the area, cooling things off about ten degrees, raining, and forcing people off the beaches and back inside. The humidity was varying degrees of oppressive. This time of year, she was looking at potential hurricane formations off the coast of West Africa. Storm-watching was an obsession in these parts, with memories of Hurricane Hugo still fresh in many people's minds. That storm had only been a Category 3, but scored a direct hit to the north of Charleston, in McClellanville, and flattened houses and trees for miles. Jordan's forecasting wouldn't make or break her career—all the TV stations were using the same models—but it would be her calm, measured delivery that assuaged viewers' fears or compelled them to action. Jordan rehearsed frequently in front of her mirror at home.

Jordan wanted to secure a position at one of the big three networks one day. She looked the part, with her dusky complexion and aquiline nose. Her surname, Santini, was uncommon in Columbia, where she had been raised. She was one of a handful of Italian families that had lived in the city for generations. Her sister, Elizabeth, became a physical therapist and was barely making a living in Myrtle Beach. Her two older brothers joined the Air Force. Nico, a technical sergeant, was bounced out of the military for alcoholism, became an electrician, and went through spells where he ruminated about murdering his ex-wife's husband. He would call Jordan's house occasionally, looking for money. If Jordan picked up, she would hang up immediately—she was having none of his bullshit. Jordan, the youngest of the four, was ambitious in a way that nobody else in the family could even imagine. She'd return occasionally for family gatherings, dressed in her TV weathergirl outfit amid the cargo shorts and print T-shirts, like a raisin in the oatmeal.

Jordan was an uncommon Zoomer, not particularly close with her parents. Her next-oldest sister, the PT, was seven years older. Elizabeth had told her that she was an *oops*—her parents were finished having children after three, her father had snuck one past the goalie, and her Catholic parents couldn't bring themselves to seek an abortion. Her parents were tuckered out from too many ballgames and awards ceremonies for her siblings, had just finished a book on free-range parenting when she was about seven years old, and Jordan was left to her own devices. She pursued gymnastics for a while, but abandoned it after she grew too tall. She switched to soccer, but could not walk on to the varsity team at Clemson. She excelled at social media, and her Instagram following became large enough in college that the thirsty DMs were a bit of a concern. Boys were a distraction. At twenty-three, she was still a virgin. In high school, she caught *9½ Weeks* on Netflix, and dreamt of being swept off her feet by an investment banker in New York who would buy her $500 scarves. This was unlikely to happen in Columbia, or even Charleston, where the men, no matter what age or income or social station, drove pickup trucks.

———————

Some of the early feedback Jordan got on her TV appearances was that she somewhat lacked energy, though she was told that this was common among beginning broadcasters. So she worked on exaggerating her speech, her inflection, and her hand gestures. It was a performance, after all. *All of life is a performance*, she thought.

By this point, she had forgotten all about Matthew Modine sliding into her DMs. She didn't expect that she would hear from him again. One DM was him shooting his shot. Two would be harassment, at which point she would go against company policy and block him. But it hadn't come to that. For all Jordan knew, he was sending DMs to Olivia over at WCBD. Olivia had too much eye makeup, highlights in her hair, and wore dresses an inch or two shorter than was prescribed. She was somebody's type. Maybe Matthew Modine just wanted to bang someone on TV. *There are people like that out there*, she thought.

After doing the 5 p.m., 5:30 p.m., and 6 p.m. shows on Wednesday night, Olivia could barely stand. A lot of energy went into those five-minute spots. After the show, she went back to her desk, and saw a Twitter notification.

> It's James again. Just wanted to try one more time, and then I'll leave you alone forever. Wanted to see if you would get breakfast with me at Page's on Sunday. All the best.

Jordan quickly navigated to his profile, clicked on the drop-down menu, and hovered over the block button for what seemed like a minute.

Fuck it.

She navigated back to his message, and replied:

Ok

She immediately regretted it. There was no way to unsend a message on Twitter. She thought she would stand him up, but she hadn't been raised that way. She could block him, but would he still be able to see her message? She started to panic.

James began to reply

. . .

Great. See you there at 9am.

Fuck. Well. Page's Okra Grill was a busy breakfast spot in Mount Pleasant. In fact, they didn't take reservations, and it was often an hour wait or more to get a table. Jordan wasn't much looking forward to standing around outside in the heat with Matthew Modine, making small talk. She would get a free breakfast out of it and go home and pet Marcus Brody, and maybe lie out by the pool. It was only an hour out of her life. She would get through it. But she couldn't quite shake the idea that it was *sex* that he was after—he watched her on TV, watched her face, watched her curves, watched her movements—and *desired* her. For all she knew, he was whacking off while watching her. People will whack off to anything. And just because he was a doctor, didn't mean his conduct was above reproach. Doctors were sex offenders, too. She made a mental note to check the sex offender registry for a certain James Hickey.

Also, Matthew Modine was significantly *older*. Jordan was just twenty-three. She reverse-engineered his age by looking at his LinkedIn profile, and concluded he was thirty-eight, a clear violation of the half-your-age-plus-seven rule. A thirty-eight-year-old man was set in his career and his ways, and old enough to be cranky about certain things. Had he been married? Did he have children floating around out there? Was he hard to get along with? Was he abusive? Was he a drunk? Did he get caught at massage parlors? Jordan felt her mind sinking into the depths of obsession, and reminded herself that the vast majority of men were not weirdos, and little harm could come from an omelet at 9 a.m.

Jordan spied Sharon walking across the newsroom out of the corner of her eye, and approached her, waving.

"Hey, remember that guy who messaged me last week?"

"Of course I remember."

"I'm having breakfast with him on Sunday morning. And before you congratulate me, this is a terrible idea." Jordan added: "A *really* terrible idea."

"Did you do your due diligence on him?"

"He is who he says he is. He's a GI doc. He lives up in Brickyard Plantation. Like I said before, just because he's a doctor, doesn't mean he's not a nutjob."

"I'm sure he's very nice. He likes you. Worst-case scenario is that you get a free breakfast."

"That's my thinking. Thanks for the advice—I guess?"

"You never know. Maybe you fall in love and have a drive-thru wedding in Vegas."

"My decision-making up to this point has been pretty good. So probably not."

———————

If it were winter, Jordan would have worn an enormous sweatshirt to her breakfast date, to hide the outline of her bust. James was obviously attracted to her form-fitting TV dresses, so she decided to dress down—a huge T-shirt and a pair of ratty shorts. Her legs would be under the table.

Jordan decided that this would be the one time in her life when it was acceptable to be late. The date was his idea. He was the superfan, he could wait for fifteen minutes. She would arrive at 9:15, and blame her tardiness on traffic, which would be ludicrous—there was no traffic on Sunday morning. Let him sit there and wonder if she was actually going to show up.

While driving, she saw her phone light up on the passenger seat next to her. At a stop light, she held the phone up to her face while it did its facial-recognition thing, and a message appeared from James:

> Got a table near the front.
> See you soon.

She looked at the clock on her dashboard: 8:45. If he had already got a table, he'd been there since 7:45 in the morning. *Fuck.* The image of him jerking off in front of her weather forecast reappeared in her mind. She declined to answer the message—she would be there soon enough. He would have thirty minutes to stare at his phone with sweaty palms and a woody.

After navigating a series of intersections with long traffic lights, she eventually arrived at Page's, and rolled into the gravel parking lot, bringing the car to rest between two $80,000 Chevy Silverados. She hopped out of her car, and walked towards the restaurant, crunching the gravel beneath her sneakers.

She spotted him instantly upon walking through the door—the whitest man she had ever seen. He was wearing a blue-patterned polo shirt with pleated khakis—hunched over his phone, possibly thinking she might not show. He saw her and quickly stood up. He was very tall—a good six-foot-three, and seemed to be fantastically uncoordinated, stubbing his toe on the leg of the table and half-tripping over the chair. He smiled, and extended his arm. Jordan waved off the women at the hostess stand, walked over to James, and delicately shook his hand. She sat down at the table with him, reluctantly.

"I'm so glad you took the time to do this," James said. "I've been watching you on TV for the last year."

"So I gather."

"I suppose I should explain myself. I'm a—*hrm*—gastroenterologist at MUSC. I moved here four years ago after completing residency. I live in Brickyard Plantation."

Jordan sat silently.

"I'm not married. I've never been married. I find meeting people in Charleston to be difficult. *Hrm hrm.* I have a French bulldog named Giorgio."

Jordan perked up a bit. "I have a cat, but I like dogs too. Where is Giorgio right now?"

"He's at home, in the crate. I took him for a walk this morning."

"You're not one of these crate people, I hope? Dogs aren't meant to sit in a cage all day."

"*Hrm.* He has plenty of time outside. I walk him in the morning, and then again when I get home from work."

"So you let your dog out a couple hours a day?"

"It's good for training. He's perfectly happy."

Jordan could feel her anger rising. "Let's change the subject. What kind of watch is that?"

"Oh, you noticed. That's my poop watch."

"A poop watch?"

"Yes, look—it has the poop emoji on it." James proudly displayed his watch to Jordan, reaching across the table and turning his wrist sideways. "I'm a gastroenterologist. I do—*hrm*—colonoscopies all day long. I have a poop clock at home, a poop pool float, poop throw pillows—and even—*hrm*—poop business cards." He dug into his pocket and produced a business card holder, and handed one to Jordan. It had the poop emoji on it, with its googly eyes and grin.

"That's... amazing."

James ordered his eggs. Jordan ordered oatmeal, plain. "Right? I try to make work fun."

"Sure, but I'm not certain I would have my entire identity wrapped up in farming in other people's shit."

"Most of the time it isn't too bad, if people have done the prep properly. It's when they've eaten a—*hrm*—porterhouse the night before that things get ugly."

"Lovely."

"Thanks."

"Do you have a cold or something? You keep clearing your throat."

"No, it's just a—*hrm*—tic. It comes out more when I'm nervous."

There was an awkward pause.

James volunteered, "So what's your favorite food?"

"My favorite food? I'm not three, I don't have a favorite food."

"I like *lasagna*."

There was another awkward pause.

"So do you like working at the station?'

The waitress dropped the plates on the table. "Sure, I like working at the station. I'm looking forward to my first hurricane. And we should be getting more of them, due to climate change, so that will be good for business."

"I don't think climate change causes more hurricanes."

"No?"

"No, I think we have the same amount of—*hrm*—extreme weather events that we had thirty years ago. They're just more in the news, so people think there are more of them."

"Well, I *am* the news, and I can tell you that there are more of them. We've had a major hurricane come close to Charleston each year for the last five years."

"*Hrm*. Small sample size. There's no correlation at all. I'm sure you've read some papers on this."

Jordan stared at him intently. "Are you a climate change *denier*?"

James pushed his eggs onto his fork with his finger. "Not at all. The climate has been changing for billions of years. The climate is changing now. I don't think there's enough evidence to say that it's man-made. Two hundred years of industrialization against the billions of years that Earth has existed. Not enough—*hrm*—data."

"Do you suggest that we wait until the Earth cooks before we do anything about it?"

"*Hrm*. We already are doing something about it. We're selling five hundred thousand electric cars a year. There will be private-sector solutions."

Jordan leaned over the table at him. "Who did you vote for in 2020?"

James chased his eggs around his plate with his fork, capitulated, and picked it up with his fingers and ate them. "I didn't vote for anyone. I don't vote."

"You don't vote?"

"No, never. I'm—*hrm*—morally opposed to it."

"Well, I voted for Biden."

"Cool."

"Aren't you going to tell me that I should have voted for Trump?"

"Of course not. You can vote for whoever you want. I just don't see how whoever is president affects me personally."

"There are people in this country other than you."

"That doesn't—*hrm*—concern me. I'm a gastroenterologist. I stick fiber optic cables up people's butts and look around. Then I come home and walk the dog."

"After letting him out of the crate."

"Yes."

James waved over the waitress for the check.

"You want to split it?"

Jordan visibly rolled her eyes. "Sure."

James slid the two credit cards in the folio and handed it back to the waitress. "Well, I had a nice conversation with you. I hope we can do it again sometime."

"It was a nice conversation," said Jordan, politely.

"I'll be watching you on TV. By the way, yellow looks great on you."

"We almost made it through without comments on my appearance."

"*Hrm.* Just trying to be nice."

"Goodbye, James." Jordan gave him a second limp-wristed handshake as he remained seated, then strode out to the parking lot between the two Chevy Silverados.

That was a huge fucking waste of time, she thought.

———————

Jordan was back in the station on Monday morning, on the hottest day of the year. It was eighty-six degrees at nine in the morning. She spotted Sharon from across the newsroom.

"You gave me bad advice."

"Huh?"

"Sharon, remember my *secret admirer*? The MUSC doc who slid into my DMs? I had breakfast with him over the weekend."

"And?"

"The guy was a total weirdo. And a creep. *And* he made me pay for my breakfast."

"What did he do?"

"I don't know where to begin. Let me just say that anyone who slides into your DMs *is* a creep."

"Was he dangerous?"

"No, of course not. Just annoying beyond belief. *And* a right-winger."

"Well," Sharon said, "I'm very sorry to hear that. It was worth a try. An hour out of your day. Too bad you didn't get the free breakfast."

"What a jerk," Jordan said, and walked back to her desk.

Jordan did want to get married someday, but not to a superfan rando who found her on TV. She had put zero thought into how she would meet someone—as it was, she was working at the station late into the evenings, and didn't have much of a social life. That would come later. For now, she was content with being the third-best meteorologist in Charleston, and going home and drinking wine and petting her cat. Maybe when she got hired by one of the huge stations in New York, she'd have an expansive social life and would meet a multimillionaire currency trader who wore Zegna suits. They'd get sushi at Zuma on Thursday nights, and on Friday would drive out to their house in East Hampton, taking vacations in Monaco and Mallorca.

There was a bouquet of roses on Jordan's desk.

No.

There was a note attached:

> Jordan, sorry the breakfast date didn't go so well. I was not at my best. I just wanted you to know that you're beautiful and smart and I wish you all the success you could ever want. Best of luck.
>
> Your friend,
>
> *James*

Jordan deposited the roses in the trash can, and blocked James on Twitter.

AMANDA

I TOUCHED down in the desert after spending the last fifteen minutes of the flight to Las Vegas trying to get a cell phone signal from the sky, in flagrant defiance of FAA regulations. Upon landing, I disembarked and made my way to the taxi stand, past the airport slot machines and the tourists and their cheap luggage. In the old days, only a few years ago, you ran the risk of getting *long-hauled* by the taxis—they'd take you on a big loop around the highway to earn a $60 fare instead of a $20 fare through the city—classic Vegas. The city got wise to their antics, and now it's a $25 flat rate for anywhere on the strip. Too many stupid tourists were getting fleeced.

I stepped onto the curb and scanned the usual throngs of men in cargo shorts and flip-flops, the younger ones having spent the entire flight practicing basic blackjack strategy on their tray table. I know how to count cards, but never took the time to practice because I can make more money at my job—the casinos are so good at catching advantage players that you'd be lucky to squeak out $20 an hour in front of the cameras. Before I left New York, I went to the Wells Fargo bank branch and took out $5,000 in cash—for gambling, obviously. The teller ran the money through the counting machine and handed me an envelope with fifty $100 bills. I discarded the envelope and stuffed the money in my wallet, which I then had difficulty fitting in my pocket.

My cab driver was in possession of what seemed to be a Hoboken accent; his huge biceps strained against his green mesh polo shirt. He volunteered some information about prostitution without being prompted: Nevada was famous for its brothels, he told me, but what most people didn't realize about Vegas was that the brothels, all sixteen of them, were outside of Vegas city limits. Prostitution was decidedly illegal in Las Vegas, and that law was strictly enforced. Every once in a while, he said, some tourist would get picked up by the cops with a hooker and get his face plastered on the internet— Google search results soiled in perpetuity. The strip clubs were a better bet, the driver explained. They varied in quality, but all the nasty girls who would do *an-y-thing* could be found at the Hustler Club. He offered to take me there. I ignored him. I knew all of that already. I wondered how many horny tourists went straight to the strip club from the airport, luggage in tow.

The Wynn was the best hotel on the strip for high rollers—I had learned from experience. It's a *brown* building, curved like Geoffrey Serra's "Tilted Arc," facing the morning sun so the pool in the back gets the sunlight in the afternoon. The Wynn had a reputation for having by far the richest clients, centimillionaires and billionaires, landing their private jets at Henderson to the south, where they would be greeted by a host and limousine service, courtesy of the casino. Hoi polloi could still stay there for $350 a night, but they would find the high minimums at the tables prohibitively expensive—at night it is difficult to find a craps table for less than $100. Blackjack tables are $100 minimums and up, with many of them being $500. Five hundred dollars for a hand of blackjack—*this country has too much fucking money*. I figured I would escape to the Palazzo to find some $25 tables, which were a little more my speed. There is also a topless pool—but I hadn't brought my bathing suit. The boob pool is not as advertised; it's pretty much all dudes trying to get cheap thrills. Any woman who dared to go topless in that pool would be quickly surrounded by a school of piranhas. I'd let the twenty-six-year-old hedge fund guys fight that out.

I thought of that old marketing campaign. *What happens in Vegas, stays in Vegas.* There would probably be a contingent from the conference that headed out to the strip clubs, but that never resonated with me. I turned forty last month, and was starting to outgrow rakish behavior. If you go to a strip club, one of two things are going to happen: You are going to walk out of there as hot as a pistol, or you are going to walk out of there googling, *Can I get HPV from a blowjob?* I disapprove. I was always too cheap to go to the VIP room, but back in my associate days I got stick-shifted in Lace in Times Square in the main room, through my pants. I was humiliated taking that suit to the drycleaners the following week. Not one of my better moments.

My wife saw me take $5,000 in cash to Las Vegas without batting an eye, despite things not going so well between us. Any marriage waxes and wanes, but lately it seemed as though everything was a fight. To *exist* was to piss her off. There was the issue of her infertility, but that was settled science—we abandoned the idea and decided not to have kids years ago. We didn't see much of each other—she worked at one of the big PR firms and put in even more hours than me. When we weren't working, we had a full social schedule, and were the smiling, happy couple, but displays of physical affection—public or private—tapered off about a year ago. The sex became so missionary and so mechanical that, in recent months, we hadn't made the effort. I worried for our future. We were lovers before we were friends, and the friendship never blossomed. Our closest friends, Bill and Jody, were like drinking buddies. The last time we were in their apartment, Jody put her tongue in Bill's ear, and the two of us stared blankly, knowing they had something we did not. There is such a thing as a marriage of convenience when there's no real reason to get divorced—no addictions, no infidelity, no violence. At that moment, we were just not terribly fond of each other.

The EQD conference was the annual get-together for those involved in the equity derivatives business. It wasn't a traditional Wall Street conference where you get the cookie-cutter Ivy League guys with Ferragamo ties and standard issue Wall Street haircuts. These were the freaks and geeks of the Wall Street world, a bunch of math PhDs and MSFEs who were too entrepreneurial to work in academia. They were also nuts. At the last conference, before the pandemic, a fight broke out on stage over one fund manager's claim that a short volatility exchange-traded fund would blow up. It turned into a giant screaming match. Less than six months later, the fund in question did blow up, losing substantially all of its value in a day. It was a memorable moment in what was ordinarily a peaceful gathering of nerds talking about things like forward starting variance.

I run the derivatives desk at one of the large Wall Street banks that executes the trades and warehouses the risk for these eccentric dingbats. I started out as a junior trader in flow derivatives, making markets in the options of small industrial concerns like Polaris Industries, small-cap stocks where information is a huge advantage. After twelve years of service, I was rewarded with a management position. Now, I'm more in a sales role, gripping and grinning and smiling and dialing, trying to increase our market share, hopefully not at the expense of profitability. Having the conference in Vegas was a big bonus: America's playground.

I checked into my deluxe king room at the front desk and wheeled my bag across the hotel lobby when I spotted BJ, the proprietor of a volatility hedge fund and an agitator at these conferences. It would be an understatement to say that BJ dressed poorly. Today, he was wearing a red-and-black lumberjack shirt with a bolo tie. Underdressed people typically don't succeed on Wall Street, but BJ was the exception. He had been putting up eye-popping returns in his fund for three years, so his appearance went mostly overlooked. I gave him a fist bump, and we exchanged a quick bro-hug, my right shoulder touching his.

"What's up, my friend?" I said, grinning.

"Living the dream. Ready for some fireworks this year?"

"Nothing can beat 2018."

BJ looked around, smirking. "I have a feeling that some people are going to *tear it up* at this conference. It's the first one since being locked up for two years because of Covid."

"You first," I said, patting him on the shoulder. "I'm going to play some craps and fire up the duck at Wing Lei. Then I'm going to bed."

"Keep telling yourself that. A hundred bucks says you'll be drinking champagne at XS at three in the morning."

"I just turned *forty*. Leave that to the young guys."

"Want to throw some dice?"

"I just got here—can I put my bags away?"

"No—you're coming with me." BJ grabbed me by the arm and headed in the direction of the casino, my bags rattling behind me.

When walking on the casino floor of the Wynn, you could practically *smell* money. Yes, there were some cargo shorts and flip flops, but the people in cargo shorts and flip flops were gambling at the $500 minimum tables. I didn't underestimate people when I was at the Wynn. I'd seen droopy, tired housewives wearing mom jeans bet $5,000 on a hand of blackjack. Last time I was here, I saw a guy wearing gym shorts and a T-shirt with at least twenty grand on the craps table, yelling *horn high yo* and doing all the prop bets, and hitting them. The guy next to him lit up a cigarette, and the dude politely asked him to put it out, saying that he was a boxer. He must have been a very good one, with that kind of bankroll.

We sidled up to a rare, sparsely populated $25 craps table and each threw down $1,000. The dealers counted it out and gave us our chips—a few black, the rest green, and some reds for change. We each put down a green $25 chip on the pass line and waited for the come-out roll, thrown by a solitary codger at the other end of the table. It was a gentle throw, but the dice bounced unpredictably across the hard surface and came to a stop.

A seven. We made $25.

"Off to a good start," I said, golf clapping.

"Don't jinx us," said BJ.

But I didn't. The next roll was a four, we both took max odds, threw some place bets on the six and the eight, and immediately hit the point on the next roll. We made five points in succession, hammering a bunch of sixes and eights, making about $2,000 each.

A couple of Jersey-Shore-type guys wandered in from the strip, possibly attracted by the Ferrari dealership. They looked confused. They squeezed us down to the far end and threw hundreds all over the table. The dealers collected and counted them, then slid a few stacks of green chips in their direction. They picked up the chips, looking like stunned mullets, laying down a couple of pass-line bets before the stickman slid over the dice. Anyone this clueless had to be lucky.

The table was hot before, but it got even hotter with the Italians straight out of central casting. Their girlfriends showed up—the one nearest to me was a four-eleven beauty named Marisa. Macho Man took the dice and bonked it off his girlfriend's forehead before chicken-feeding it down the length of the table. They hit point after point after point, playing all the hard ways and even the feature bets, high-fiving us after every score. We ordered double vodkas from the buxom cocktail waitress and tipped her with green chips. It was an orgy of winning.

After the last of the Jersey Shore guys sevened out, we colored up our chips with ten bananas, and headed off to the cashier's cage.

"*That* was pretty freaking great," I said.

"Yeah, that didn't suck. Aren't you glad I dragged you out here?"

"I almost forgot my luggage."

At that moment I felt something brush my left hand as a young woman passed between the two of us. We both stopped and look at our palms, each finding a black business card there. We looked at the woman, a petite brunette in a short skirt and high heels. She smiled and blew us a kiss, and walked off, the skirt bouncing behind her.

I read the card:

sexyamanda702@gmail.com
(702) 389-4021

"*That* just happened," BJ said.

"I didn't know they had pros in the Wynn."

"Buddy. Are you naïve or something? They're everywhere. They probably all drove in for this conference."

"You'd think they'd try to keep the riffraff out."

"She didn't look like riffraff to me. That'll probably set you back three grand at least."

BJ placed the business card on the tray of a cocktail waitress passing by. I placed mine in my pocket.

"Did you just put that in your pocket?"

"Yeah."

"Are you going to *call* her?"

"Just keeping my options open," I said, smiling.

"Maybe it'll be good for you. Get it out of your system."

Maybe, I thought, as I took my bags and headed up to my room.

———

A hotel room represents possibilities. *Think of all the things we can do in here.*

I was a frequent traveler, and methodically put away all my stuff. I'd be here for three nights, so I took my clothes out of the suitcase and placed them in the dresser drawer. I hung my jackets in the closet, and systematically arranged my toiletries in the bathroom. I didn't have anywhere to be until the opening reception tonight, so there was time to think.

I took the card out of my pocket and looked at it again. *Amanda.* I had a high school girlfriend named Amanda. She was a little high-maintenance. Also, I had never met a brown-haired Amanda. This was new to me.

Well, now I had $10,000 to go along with the $5,000 I brought, for a total of $15,000. Money was not the issue here. I could afford Amanda. I could come home with $12,000 and my wife would be none the wiser.

And there was virtually no chance of getting caught. I spent a few minutes staring at the business card. I held it up to my nose—*it smelled good.*

When you come to a fork in the road, take it.

———————————

I decided to take a shower, even though I knew I would be taking another in an hour. I washed my hair, my armpits, my butt crack, and paid special attention to the boys, scrubbing vigorously, knowing she'd be close enough to smell them in less than an hour. I ran a touch of pomade through my hair, which was well-behaved in the desert air. I brushed my teeth with the travel size Aquafresh toothpaste that I had in my toiletries kit. I rubbed a stick of Secret deodorant under my arms—the key to deodorant is that the women's stuff is much more effective, and I imagined I would be sweating profusely. For cologne, I had a sample of Byredo's "Mojave Ghost," which had been rattling around in my bag for over a year, that I saved for special occasions.

I thought about what to wear, not having much in the way of options. I could answer the door in a suit, in gym gear, or totally nude. I imagine some perverts went behind door number three—hookers have probably seen it all. Gym gear seemed too informal. A suit it was, without the jacket. I had heard enough stories about prostitutes stealing watches and wallets and anything not nailed down, so I put all my valuables, including my laptop, in the safe. I figured if I had to get up to go to the bathroom, I would make her clap. Just to be safe, I wiggled out of my wedding ring and put that in the safe, too. I pressed 1 9 1 9 LOCK and the motorized lock did its thing.

The clock read 5:50 p.m. Ten minutes. I fully expected her to be late, but at the same time, this was no streetwalker—she had a business to run and was probably used to dealing with picky clients at the high-end casinos. The agreed-upon price was $3,000, as BJ had predicted. I had little doubt that I would be able to use the full hour—I was never one to shoot before the squad was ready. The truth was: I wasn't that horny. Amanda was attractive—petite brunette, my type—but my relationship with sex was a relatively healthy one. This would be my first prostitute. I never was particularly obsessed with pornography. I wasn't one of those guys whose head was snapping around like a typewriter on the streets of New York City in the summer. I regarded Amanda as a new experience, and I liked new experiences. It would be unforgettable.

A knock on the door. Four minutes early. *I like this girl.*

Amanda was smart. She knew that if she traipsed through the lobby of the Wynn wearing platform heels and fishnet stockings, she would be quickly escorted out into the desert heat. She was wearing a *gown*, a black gown, with drastic decolletage and silver hoop earrings. I had only seen her a few hours ago, but she looked as if she had spent at least that much time on her hair.

"Can I come in, *honey*?"

As she passed by me into the room, I got a noseful of Victoria's

Secret body spray, and immediately began to vulcanize. Amanda smoothly picked up the envelope of cash on my nightstand and put it in her purse.

She turned and looked at me. "What do you want to do, *honey*?"

"I don't have much of an imagination. I just thought we'd have some fun."

"Where are you from?"

"I'm from New York," I said. It was pointless to lie, and I didn't have the energy. "I live in the city."

"*Nice.* I'm from *Puerto Rico*," she said, letting her accent hang out.

"I've actually never been."

"You should go! A lot of money going there now—people just figured out that there are no taxes."

"Are all the girls in Puerto Rico as beautiful as you?"

God, that was stupid.

"No," said Amanda, smiling. And she walked over to me and put her hands on my chest.

It had been a while—*a long while*—since I stood face to face with a woman and looked directly in her eyes. This business of prostitution is so weird; I was already developing feelings for her. It's an old saw that prostitutes don't kiss on the lips, but she stood on her tiptoes and did just that. And there we were, making out in the middle of my hotel room, with the sun dipping in the distance.

Amanda wiggled out of her dress, letting it fall to the floor, unhooked her bra, and threw it on the bed. Large, brown, perfectly round breasts. Implants. She was so flawlessly formed that there was little chance she didn't have an OnlyFans page. Some men have an aversion to implants—I didn't. In fact, I preferred them. Bring on the unrealistic standards of female beauty. Amanda had it all. It occurred to me that, up until this moment, I had never been with anyone truly *hot* in my entire lifetime. My wife, Anna, was a handsome woman. Tall, with broad shoulders, and strong bones, a runner's physique—all right angles where there should have been curves. She looked outstanding in a woman's suit. Out of it, she looked like a steeplechase racer.

"What do you think?" she asked, curtseying in a minor way.

"*Gorgeous.*" I went to feed upon her breasts and was greeted with her open hand to my crotch. I was sideways in my pants like I was parallel parked.

"Big ten pounder!" she said.

She was being charitable. I knew the statistics on penis size, and I knew that I was above average, but not by a lot. I was no Lexington Steele. It occurred to me that half of her clients were below average.

"Take off your pants and sit down on the bed, *honey.*" I obeyed, with my shirt still on. "Take off the nice shirt, too, *honey*, we don't want to get anything on that." And she promptly took a small bottle of baby oil out of her purse, dribbled some into her hand, and began to stroke. At this point, I was pot-committed—I wasn't about to kick her out mid-handjob. She stared at it, then looked into my eyes. Stared at it, and looked into my eyes. I had underestimated how *fast* this would progress; it took me two minutes to be close to an explosion.

"You want to do it, *honey*?"

I really didn't. The handjob was hot beyond imagination, and actual intercourse seemed a bit too intimate, something that should be reserved for someone special. But I was in Vegas. *If you're going to fuck a hooker, then fuck the hooker.* "Okay." She went to her purse on the other side of the room, still wearing her heels, and produced a condom. She unwrapped it, and applied it expertly in one motion with the agility of a Chinese table tennis player, then lay down on the bed, arms outstretched. "Come here, *honey.*"

I straddled her and looked down. It was a vagina, all right.

Sex or death, pick your poison, and I was in, thrusting, and the smell of her sex filled up the room.

"That's nice. Give me that ten-pounder."

In my marriage, or previous encounters, I'd let my mind wander to delay orgasm to maximize the pleasure of my partner, prolonging the act as long as possible. Today, this was not a concern. I was sprinting towards the finish line, in a run for the roses. But I wanted to try something I couldn't try at home.

"I want to—I want to come on your face," I said, panting.

"Just like the movie? That's another thousand dollars, *honey*."

"What?"

"I'll have to redo my makeup!"

"Okay."

"No, you have to get the money *now*."

Dammit. I exited her, making a soft yet audible *schlop* sound, jumped off the bed with my dick flopping around, dropped to my knees, opened the safe, fished ten more $100 bills out of my wallet, pressed 1 9 1 9 LOCK and placed them on the nightstand.

"Okay?"

"Okay."

I jumped back on the bed, straddling her chest, yanked off the condom, and began flogging my nude eel, trying to get my non-dairy creamer going. But the moment had passed. I sat on her chest, furiously jacking off for a full five minutes.

"Show me! Show me!"

It was a sad ejaculation, dribbling out and pooling on her neck, missing her face entirely.

"Good boy," she said, grabbling a Kleenex, wiping off her neck and the end of my penis.

I looked at the clock. The encounter had lasted eighteen minutes.

————————

Each year, the EQD conference began with an opening cocktail reception, filled with all the big names from the volatility world, from tail-risk managers, to long vol and short vol hedge funds, and the dealer desks at the big banks. This was a target-rich environment—my purpose here was to persuade all these funds to trade with my firm, though most of them did already. I rather liked cocktail receptions—I go to see people I hadn't seen in a while, like Micah, who started a quant vol hedge fund in Marin County after getting his economics PhD from Berkeley. He was a big-time lefty, which didn't quite square with the typical ideology of a swashbuckling hedge fund manager. But I didn't see him—I wondered if his performance had been lagging and he had feelings of inadequacy and decided to stay home.

I instantly spotted BJ—he was hard to miss. He saw me, and came walking over, completely disheveled, holding four chickens-on-a-stick and what appeared to be a vodka soda. He was pretty tuned up this early in the night. I was, in effect, paying for his drinks—my firm was a diamond sponsor of the conference.

"You look... different," he said. "Your hair is wet. You took a shower.

I smiled.

"You didn't."

"I did."

"My man. I didn't think you had it in you."

I snatched BJ's drink out of his hand and took a sip. "It was fucking weird. I think that's a one and done for me."

"But she was hot, right?"

"Yeah, but—"

"She did *anything*, right?"

"Yeah, but—"

BJ shook his head. "I don't know why you're such a crybaby about it."

My phone rang in my pocket. It said ELAINE. I showed it to BJ. "*This* is the source of my consternation." I muted the call.

"Ah, you'll get over it. Good memories. One for the spank bank."

"It was *weird*, man. I started to really like her, you know? The whole thing is just bizarre. I don't know how people do this."

BJ leaned over. "Let me tell you something, dude. I'll give you a statistic. Fourteen percent of American men have paid for sex at some point in their lives. You are now part of that fourteen percent. *I* am part of that fourteen percent. I get a pro every time I travel. I'll get one while I'm here. It's good, clean fun. I can afford it, and I don't have any hang-ups about it. It's a hobby."

"A hobby."

"Yes. I go online and read the reviews and do my research. I'm in a forum with a whole network of guys. If you're interested, I can get you hooked up."

I polished off the rest of BJ's drink. "I need to get another drink." I lifted my arm to my nose. "I took three showers and I can still smell her on me."

"I know, it's amazing, right?"

I saw a waiter walking by with a tray full of sandwiches. "Yo, I have to get something to eat." I walked a third of the way across the room and mugged the hors d'œuvres guy, taking half the mini-sliders off his tray and munching them in silence.

I had better call Elaine before she gets suspicious. I took my cell phone out of my jacket and hit her button in the favorites, getting burger grease all over my phone.

"Hello?" she answered.

"Hey."

"You make it to Vegas?"

"Smooth as a gravy sandwich."

"What's the matter?"

"Nothing's the matter."

"It sounds like something's the matter."

"Nothing's the matter. I'm at the opening reception, and was just talking to BJ when you called. I'm calling you back."

"I hope you haven't been getting into any trouble," she said.

My neck tingled. "What trouble could I possibly get into in four hours? I did throw some dice. Going to Wing Lei tonight. You remember the duck."

"I forgot to show you the carpet samples for the summer house. I'm going to text them to you. Let me know which one you like."

"Which one do *you* like?"

"I like the slate."

"Then let's do the slate."

"But I want to know what you think."

I wanted to say, *it doesn't matter what I think*, but instead said: "I trust your judgment."

"You never want to be a part of these decisions. I have to do everything myself. It's all on me."

"Maybe it's not important to me. Maybe it's important to you. So you can decide. I can decide other things that are important to me. We're a team."

"Okay."

"I'm going to get back to the reception, I'll talk to you later, okay?"

"Okay." Elaine hung up. We had stopped saying "I love you" when getting off the phone about a year ago.

This was the most disconnected I had ever felt from my marriage. Maybe BJ was right about paying for sex—a few thousand bucks, get it out of your system, no fuss, no muss, no muting notifications from your mistress texting you, no washing your dick off before you get home so it doesn't smell like latex, just clean, transactional, no-strings-attached fun. No getting into a fight about carpet samples across the country. No emotional terrorism. No psychological warfare and intrigue.

Amanda did something that nobody had done in the last ten years—she *paid attention to me*, if only for a half an hour. She cared about me, even though I paid her to do it. It was worth it.

I still had $11,000.

Fuck this cocktail reception.

I slam-dunked my napkin on the tray of a passing waiter and headed back towards the casino.

Maybe I'd go to the Chandelier Bar at the Cosmopolitan. There had to be some pros there.

As I walked past the luxury watch stores and the roulette tables, I saw Amanda headed in my direction. She was looking down. As I got closer, I waved, and smiled—

—and she just kept on walking.

LEFT OUT

FASTBALL count, two and oh. Middle-middle. Then, over the centerfield fence.

Henry had barreled up on his fourth ball of the game. In the second inning, he pulled a home run down the left-field line, just inside the foul pole, then a double off the fence in the third, then a triple in the gap in the fifth. This last home run, a three-run shot, gave him six RBIs on the day. About halfway through the season, Henry had insisted on being called Hank, in honor of the best slugger of all time, Hank Aaron. His father, Brendan, called out to him through the chain-link fence:

"All you needed was a single for the cycle!"

Henry called back:

"Isn't a home run better?"

The Braves had won. It was off to Dairy Queen. Henry got the same thing after every game: a Reese's Pieces Blizzard.

"You're going to make the All-Star team this year," Brendan said to Henry between bites of Reese's Pieces.

"I made it last year!"

"Yeah, but you're really going to make it this year. And this

league is stacked. This team could go all the way to the Little
League World Series."

"Really?"

"Think about it. You have two pitchers—Mike and Kris—
who throw 70 miles per hour. You're one of the best hitters in
the league, but you've got some even bigger power hitters, like
Big Jon, who hit 20 home runs this year. He's one of the best
hitters in the whole country. This team is going to be loaded
with talent. And you're going to be on it, and you'll be going to
Williamsport. You'll be on ESPN!"

"Dad, really?"

"I'm being serious. Look at the statistics. A .413 batting
average with eight home runs and 29 RBI. Not to mention, 25
walks. You've got an OPS over a thousand. Statistically speaking,
you've got to be one of the top three or four players in the league.
And Westport is going to be the team to beat."

"Thanks, Dad."

"I'm proud of you, Henry."

"Hank."

"Hank Kelley. Has a ring to it. I like it."

Henry was Brendan's only child. He couldn't have asked
for any more in a son: Henry was smart, got good grades, got
along with all the kids in school, did his homework, and didn't
play much in the way of video games. There was that bullying
incident a few years ago, where Henry had been imitating the
gait of one of the special needs kids, but Brendan was convinced
he didn't have a mean bone in his body. There were long
conversations in the living room about that incident, and when
Brendan was satisfied that Henry understood the importance
of it, he let it drop. Brendan knew some parents with some real
stinkers for kids, Mountain Dew-addled *Call of Duty* players
who disappeared into their bedrooms with their phones, and
took up vaping at age eleven. Antisocial fuckers. Henry was the
type to go on to be prom king, class president, and maybe even

president. He had that effect on people, looking them in the eye and calling them Mr. and Mrs. so-and-so, and giving them firm handshakes like a grownup.

"Dad, who's going to be the coach of the team?"

Brendan hadn't considered this. "Probably Mr. Ahearn. He's been coaching the longest and has won the most championships.

Brendan had known Jed Ahearn since he moved to Westport from the city twenty years ago. Ahearn had been a star trader at J.P. Morgan, making markets in the bank stocks, when he inexplicably had an affair with an administrative assistant which was *caught on camera* in an otherwise unoccupied conference room. Ahearn really went through the wringer, losing his job, his wife, and his house, moving into a smaller one far away from the beach. Word of his indiscretion traveled fast around Wall Street, and even within Westport social circles. He was a pariah. Jed Ahearn had texted Brendan one night in the depths of it—he was in the interview process for a second-tier broker-dealer and was looking for a reference. Brendan left him on read. Ahearn was toxic, and Brendan didn't want to be seen helping him out. Ahearn didn't have much to say to him after that. He did end up getting that job, a sinecure that allowed him to spend the majority of his time coaching Little League. His pay had been cut in half or more, but he got his life back. He would tell anyone who listened that things ended up turning out for the best, that he was the happiest he had ever been.

"Is Mr. Ahearn nice?"

"He's nice. Talk to the kids on the Brewers, they all seem pretty happy."

"Do you like Mr. Ahearn?"

"I like him just fine. He's done a lot for the league."

"Do you think he'll pick me?"

"He can't *not* pick you, Henry, you're one of the best players in the league," said Brendan, though he was secretly worried about this. "If he doesn't pick you, he's an *idiot*."

"Some people are idiots," said Henry.

"Yes, they are," said Brendan.

———————————

Brendan wasn't much of a ballplayer himself. He played football in high school and college as a left tackle. Back in his college days, he was pushing 320 pounds, but had slimmed down to 280 as an adult, still big enough that he had difficulty finding suits that fit. With his large abdomen and his Chris Farley hair, he sometimes had a difficult time being taken seriously. Size was important for a man. It was good to be physically large, which garnered respect, but there was a dumb football player trope in the business that Brendan found hard to shake. Brendan's football career ended with an ACL rupture that was so severe that his leg was disfigured. This was prior to arthroscopic surgery—the surgeon fileted his knee wide open. He spent weeks in the hospital, and it took him a full year to recover. Brendan was incredulous that football players today could have an ACL tear and be back on the field in four months. For him, it was a career-ending surgery that left him half-crippled.

Brendan and Grace moved to Westport upon becoming pregnant with Henry—the Upper East Side, as tranquil as it was, was no place to raise a child. People did it, and ended up with overly precocious kids who were clubbing and doing cocaine at thirteen. Westport was an obvious choice—the property taxes were too high in Westchester, and a real estate food fight was always happening in Greenwich. There was less dick-measuring in Westport, too, though there was still plenty of that. Westport also had its own public beach, on the sound, exclusive to city residents, and the commute to the city wasn't too bad, either.

Henry learned baseball the way most kids did—playing catch in the backyard with his father. At the age of five, Henry could throw the ball the width of the backyard, and do it with such precision that Brendan knew that he had been born with a natural talent. He would hit the ball off a tee with an audible *whop*, sending it well into the outfield. Live pitching at seven never presented much of a challenge to him—he never had to be taught to keep his eye on the ball. Brendan watched early videos of Henry hitting, seeing him watch the ball all the way to the bat, squaring up on it. He hit his first honest-to-goodness over-the-fence home run at the age of eight, not one of those Keystone Cops inside-the-park Little League home runs with fourteen errors. He knew he hit it—Henry did an outrageous bat flip like the South Koreans he had been watching on TV.

Brendan thought that most fathers got to live a second life through their sons. For him, playing football in high school was a lonely affair, with no parents or family in the stands. They would read about the outcome in the paper the next day. Brendan vowed not to repeat his parents' errors, and went to every single one of Henry's ballgames, and most of his practices. In the summer, they traveled all over New England, staying in Homewood Suites and Hampton Inns. Brendan got to know Henry's likes and dislikes—there was a girl, Lauren Reiner, who he stole a kiss from in fifth grade. His teammate Mike Lavache, the five-foot-eleven pituitary freak pitcher, doctored up the ball with sandpaper, because at the Little League level no one was checking. He also heard that Dave Lieder, the Robert Redford-looking first baseman, had a party at his house, with beer. Henry was invited, but gave him the hard pass. They ate in Denny's and IHOP and Perkins, as Henry was a big fan of pancakes at all hours of the day. Soon, perhaps within a year or two, Henry would be embarrassed to share a hotel room with his father. Brendan was enjoying it while he could.

———————

Brendan sat on the couch with his iPad and opened his email.

2023 Westport Little League All-Star Team Selection

He opened his mouth to call Henry over, then thought better of it.

He tapped on the email and scrolled down.

We are pleased to announce the members of the 2023 Westport Little League All-Star Team!

Jake Lingle

Bobby Lingle

Mike Lavache

Conrad Sauer

Kris Ricchiuto

Chad Pollock

Jeff Mann

Rick Alberti

Dave Lieder

Steven Bower

Jay Lamoureux

Jon Baker

Dustin Bland

Brendan scanned the list a half-dozen times. No Henry. He slowed down, reading the names one by one, mouthing them. No Henry. He counted the names—one, two, three, four, five, six, seven, eight, nine, ten, eleven, twelve, thirteen.

The Little League World Series allowed fourteen players on teams. There were only thirteen here.

That skunk Ahearn.

Brendan immediately went to his text messages and pulled up Jed Ahearn. To his dismay, he saw the last text was from 2019:

Brendan, I'm close to a job at Janney. Could really use a reference.

As you know, things have been tough lately. I need your help.

Brendan dove in anyway.

Jed, what the fuck? Henry belongs on that team and you know it.

And you only have 13 on that team—you have room for one more.

Brendan saw the (. . .) appear. Jed was at his phone.

I don't think Henry has performed well enough to make the team this year.

He can hit, but he's a defensive liability in the outfield.

And he's not a team player.

You mean I'm not a team player.

> Can we have a phone call please?

Brendan called. Jed answered on the first ring.

"Hello?"

"Hey, Jed."

"Hey, Brendan."

"Look, I don't know what you're trying to do here, but this is outrageous. Henry has the third-highest batting average in the league, the third-most home runs, and the—"

"Second-most RBIs. I know."

"This wouldn't have anything to do with me not helping you out four years ago, would it?"

"It might have something to do with that."

"Well, don't take it out on him, take it out on me."

"I am taking it out on you—this means more to you than it does to him."

"You arrogant fuck."

"Look, Brendan, we've been friends for twenty years. I needed something from you four years ago, and you weren't there for me. You need something from me now, and I'm not there for you. It's as simple as that. A real friend would have made that call. You showed your true colors. So I owe you nothing."

"Jesus Christ, Jed, you only have thirteen players on that team. It would cost you nothing to add Henry. You don't even have to bump anyone."

"Which is precisely why I'm not adding him. You are going to learn something from this, Brendan."

"You know what? Fuck you, pal. Suck my dick till my ass caves in."

"This is definitely helping your cause."

"You can play your political games as much as you want, but this team is going to lose, and it's going to be because of your stubborn ass. Everyone can see what you're up to."

"The parents in this town trust my judgment. Talk to whoever you want—it will go nowhere."

"Fucking kill yourself, Jed."

"Thank you."

Brendan hung up.

"Dad?"

Brendan whirled around.

"How long have you been standing there, Henry?"

"I just caught the end of that. I didn't make the All-Star team?"

"No."

"Why not?"

"Because of politics. Because Jed Ahearn is an idiot."

"Is this because I didn't lay down a bunt that one time against the Diamondbacks?"

Brendan remembered the incident. Henry's coach, Rob Morehead, gave Henry a bunt sign with runners on first and second with nobody out. Henry disregarded it and cranked it over the right field fence for an outrageous oppo taco, winning the game. Morehead was furious. Word of the incident undoubtedly got back to Ahearn. But that wasn't what this was about.

"No, this about me and Mr. Ahearn."

"I thought you guys were friends?"

"I thought so, too."

"Now what?"

"How's your chess game, son?"

Ahearn was right. He was the mafia don of Little League in Westport. Brendan was sure that some of the parents would find it odd that Henry didn't make the team, but nobody would question Ahearn's acumen at coaching. Nothing could be done. Brendan went back through his texts with Ahearn, and noticed that Ahearn had skillfully switched the conversation off text and onto the phone, so there would be no historical record of the conversation. Ahearn wasn't going to put it in writing that he was leaving Henry off the team because he thought Brendan was an asshole. *Slimy little bugger*. Brendan began to have violent revenge fantasies where he cold-cocked Ahearn in the left temple with the force of his 280-pound frame, and sent him to the emergency room with a brain bleed. Maybe he could hire someone to take his kneecaps out with a tire iron. But the last thing Brendan wanted to do was to end up with a mark on his U4 and be panhandling for jobs like Ahearn was a few years ago.

Instead, he would root for them to lose.

———————

Westport had powered through regionals, beating Wilton 13–3 in four innings (mercy rule) and Trumbull 10–0 in five innings (mercy rule). Brendan imagined that Mike L. was doctoring up the ball for the second game, throwing wicked sweepers with an 18-inch break, with the aid of a bit of sandpaper in his glove. The bats were alive. The Lingle twins, third baseman and shortstop, went back to back off of some sissy from Wilton, opening up a six-run lead in the first inning. The team was doing fine without Henry so far, but Henry played the game with a level of hustle that the other kids didn't, beating out grounders, sliding headfirst, and breaking the pitchers' rhythm with his aggressive baserunning. He would be missed, eventually. For now, Westport was padding its stats on the weaker teams from Western Connecticut.

On the day that Westport was due to play the state championship against Glastonbury, Henry wanted to go to Six Flags in Massachusetts. Henry had never been a roller coaster kid, and Brendan hadn't set foot in an amusement park in decades. He wondered if he would exceed the weight limit on some of the rides. Brendan indulged him. They made the drive up 84 to 91 to Agawam, just south of Springfield, where they parked in section Q3 of a truly enormous gravel parking lot. Brendan saw the twisted metal of the roller coasters in the distance, forming loops and corkscrews and 80-degree drops, and wondered if he had made a mistake coming here. He was six months shy of 50 years old, and his weight had been putting pressure on his left hip, making it painful to stand for more than ten minutes at a time. He hadn't thought about standing in long lines all day. Maybe he could find a bench to sit on while Henry rode the rides.

"Are you going to ride the Batman ride with me, Dad?"

So much for that.

Tickers were $40, or $50 with unlimited soft drinks. Brendan opted for the latter, and handed over a $100 bill to the attendant. Not egregiously expensive. He figured they would get him on the food.

"The Batman ride is this way, let's go!" Henry set off jogging in that direction, Brendan lumbering behind. When they arrived, they found that there was already a 45-minute wait. Brendan inspected the sign—nothing about weight limits. You had to be 54 inches tall to ride the ride, and Henry was pushing five-two on the cusp of puberty.

Brendan leaned against the rail to take pressure off his hip. "The Glastonbury game is at noon."

"I know."

"Don't you care?"

"I've moved on."

"I haven't."

"You should. It's no use thinking about it."

This kid.

"They've got Sauer pitching today. That kid is a walk machine," said Brendan.

"Dustin was doing pretty well towards the end of the season," Henry said.

Dustin Bland was the backup outfielder who had been thrust into right field with Henry's absence. The kid could play a little—but he was no Henry.

"Dustin would be last pick for my foxhole. I've seen him cry twice after getting hit by a pitch."

"Well, he did get drilled in the ribs by Bryan Duncan. That would make *you* cry."

"I don't know how people look at this and even think for a second that Dustin is a better player than you." Brendan bent over at the waist—his hip was killing him.

"Maybe people don't like us."

"What?"

"Maybe people think I'm a showoff and you're a big bully."

"You think I'm a big bully?"

"I don't know."

This kid. "When have I ever bullied anyone?"

"You tried to bully Mr. Ahearn."

"That's because he's a jacknuts!"

They moved forward in line. Henry looked in the direction of the twisted metal. "I'm starting to think the best people don't always win. I'm starting to think politics matters more."

"You're a little young to be thinking that, but maybe it's good you're learning this lesson now. It's true. Somewhere out there is a player who's better than Aaron Judge. And he's sitting in the minor leagues, because people think he's a bully."

"So?"

"So be nice to people. That matters more than being the best."

"Thanks, Dad."

"Good talk, Henry."

They entered the loading station for the roller coaster. Just a few more minutes. At once, the air was filled with sound of screams, laughs, and cars screeching to a halt with the *hissing* of hydraulic brakes. Two older phone-addicted teenage boys had been ahead of them the entire time in line—one of them had back acne creeping up his neck, visible above his T-shirt. They were hyperactive in a way that was uncommon even for seventeen-year-olds. They had those little dog haircuts that boys get. Brendan had been eavesdropping while having his heart-to-heart with Henry—they were talking about weed. Brendan had laid down the law on that two years ago—cannabis was an ambition-killer. Henry would never achieve what he hoped to achieve if he tried it. It was present, at school, even in sixth grade. Henry knew where it was and how to avoid it.

The coaster screeched to a halt in front of them. A *hanging* coaster. Henry got in first, and Brendan followed. He struggled to get the shoulder restraint down over his enormous chest, straining until he finally heard a *click*. The attendant came around and buckled everyone's straps, gave a wave, and they lurched forward.

Bad idea. Brendan and Henry were three rows from the front. Brendan thought the Glastonbury game would be starting about now, without Henry in right field. The Glastonbury team had a five-eight flamethrower who went 10–0 during the regular season, striking out 2.25 per inning. Henry loved the hard stuff—he could hit the fastball. Dustin Bland would be standing at the plate, quivering like a bowl of Jell-O—an automatic out. *Fucking Jed. It's not my fault he was deep-dicking a secretary in a conference room.* Brendan looked at Henry as they crested the first hill, his mouth open in ecstasy. The coaster made a quick turn, and the bottom dropped out, accelerating with the gravitational force vector of 280 pounds of payload.

He had to admit—this was fun.

———————

Brendan got the news when he got home. Westport won 4–3. Glastonbury scored all three runs on a bases-clearing error by Dustin Bland, when a routine fly ball clanked off his glove and rolled to the fence. Bland also went 0-for-4 with four strikeouts, the golden sombrero. Westport played some small ball in the final inning, with a couple of walks, a hit by pitch, an error, a safety squeeze, and a wormburner up the middle by the slugger

Jon Baker that barely eluded the infielders. They got lucky. Brendan thought about shooting a text to Jed, hectoring him about his decision to leave Henry off the roster. So much for Henry being a defensive liability—the Bland kid was worse.

One evening, after dinner, Brendan went through all the statistics and found that Dustin Bland had gone 1-for-13 in the tournament with ten strikeouts, and the one hit was a swinging bunt with the bases empty that caught the infielders back. Now they would be headed to regionals, to play against some really tough teams from Northern New Jersey.

An email landed in his inbox:

Westport Little League

Connecticut State Champs!

There will be a gathering of parents, players, coaches, and friends at 6 p.m. at the Moriarty School gym on Sunday to celebrate the Westport All-Star team's state championship and advancement to the Regionals! Refreshments will be provided.

Brendan heard Henry walk down the hall behind him. "Henry! Come here! You want to go to this thing?" He held out his laptop.

Henry scrutinized it. "Dad, I don't think that's a good idea."

"What? You still have friends there. Don't you want to hang out with your buddies?"

"I'm worried about *you*."

Brendan smiled. "I'll be on my best behavior, I promise."

"Whatever you say, Dad."

They went. Henry was silent in the car. They walked into the gym and saw a crowd of about a hundred people, high-fiving and back-slapping. There were fathers and mothers, sisters and brothers. The team went in uniform, with WESTPORT emblazoned across their chests.

Brendan broke away from Henry, bypassed the cookies and punch, and walked right up to Jed Ahearn.

"Jed."

"Brendan."

"You still have a chance to change the roster before the regionals."

"This is the team I want."

"That Bland kid almost blew it for you. He's been terrible."

"He'll come around."

"*Goddamnit* Jed, you are everything that is wrong with youth sports these days. Forget the politics. Put the best team on the field."

A small crowd began to form around the two of them. "I have the best team on the field."

"That's horseshit and you know it."

"We agree to disagree."

Brendan took a step forward, encroaching on Ahearn's space. He towered over him.

"Brendan, don't touch me."

"Was I touching you?"

"You look like you're about to touch me."

"I'm not touching you."

"Brendan, I'm going to have to ask you to leave. You're being belligerent."

"You're going to regret this, Jed, I promise you." Brendan turned around and called after Henry, who had been watching from a distance.

"*Dad*," said Henry, "I told you this was a bad idea."

Brendan harrumphed. "It was a great idea."

Henry asked: "So did you get me on the roster for the regionals?"

––––––––––

The Westport All-Star team cruised through regionals, culminating in a 10–4 win over Toms River, New Jersey.

Westport, Connecticut, would represent the East at the Little League World Series in Williamsport, Pennsylvania.

Dustin Bland was hitless throughout the entire tournament.

There was another party at the gym. Brendan declined to attend, and remained mute throughout regionals, although he did engage in texting with some of the other dads about the hapless Dustin Bland. Brendan realized that physical intimidation had backfired—that skunk Ahearn would probably sue him if he so much as poked him in the chest. When he was a young left tackle in his early twenties, he played peacemaker in bars by inserting his 320-pound frame in the middle of a fight, and he'd used *might makes right* to great advantage professionally, intimidating people with his mass. But it wouldn't work on Ahearn. He may have been dumb enough to get some trim in a conference room, but he was wily, and if Brendan had even breathed on him in a room with a hundred witnesses, he would be sitting in jail. Ahearn was well-versed with the legal system after being raped by lawyers hired by his ex-wife and former employer.

Brendan thought about telling Henry the sordid story about Ahearn, to give the situation some context, but he decided not to, because he was embarrassed at his conduct in not helping him get a job. Ahearn was doing quite well at Janney, and the whole firm was rooting on the small, dark Little League coach who had gone all the way to the Little League World Series. The news had even made its way to Bloomberg. If they won, he was sure to get a writeup in the *Wall Street Journal*, with his pointillistic portrait accompanying the article. Ahearn had a third opportunity to add Henry to the roster at this point, but Brendan had burned that bridge two weeks ago.

The first game was against Japan. Japan had won eleven Little League World Series titles, but hadn't won since 1996. They weren't a power-hitting team; they were undersized with good pitching and Ichiro-style slap hitting. They put wood on the ball. Lavache was the starting pitcher—Brendan wondered if he would try to get away with his sandpaper trick on national TV.

"Henry, don't you want to watch?" Brendan called across the room.

"Not really, Dad!"

"Get in here, let's watch."

Henry flopped on the couch, begrudgingly, and took off his socks.

The game went about as expected, with Lavache scattering ten hits, all singles, over four innings before getting chased from the mound. Death by a thousand paper cuts. Kris Ricchiuto came on in relief, and threw a bunch of junk balls that looked like strikes, the Japanese swinging wildly. The big bats woke up in the fifth inning, with two triples by the Lingle boys, and an unlikely home run from the light-hitting, slick-fielding second baseman Jeff Mann, who took Watanabe deep on an 0–2 count. Westport won, 6–4.

"Dad, who are you rooting for?"

"I'm rooting for Westport."

"Are you sure?"

This kid. "Okay, I'm not rooting for Westport. I'm rooting for whoever Westport is playing."

"Are you sure that's healthy?"

"If there is any karma in the world, Jed Ahearn will get what's coming."

"Dad, I think you should let it go."

"Son, you'll be playing senior league next year, and I want people to know that you could have helped them win it all. Like I always tell people at work: I want you to agree with me—*later.*"

"Okay, Dad. Whatever you say."

———————

The semifinal match was against Akron, Ohio—big blond farm boys, power hitters, all of them, who had slugged their way into the Little League World Series. They were not known for their pitching. Paradoxically, the Westport-Akron game turned into a pitcher's duel, scoreless until the last inning. Even more improbably since the third-string Chad Pollock was the starter. He pitched a gem, changing speeds and arm angles, keeping the farmhands guessing. Jeff Mann bunted for a hit, stole second and third, while Akron brought the infield in. Rick Alberti hit a slow roller to second, and Mann beat the throw at the plate. It was pandemonium on the field—Westport was going to the finals against Venezuela.

Venezuela was good at two things, Brendan thought—beauty pageants and baseball. Each year, major league scouts flew to Caracas to scare up the best baseball players in the country. Some of them were sixteen. Some of the kids on the Little League team looked to be sixteen. That was the thing about Latin American Little League baseball—you could never be too sure about the birth certificates. There was that Danny Almonte incident from years ago. Some of these kids had beards.

Lavache was pitching in the final, Westport's number-one starter. Even without the abrasion, he was the best pitcher in all of Little League baseball—tall, lanky, hard-throwing—he *looked* like a major league pitcher. He was matched up with Villeneuva, who had clocked the fastest pitch in the tournament. Brendan parked himself on the couch, and physically forced Henry to sit next to him. Henry wanted to go out and skateboard in the driveway. He was watching the championship game against his will.

Westport, the home team, staked an early two-run lead with three straight doubles, the Lingle boys both touching up Villenueva's high heat and Lieder sending one down the third base line into the corner. But that would be the offense for the entire game, after Villenueva settled in, with Venezuela chipping away at Lavache, getting a run in the second, third, fourth, and fifth innings. Going into the last inning, the score was 4–2, Venezuela.

Ricchiuto struck out the side in the top of the sixth, and it was Westport with last licks. After two quick strikeouts, Westport was down to its final out. Lamoureux hit a pinch-hit double in the gap, and the Venezuelan manager elected to walk the light-hitting Bower to get to Dustin Bland, who by this point, was 1-for-30 in the tournament. They put his batting average up on the screen: .033. There was nobody on the bench—Westport was out of substitutes.

"Oh boy, they're sunk," said Brendan, rubbing his hands together. "Bland is going to fuck it up." Brendan caught himself. "Sorry, Henry."

"I've heard it before."

"Imagine if you were coming up in this spot."

"I'd hit it into next week."

Bland watched helplessly as the Venezuelan pitcher painted the outside corner with two vicious curveballs. He was completely overmatched. He looked like a deer in the headlights on national TV.

Then the pitcher inexplicably grooved one right down the middle of the plate—

—and Bland connected with such force that he dented his bat. The ball was still going up as it went over the fence. It was the hardest-hit ball of any Westport player all year.

Brendan and Henry watched as the team poured out onto the field, Bland pumping his fist while doing his home run trot. He jumped onto home plate in a sea of bodies, and they went berserk, hugging him, tossing him in the air, and carrying him on their shoulders. Out came the buckets of Gatorade. Brendan saw Jed Ahearn running out of the dugout, celebrating with the kids, and holding the trophy high above his head.

"Turn off the TV, Dad."

Brendan turned it off.

Henry was crying. "I want to play golf next year, Dad."

DISAFFECTED

———————————

J EFF turned onto Possum Hollow Road, down the tree-lined street and into his driveway, past the three giant spools of fiber optic cable on his front lawn. He parked in front of the garage door, because the garage was full of optical networking equipment and could not accommodate a vehicle. He collected his keys and his legal documents and walked around to the front door, inserted the key, wiggled the doorknob from eleven o'clock to six o'clock, and pushed. He was greeted with the smell of butter chicken.

The primary benefit of Jeff's marriage was excellent food, and a secondary benefit was excellent sex. Jeff was the last in the band to marry, if you didn't count Tyler; he met Anjali when she got a backstage pass at a House of Blues reunion tour in 1999. It was odd, seeing her there—Disaffected was the name of his band, but also perfectly described their demographic, predominantly white, lower-middle class residents of economically struggling Midwestern towns, mostly smokers. There wasn't much in the way of drugs at their concerts—the odd spliff, and lots and lots of hard drinking. In the early days, there were mosh pits, and the mosh pits would turn into fights, the skinheads in their Doc

Martens would be windmilling their fists counter-clockwise, and some guy would end up getting a beer bottle busted over his jaw. Those were the days. By 1999, their fans were in their thirties, and the hooliganism had mostly subsided. Anjali was in college when their single "It's Not Over" went double platinum, but never made it to a show until the House of Blues concert in Boston. She'd bought a vintage "Straight Outta Harrisburg" T-shirt off eBay and wore it to the venue, where she was spotted by the PR team, and invited backstage with her two friends, interchangeable white girls with damaged hair. When Jeff saw her, he imagined that she would have large, dark nipples like gumdrops. That turned out to be the case.

"Did you get the paperwork?" asked Anjali.

"I got it," said Jeff.

The paperwork was a lawsuit from Jeff, the bassist, Mark, the drummer, and Jared, the guitarist, against Tyler, the lead singer, for double-dealing. Tyler had been holding himself out as Disaffected and secretly booking solo gigs. The amount of money in question was inconsequential—it was the principle of the thing. Tyler had been the quintessential lead singer prima donna, and he still was, eleven years after their big break. The preening, the peacocking was functional in 1992—in 2003, the act was tired. He was constantly in the gym, working on his abs—he always took his shirt off at shows, though the long, thrashing hair had given way to a chrome dome, due to alopecia. Jeff had no abs to speak of, and neither did Mark or Jared; they had all settled into middle age with their kids and families, moving back to their hometown of Harrisburg, Pennsylvania. Harrisburg wasn't much of a town—just the state capitol building surrounded by rolling hills and artisanal Amish farms growing corn and tobacco. It was hard for the band to remain angry in these surroundings.

But it wasn't just the double-dealing. By the time Disaffected had stopped touring, the nation was in the grips of the dot-com bubble, and Tyler had been obsessed with an optical networking stock called JDS Uniphase. He told Jeff about how optical networking would be "Moore's Law squared," and that the band should return to Harrisburg and make it the data hub of Pennsylvania. They formed a corporation, and each of the band members contributed a million dollars, substantially all of their savings. Tyler hastily signed a purchase agreement for some fiber optic cable and associated equipment—they agreed it would be stored at Jeff's house until it could be deployed. But the permit process proved to be more complex than they imagined, and they were unable to obtain rights of way, so three giant spools of fiber optic cable had sat on Jeff's lawn for the last three years. Meanwhile, there had been such a gold rush in optical networking that prices of fiber had crashed, so the spools that sat on Jeff's lawn, mocking him, were next to worthless. Jeff couldn't bring himself to hire a flatbed truck to take them to the dump. They stayed as a reminder of Tyler and his big fucking ideas. There was nothing to sue over—there was no law against being stupid. But most of their wealth had vaporized.

There was also the issue of the girl Mark had fucked who allegedly belonged to Jared, but that was ancient history by this point. They got into a fistfight outside of the tour bus over that one. Jared was drunk, swinging wildly and missing— he was intoxicated for the vast majority of their gigs. Then there was the time that Jeff accosted Tyler over his incessant peacocking, which got him left out of the band introductions during a concert. There was a fight in the parking lot over that as well. There was Mark's perfectionism in the recording studio, and how they ended up spending three times as much as they intended recording their third album, which sold ten percent as much as the second. There was the time Tyler had an encounter with two girls after a show, barely sixteen, that had him paranoid and listening for police sirens for months. There was the time Tyler told Jeff that he sucked at playing bass. There was the time Mark told Jared he sucked at playing guitar. There was the time Tyler told them they all sucked, and walked off the stage halfway through a show. There were the numerous times Tyler showed up an hour late to rehearsal, and there was the time Tyler showed up two hours late to their biggest show yet. But they had remained friends until the double-dealing incident, which was a bridge too far.

"Come, sit down, eat," Anjali said. "How does the lawsuit look?"

"It's fine. My guess is he settles for eighty thousand or so and we each get twenty to thirty grand."

"That's not nothing."

"It's fine."

"Honey, you need to get a job. You can't sit in this house day after day and think about who did what to whom."

Jeff took a bite of the butter chicken, shoveling some of the basmati rice on his fork. *God, this is good.* "We've talked about this before. I have no skills. What does a thirty-three-year-old rock star do?"

"You made some money during those reunion tours, but that's no longer an option. I can get you a job at the capitol."

"You work for a Republican state senator."

"*It's a job.* I don't think about the ideology. You have to do *something.*"

"Maybe I could open a guitar store."

"Maybe you could work at one first, and see how it goes? There's Owen Grace Music up at the mall."

"I don't know. Let's go to bed. I'm horny."

"Jeff."

But she led him upstairs to the bedroom, and lifted her shirt above her head.

Those nipples. He stripped, mounted, and commenced to dump bucketloads of his no-good sperm in her. No good, on account of the varicoceles. They would never have children.

———

"Christ, it's like Fort Apache in here."

The three rugrat boys chased each other through the house with plastic tomahawks, jumping on chairs and sofas and tables.

"Hey, knock it off, kids. Go outside."

Jake stood on his tiptoes to reach the doorknob, and in a rush they were all on the front lawn, scalping each other. At least they stayed away from his drum set—fourteen spankings had been required to achieve that.

Mark needed money, in a way that most people think of when they think of debt-strapped Americans living paycheck to paycheck. Mark was living off of Tammy's paycheck. Tammy, a hairdresser, could have used some guidance on her own hair, with the same teased bangs and frizzed-out look that was popular in those parts in 1992. She had been Mark's on-and-off girlfriend through the early years of the band, high-school sweethearts for a moment in the eighties, but drifted apart during the hedonism of blowjobs on tour buses. There was $30,000 to go around among Mark and Tammy and the three boys. Mark had brought in a small fortune during the last reunion tour, but they had blown through most of that on home improvements and body art. Mark had no tattoos during the Disaffected days, but got some in a fit of pique after losing the optical networking money, two full sleeves, as well as across his chest and back. With his long hair, he was the last member of the band that actually looked like a musician, a fact that precluded employment at most respectable places. He wondered if the band could reunite and retool their sound, as Nickelback had been having some success with their song "Someday." It wasn't too late. Mark liked this idea, but Mark and Jared were family men now—also, Jared was still sore at him over the Tiffany incident from years ago. Tyler would be game, but Mark was suing him. With the boys outside, Mark sat down at his kit and started wailing away—he still practiced almost every day. He'd form a new band, but knew of no other capable rock musicians in Harrisburg, outside of skinny high-school guitar players struggling with barre chords.

"Jesus, Mark!" Tammy arrived with two armfuls of groceries.

Mark put his sticks down. "Can I help?"

"Are you even watching these kids? They're out there eating caterpillars."

"It's my parenting style. Is it working?"

Tammy kissed him.

"There's a fifty percent chance that I got an overdraft on my debit card."

Mark looked in the shopping bag. "Three more boxes of cereal? We already have, like, eleven." He put the Cocoa Puffs in the cabinet.

"They go through them like crazy," said Tammy, putting a plastic bottle of mustard in the refrigerator. "Have you heard from Jeff?"

"I haven't. I doubt I will. I haven't talked with him since we were in the attorney's office two weeks ago. He's handling it."

"You guys are so fucking weird. You've known each other since kindergarten, and you don't talk."

"We've known each other since kindergarten, so we always know what we're thinking."

Tammy smiles. "You want to go out to eat tonight? Get a babysitter?"

"We don't have the money for that."

"We will soon."

"Don't count on it. I wouldn't be surprised if Tyler spent all that gig money on whores or something. We might never see a dime."

"Well, I feel like going out. Want to go to Brown Thompson?"

"Jesus. That's going to be like a hundred bucks." Though Mark was thinking about the deep-fried ice cream, their signature dish. "Okay. Call Katy. She's the only babysitter left that the boys haven't eaten alive."

Tammy clapped her hands. "Yay!"

"I don't know why I'm agreeing to this. We're fucking poor as shit."

Tammy put on a dress sweatshirt, and Mark a long-sleeved tee to cover up his tattoos. Tammy told Katy in no uncertain terms that the three little jerks had to be in bed by 8:30. Anything on TV was fair game, except for MTV and HBO. They rattled down Fox Creek Road in their PT Cruiser and landed in downtown Harrisburg within twelve minutes. Mark dropped a few quarters in the meter and they went inside.

The maître d' immediately recognized him. "Mr. Snider! To what do we owe the pleasure?"

"We have a reservation. Six-thirty."

"You don't need a reservation here, Mr. Snider, we always have a table for you. Come this way." He led them through a maze of white and blue dress shirts to a table by the window, looking out over the city. "Angela will be your server, please let me know if you need anything."

"They rolled out the red carpet for you. One of the perks of being a rock star."

"*Old* rock star," said Mark. "A has-been."

Nobody could have been more surprised that the band landed back in their hometown than the band themselves. They recorded their second album in Los Angeles, and they took to it, going to parties in the Hollywood Hills, skateboarding on the Strand at the beach, and nightclub-hopping downtown. This was before they were celebrities, but there was something magical about Paramount, their recording studio, and there was something intoxicating about being around all the beautiful people, so that they knew, deep down, that their album would be a huge success. They sold millions of records. The video for "It's Not Over" was filmed in a warehouse in El Segundo—they spent barely $100,000 on it, but it was in constant rotation on MTV for over a year. Tyler took to LA more than the rest of them, obsessively focused on his appearance, even lifting weights at Venice Beach.

After their disappointing third album, Jared, Mark, and Jeff thought it best to move back to Harrisburg, where the schools were good and the property taxes were low. The town treated them as something of a curiosity, rockstars in cornfields, but they were famous enough to get dinner reservations. After a few years, the locals got used to seeing them, and the pointing and waving died down. There were no groupies—the women were married and the high-school girls had no recollection of who they were. Mark had signed one autograph in the last six months.

"You're *my* has-been. Speaking of which, we don't make love anymore."

"We have three animals. Plus four pets."

"The animals go to bed at eight-thirty."

"I'm really more of an afternoon delight kind of guy."

"Is it because—"

"Your twat is tired."

"I hatched three kids. It's not my fault."

"There's no mystery anymore. I know what a vagina looks like. I've seen plenty."

"If we could take a romantic getaway—"

"We could, if we had money—"

"Then maybe we could try."

"I promise to."

Tammy took a sip of white wine.

"You need to be playing music."

"I know."

"There must be a band looking for a drummer."

"It's 2003. People don't listen to bands anymore. It's all bleeps and bloops, Venga Boys and Alice Deejay. I belong in a museum."

Tammy folded her hands and looked at Mark. "Do you ever think you'll make up with Tyler?"

"Honestly, if he'd just apologize, I think we'd probably drop the lawsuit. We'd make a lot more money touring than fighting over scraps."

"Do you think he will?"

Mark thought about the time that Tyler was two hours late to their biggest show at the Time Warner Center in Charlotte. He walked out on stage and grabbed the mic as if nothing had happened.

"Not a chance."

———

The first time Jared drank during the day, he was home from his first tour, a pile of Christmas presents in his living room. A few weeks passed, and his mother scolded him, telling him that even rock stars had to write thank-you notes. So he tapped the box of wine in the fridge, and began writing notes to Grandma and Grandpa and Aunt Shirley and Uncle Jack and Cousin Gina. He finished a glass of wine after each one, and by the ninth thank-you note his handwriting had turned loopy, like that of an eighth-grade girl. Proud of his handiwork, he stumbled out the door in his bare feet, crunching the snow, put them in the mailbox, then hurried back inside to take a triumphant piss.

He had long since abandoned his aversion to day-drinking, but these days he was flirting with morning drinking. A bottle of Yuengling beckoned to him from the fridge. It was 10:30 a.m. *What the fuck*, he thought, and grabbed the bottle, snapped the top off, and sucked down half of its contents. *It's five o'clock somewhere*, he thought, and strained his knowledge of time zones to think of where it actually was five o'clock.

Jared was sick, having woken up with a case of the crud. He called work and sent his regrets. At work, he was the Ctrl-Alt-Del guy—the IT worker who got called when someone's computer froze up. Usually, it was as simple as hitting Ctrl-Alt-Del and starting the task manager, then euthanizing the offending process. He was paid good money for his efforts. When the band eventually settled down in Harrisburg, Jared knew that he needed a plan, so he took some IT classes at the local community college. He was drunk for half of them. His co-workers found it odd that the virtuoso guitarist for Disaffected was tending to personal computers, clean-shaven, with a burgundy shirt and a company man haircut. It was as if his previous life never existed. On the last reunion tour, the fans didn't even recognize him, and thought that the band had hired some mercenary guitarist. He couldn't play unless he was drunk—it was a matter of state-dependent learning. The night that Jeff met Anjali backstage, Jared was passed out on the couch, and remembered none of it.

Jared thought it might not be a good idea to be drunk and sick, so he resolved to pace himself that day. Courtney was teaching ninth grade civics by rote memorization, about the number of representatives in the House and the length of a senator's term. Mark was the one in the band to be fulminating about politics, though he didn't know a damn thing about politics. He had the rage of Tom Morello without the education of Tom Morello. None of them had gone to college. Jared became obsessed with the guitar at a young age, stretching and contorting his fingers to make the chords, memorizing the shapes. Out of everyone in the band, he was the only one who knew what Mixolydian meant. Jeff told him he must have been Joe Satriani in a former life, with his wanky riffs and whammy stick, and added that he should dial back the hot dogging, as this was a grunge band, for Pete's sake. Jared was bored with the power chords, but had a nose for the direction music was heading—as of 1990, hair metal was on the outs, and this new band from Seattle had appeared on the scene that was capturing everyone's imagination: Pearl Jam. So he played the power chords and shut the fuck up.

Beer number two. He grabbed it from the fridge. Three. He drank them both in quick succession. Another. Four. He thought he'd give Courtney a call, which was a profoundly bad idea.

"Hello?"

"Hey. How's work?"

"I'm in the teacher's lounge. How are you feeling?"

"I'm okay. I probably could have gone into work today."

"Are you drinking?"

"I had a beer."

"Then I guess you're not picking the kids up from daycare today."

"Oh."

"Ja-red. What the hell? It's not even noon."

"Sorry."

"You're always sorry. I have to go."

Five.

Courtney had started out as a groupie superfan, following the band around from show to show with her friends. She was from just to the south, in York. She didn't have much in common with other Disaffected fans—she was smart, went to college, had goals, and didn't smoke. Jared had seen her at a bunch of shows, and at the end of one in Cleveland, he jumped down from the stage with his guitar and asked for a kiss. Though she liked Disaffected, she really liked the *idea* of Disaffected, and didn't have an appreciation for the music. She never listened to music—not in her car, in the house, during dinner, working out—when Jared wanted to play, she banished him to the garage, and would tell him repeatedly to turn it down. The only sound she tolerated came from a white-noise maker while she slept. Jared thought she had selective musical anhedonia.

Jared was out of beer in the fridge. He went into the garage to get a case sitting by the lawnmower. He would drink it warm. Yuengling wasn't the worst beer to drink at room temperature, though this beer was hot. He took the case to the living room, opened a sixth, grabbed his guitar off the stand and sat down on the couch to play some scales. He was a little rusty, but it came back in a minute or two. He loved the complex chords, the suspended chords, with texture and nuance, but he didn't have much opportunity to play those in the band. Within a few minutes of strumming, he had a chord progression he thought he could use in a song. For a moment, he got excited, thinking he should call up the other band members for a rehearsal, when he remembered that they were suing the lead singer and the band was effectively neutralized for the foreseeable future.

Jared continued to play, and drink beer, and play, and drink more beer, and then he was sloshed, fucking up his riffs. He put the guitar back on the stand with a little more force than was necessary, sending the instrument and the stand crashing to the floor.

He decided to lie down on the couch, and then he thought it would be a good idea to call Tyler and mend fences and get the band back together, but he couldn't reach the phone. He could hear his heart beating in his chest. The second he lost consciousness, Courtney walked through the front door with the kids, and frowned.

———————

Tyler had enjoyed a half hour of languorous sucking when it hit.

"Stop!"

It was too late. With an *uhh uhh uhh* he exploded in her mouth. Ella watched him throughout, then drooled it back out onto his balls.

"That's so fucking hot. How are you so good at this?"

"Just a natural," she said.

"Fry me an egg, you cunt."

"What?"

"Never mind, I'll do it."

Tyler stood up from the couch, his dick wet and swinging, produced a frying pan from the cabinet and a dozen eggs from the fridge. Ella came up behind him and grabbed his bare ass, her flat chest against his back.

"Are you sure you're only eighteen?"

"You insisted on seeing my driver's license." She rubbed his bald head.

"Standard operating procedure. I bet you can't name three of my songs."

"I've watched three of your videos."

"Back when I had hair."

"I like you like this."

"Want to hear the Red Rocks story again?"

"Where you were crowd surfing? You told me that one."

"How about the Madison Square Garden story?"

"You told me that one, too. When are you going to make new stories?"

Tyler grimaced. "The other guys are pissed at me. Not anytime soon."

"Why are they pissed at you?" She licked his ear.

He turned to face her. "Long story. Don't you have to go to school?"

She slapped him lightly. "I graduated *last year*, dummy. But I have to go to work soon."

"Delia's? At the mall?"

"You listened." She bent over to pick up her panties and shimmied into them.

"At least stay for breakfast?"

"I have to go in early. Inventory stuff."

"At least leave me something that smells like you."

Ella shimmied back out of her panties and tossed them to him. "Here. Wash them when you're done."

Tyler tilted his head back and draped the lacy underthings over his face, breathing deeply.

"You're a tool. I'm leaving now, okay?"

Tyler gave her a peck on the cheek. "Goodbye, sweetie." And Ella was out the door into the stifling Harrisburg air.

Tyler was naked, but he didn't particularly feel like putting on clothes. He could be naked. He went into his office, opened up the clangy file cabinet, and pulled out a file named BERNIE. Bernie was his manager. Of course, Tyler wasn't supposed to have a manager. The band had a manager. They were both named Bernie.

Tyler had reached out to Bernie around the end of their last reunion tour, thinking that he could ditch his loser friends with their bellies and bad clothes and have a solo career. He erred in calling his act Disaffected, which amounted to a breach of the contract that the four of them had signed with the other Bernie years ago. Tyler reflected that if he had just approached the band about a solo career, they probably would have approved, so long as he did not hold himself out as Disaffected. But you can't put the toothpaste back in the tube. Tyler had played two solo gigs in Washington before word got back to the band— with the internet, it was impossible to keep anything a secret. Anjali had noticed an advertisement for one of his shows on a message board, and spilled the beans. That led to a series of angry phone calls from Jeff and Mark, with Jeff showing up at his door, panting, yelling about fiber optic cable. He hadn't heard anything from them since, which made him uneasy. Not even an email. He wondered if they were plotting, or if they had simply given up on the friendship entirely. But Tyler was up to his eyeballs in pussy, and continued to work with Bernie for more solo gigs, this time going out as Tyler Kuhner. Tyler wondered if he could go to the gym naked.

He picked up a pair of 35-pound dumbbells and stood in front of the mirror. He began doing hammer curls, watching the veins in his biceps bulge and curl into tendrils. The refractory period had passed and he began to get another erection, and found that lifting weights in the nude was strangely autoerotic. He gave it a few strokes, but his balls were still throbbing with dull pain from the marathon morning blowjob, so he quickly abandoned the idea. He did lateral raises, one-armed rows, front raises, and shoulder presses, and forgot all about his penis.

He stood at the mirror and stared at the result. *Fucking stud.* He couldn't wait to do another show and take his shirt off on stage; he looked even better than he did when he was twenty-four. He added fifty push-ups for good measure, his dick brushing against the carpet.

The doorbell rang. Tyler quickly stood up and looked around for a towel. He grabbed his T-shirt, covered his package, and opened the front door. There was a man in a suit. He handed him a brown envelope.

"You've been served, Mr. Kuhner."

"Thanks?" He checked to make sure that he was covering his crotch.

He closed the door, dropped the towel, and took the envelope over to the kitchen table and sat down. It was from a law firm he didn't recognize. He opened the envelope with a knife leftover from breakfast, and emptied the contents: a ten-page document. He began to read.

> Plaintiffs Jeff Snider, Mark Aughenbaugh, and Jared Taylor ("Plaintiffs") by and through their undersigned attorneys Brady Kepper Bauer LLC, as and for their complaint against Tyler Kuhner, respectfully alleges as follows...

What followed was a list of complaints about Tyler's business dealings with Bernie (his manager) and the two gigs he did in Washington, along with a cease-and-desist order to prevent him from booking any solo gigs under the Disaffected name in the future. The damages sought were $500,000.

Well, this is all about the optical networking stuff, he thought. But it only covered a fraction of what they all lost in that venture. Maybe it really was about his solo gigs—he didn't think it was that big of a deal. Though, deep down, he knew it *was* a big deal, because he had been sneaking around to do it. He hadn't allowed himself to believe that he was deceiving his bandmates.

This could all be handled with a phone call.

Tyler looked at the phone.

He was going to have to hire an attorney, but he didn't know where to start. He walked over to the kitchen and got the *Yellow Pages*, and looked under L for Lawyer, which referred him to A for Attorney. All real estate attorneys and injury lawyers. What was the kind of lawyer he was looking for? *Litigation*. He found a few, but didn't know which to choose.

Flummoxed, he grabbed the phone and dialed Jeff's number.

"Hello?"

"Hey, this is Tyler."

Jeff abruptly hung up.

Tyler looked at his phone. *After all these years, it comes down to this*. Waves of remorse washed over Tyler, and he allowed himself to feel genuinely sorry for what he'd done. He wanted to apologize, but Jeff would clearly have none of it, Mark needed the money, and Jared was drunk by that time of the day. Maybe he would write an email. For this, Tyler put on pants.

From: **rockstar68@aol.com**

To: **msnider@cs.com**; **jaredguitar@earthlink.net**; **bassman@aol.com**

Guys,

I wanted to apologize for booking those two gigs in Washington—I've been a monster. Not just about this, but everything. I hope you will forgive me. I'll give you all the money I made off those gigs. You don't need to sue me. Let's get together soon.

Tyler

His fingered hovered over the mouse for a moment. *Send*.

Tyler spent the next few minutes trying to find that Zara White scene he found last week, when an email arrived.

From: **bassman@aol.com**

To: **rockstar68@aol.com**

Cc: **jaredguitar@earthlink.net; msnider@cs.com**

Tyler,

You fucking lost all our money in that fucking optical networking deal and then you have the balls to fucking steal from us. Fuck you, you fucking fuck. We're all tired of your shit. See you in fucking court.

Fuck you,

Jeff

Tyler found the Zara White scene, and turned up the volume, so he could hear her squeaky voice, begging for it.

SEABOARD STREET

THE tattoo was going well enough until Lyle moved from the muscle of her calf to her shin, at which point the pain, which had been trivial, became intolerable. Olivia writhed in the chair, holding her hands on her forehead, grimacing. She tried to focus on the artwork on the walls—one piece made use of a small swastika placed upon a crudely drawn demonic figure. A tear fell from Olivia's eye and rolled down her right cheek.

"You're crying?" asked Lyle.

"No, it feels good, I'm just—all emotional, and wrung out!"

"That's what small amounts of pain over long periods of time will do to you. Some people find it enjoyable."

Olivia did find it enjoyable. She understood now why people became addicted to tattoos—the *experience* of getting a tattoo was thrilling. Olivia had wanted a black widow spider on her leg since she saw one on a goth Instagram model she followed. The model frequently wore bikinis shaped like bats. Olivia thought of herself as a large, poisonous spider—beautiful, silent, and deadly. She had been thinking about it for a year until the day she turned eighteen, which was on Tuesday. She was no longer jailbait, but she had been drinking since thirteen and tried smoking at fourteen, though smoking disagreed with her—that habit didn't last longer than a few months. She had carnal knowledge at fifteen, sticky fumblings that resulted in a pregnancy scare, which resulted in a large investment in prophylactics. The tattoo, she thought, would make her look *hot* and *dangerous*, and given that it was shorts weather in Myrtle Beach nine months out of the year, there would be ample opportunity to display it. All the tattoo parlors—all of them—had been zoned to a two-mile stretch of road known as Seaboard Street, which was also home to two strip clubs, a few piercing pagodas, and an Alcoholics Anonymous clubhouse. On Friday nights, all the kids would drink in parked Dodge Challengers and get inadvisable tattoos, from places like Bulldawg, which is where Olivia was currently. These were not high-end tattoo parlors—they were the types of places where you'd pick a piece of flash off the wall and some convict would inexpertly apply it to your body. Lyle had a better reputation than most.

Olivia watched as Lyle methodically dipped the needle into a tiny thimble of black ink, then resumed work on her leg.

"Almost done—just have to do the red."

The door to the studio opened, the bells hanging above it clanging wildly.

"Hey, Lyle."

"Hey, Rowdy."

A burly man with a thick red beard and a flat-billed cap stood over them. "What do we have here?"

Lyle wiped his nose with the back of his right hand. "This is Olivia. She's getting this black widow here on her leg."

Rowdy inspected it. "*Very nice.* I like the detail. Lyle, you owe me a hundred bucks."

"Did you come all the way here for a hundred bucks?"

"You lost a bet. It's not my fault you picked the Gamecocks."

"I'm sitting on my wallet right now, and I have my hands full. Just take it out of the register. Hit the button. I'm fucking watching you, man, don't take more."

Rowdy squeezed behind the counter and removed five $20 bills from the cash register, and shut the drawer. "Olivia, you want to come to a party tonight?"

Olivia looked up from the chair, evaluating the opportunity. "What kind of party?"

"A fun party."

"That's not a lot to go on."

"That's all I got. What else do you have planned?" He took two fingers and pantomimed finger-banging himself, while whistling.

"Very funny. Sure, I'll come."

"Great. It's at 597 Yaupon. Come on over whenever." He turned towards the door. "Smell you later, Lyle."

"Fuck yourself," said Lyle. The door closed, the bells ringing for a second time.

Lyle put down his needle. "We're done. Go walk over to the mirror, tell me what you think."

Olivia got up slowly, stiff from spending three hours in the chair, and walked to the full-length mirror, turning from facing the mirror to a three-quarter rear view.

"That's one big fucking spider," said Olivia.

"Isn't it great? Look at the detail."

"It's beautiful. Thank you!"

Lyle put away his needles and ink. "Get back in the chair for a minute, let's get that fixed up." He grabbed a bottle of antiseptic solution, squirted it into a paper towel, and wiped down the tattoo where the surrounding area was red and swollen. He then unrolled a length of Saran wrap, spun it around her calf, and tore it off.

"What's that for?" asked Olivia.

"Germs. Don't take this off for twenty-four hours. You're good to go."

"How much do I owe you?"

"Four hundred bucks."

"Yeesh." Olivia reached into her purse, pulled out a wad of crumpled-up cash, and began to count it. "That's a lot of days working the drive-thru window at Dunkin' Donuts."

"Which one do you work at?"

"The one in Surfside."

"I go to the one on twenty-ninth all the time."

"Come by Surfside, I'll give you a free donut."

"You're a sweetheart." Lyle's expression changed, showing concern. "By the way, I don't think it's a good idea for you to go to that party."

"Why not?"

"You're a good kid. I don't want to see you mixed up with that bunch."

"Why not?"

Lyle sighed. "Suit yourself. You've got a spider on your leg now, you look like a badass."

Olivia blew him a kiss and sashayed out of the studio, clanging the bells.

———————

Was it 597 Yaupon? Or 579 Yaupon? Olivia figured she'd head in that general direction and look for a pile of cars in front of a house. Yaupon was on the south side of town, in the slums, though the locals didn't call it the slums. They didn't call it the ghetto, either. They didn't have a name for it—it was among the no-tell motels, where the streetwalkers roamed and the vagrants found rooms for $15 a night. It was a place her mother told her never to go, and she had obeyed, until today, the third day after her eighteenth birthday. She was an *adult*, with a big fucking spider on her leg. Her mother had stopped monitoring her movements since she dropped out of school and started earning her own money. She put "579 Yaupon" into Google Maps and the robot led her down Kings Highway South, past Family Kingdom, a decrepit Chinese restaurant, a massage parlor, and an adult boutique. She could see the lights of the hotels off in the distance. One day, she wanted to go to one of those hotels in the middle of the winter, when the rates were cheapest, ask for the penthouse, and stand naked in front of the window, overlooking the ocean. She figured it wouldn't cost more than $75. But after paying $450 to Lyle, exclusive of tip, she had $20 left. She hoped there would be free beer at the party.

As Olivia pulled her 2003 Impala up to the house, she thought that Yaupon looked much better at night than it did during the day when you could see the houses in disrepair. She quickly realized that 579 was the wrong address, after rumbling to a stop in front of single-story house with the lights off, but she saw at least a dozen cars and mopeds parked up the street. She pulled forward, parallel parking behind a rusty Ford F-150. There was a group of three men wearing flat-billed caps on the front lawn, one of them Rowdy—he was impossible to miss. Olivia approached them, the dead grass crunching beneath her feet.

"Well, well," Rowdy said, looking her up and down.

"Hi, Rowdy."

"What's up with the fucking Saran Wrap?" asked one of the men, who bore a striking resemblance to Vanilla Ice. He had gold teeth.

"She just got a tattoo," explained Rowdy. "Show 'em, Olivia."

Olivia extended her right leg, turning it back and forth.

"A bitch with a spider on her leg," said Vanilla Ice. "That's fucking gangster."

Rowdy continued to size her up, his small eyes coming to rest on her body parts. "Hey, Olivia. What are you, five-nine, 110 pounds, B-cup?"

Olivia felt a shot of adrenaline, beginning to understand the gravity of the situation. There were no rules here, no laws and no law enforcement, just the way of the street, the underworld of Myrtle Beach. A body had washed up near here a few years ago, with no head, hands, or feet. Olivia wondered if Vanilla Ice was responsible.

"That's right," she said.

"You should really talk with my friend Benji. He's inside."

"You want some heroin, bitch?" asked Vanilla Ice.

"Rick, shut the fuck up," said Rowdy. He turned to Olivia. "*Do* you want some heroin?"

"Maybe later."

"There's some inside if you change your mind. Go see Benji."

"Okay." Olivia walked toward the front door, feeling their eyes on her back. As she approached the threshold, she heard Rick say, "That is one hot cranky bitch."

Olivia knocked on the door and waited a moment, before she considered the absurdity of knocking on the door of a party where there was heroin. She turned the knob, and pushed inside.

There were about a dozen people in the living room, most sitting on the floor, slumped over, motionless. There was a flat-screen TV at one end, showing a vintage recording of a *Girls Gone Wild!* episode, with a blonde girl, probably about Olivia's age, drunk, flashing her tits for the camera. There was a crack across the middle of the screen, splitting it into a top and bottom image. The carpet was stained. The ceiling fan was on, rattling miserably. Classic rock was coming from somewhere in the room. Olivia didn't see any heroin, but the collapsed bodies were all the evidence she needed—there must have been some somewhere. There had been a girl in school who had overdosed on heroin, in her car, which she had allegedly procured from this part of town. Olivia looked down and saw one of the bodies staring at her, a kid wearing a ballcap with DERANGED in Olde English letters printed on it. She suddenly became self-conscious, and realized she had nothing to cover her legs.

"I just fucked!"

A man encrusted in tattoos and piercings all the way up to his chin came bounding out of a bedroom, totally nude, his enormous hog glistening triumphantly. He held his hands in the air, and pumped his fist.

He spotted her. "Who are you?"

"I'm Olivia."

"I'm Benji. Give me a minute." He disappeared into the bedroom, and re-emerged moments later, wearing pants. His earlobes had large gauges, and they were flapping wildly.

"Nice to meet you. Sorry, that was totally unprofessional." He extended his hand, and Olivia took it.

"Rowdy said I should see you."

"Fuck, yeah. What's with the Saran Wrap?"

"I just got a tattoo. See? It's a black widow spider."

"Dope. You want some heroin?"

Olivia shook her head.

"You want to make some money? I could get you a thousand dollars tonight. You won't have to do a thing."

Olivia stared at him.

"I'm a pimp."

"Oh."

"This will be the easiest money you ever made. Trust me—you won't have to do a thing, I swear."

Olivia considered this. She hadn't set out to be a prostitute when she decided to get a tattoo. She hadn't set out to go to a heroin party either. A trapdoor had opened and she had tumbled into what appeared to be hell, among the fiends and devils, a near-death experience that she was struggling to escape, reaching for the light. Or—she could descend a few more levels into the abyss, and see what awaited her. She felt very *adult*. She wasn't in the mood to get fucked by a strange man, but there was something so earnest about Benji, telling her that she wouldn't have to do a thing—would she be modeling clothes? Was this a guy that just liked to *talk* to hookers? Would she cuddle? A thousand dollars was a lot of money—more than she'd make in two weeks slinging Bavarian cream donuts. She could get another tattoo. She could get that hotel room she had been dreaming of. She could get that dent fixed on her car.

"Trust me," said Benji. Olivia watched the piercings on his lower and upper lip as he mouthed the words.

"Okay."

"Dope. Let me make a few phone calls and I'll let you know what to do. There's beer in the fridge."

Olivia stepped over two bodies and made her way into the kitchen, opened the fridge, and grabbed a Busch Light. She popped open the top with a hiss, then took a sip. She paused, then sucked down the entire can, gulping frantically, then reached for another.

Benji was standing behind her. "So here's what you're going to do. Go to the Breakers hotel up on the north side, and go to room 1404. You're going to see Billy. He's a longtime client of mine. You don't have to worry about a thing. He'll give you two thousand in cash. You keep a thousand, and bring a thousand to me. Don't make me come looking for you."

"Okay."

"You should bring me the money tonight."

"Okay."

"He's expecting you at eleven o'clock. Don't be late, don't be early, be there right at eleven." Intelligence flickered behind Benji's eyes.

"Okay."

"You nervous?"

"Yeah."

"Don't be. If this goes well, I have plenty of work I can give you. You can ease into it over time."

"Thanks."

Benji looked at his phone. "It's nine-thirty now. You have a little time to get a burger or something."

"I like Cook Out."

"*Love* Cook out. What's your order?"

"A big double with lettuce, tomatoes, onions, and cheese, and a huge Coke Zero."

"Baller. I'm more of a tray guy myself. Now get the fuck out of here."

Olivia thought about shaking his hand again, decided it would be inappropriate, did a volte-face and exited the house. Rowdy and Rick were gone, but the third guy, with his flat-bill cap, was smoking a cigarette, staring at her. She acknowledged him and got in her car, backed onto the dusty lawn, and swerved onto the street.

She had time. Olivia thought she would drive down Ocean Avenue at fifteen miles per hour and cruise the strip, looking at the hotels. In Myrtle Beach, the tallest buildings—by far—were the hotels. There were no office towers, no banks, no finance— just real estate and hospitality. The hotels were the lifeblood of Myrtle Beach, and had a tight grip on the Chamber of Commerce and local politics. The Grand Strand had a thousand restaurants, most struggling from the economic state known as perfect competition. The hotels weren't exactly thriving, either. As such, there was no middle class in Myrtle Beach—just low-wage workers like servers and housekeepers, commingled with a few real estate millionaires, who all lived at the Dunes Club at the far north end. Olivia's mother worked as a medical admin at Myrtle Beach Otolaryngology. She made $18 an hour. Their apartment, on River Oaks, cost $900 a month. Olivia wanted her own apartment one day, but since she was more or less emancipated, it didn't make financial sense.

There were the usual characters roaming the strip at night, mostly disaffected Ohioans wearing jean shorts and tank tops. She heard the *whirr* of a moped behind her—probably a crackhead. She slowed the car to avoid a crowd of people spilling out from Bummz, drunk, into the street. She took a left on 21st Avenue, past the Starbucks and the Soho Sushi, and took a left back onto Kings Highway, making a beeline for the Cook Out.

Predictably, there was a line of cars around the restaurant, but it would move fast—the chimney on the roof of the restaurant was chugging out meat smoke. She took her place in line, and looked at her phone—five minutes before ten.

As she was staring at the screen, the phone rang. *Mom.*

"Hello?"

"Did you get the tattoo?"

"I did, it's awesome."

"Where are you? I thought you would be home by now."

"I went to a party. A guy at the tattoo place invited me."

"What kind of party?"

"A fun party." Olivia smiled to herself.

"So, are you coming home now?"

"Hang on a sec, I'm in line at Cook Out. *Can I get a big double with lettuce, tomato, onions, and cheese, and a huge Coke Zero?* Sorry. I have to run an errand after. Don't wait up for me."

"Well, don't do anything—"

"—I wouldn't do. Of course not. Love you, Mom."

By this time, Olivia had pulled around to the drive-thru window. She put her phone down on the passenger seat.

"Olivia!"

Olivia looked up to find one of her high-school classmates in the window, wearing the customary red Cook Out polo shirt.

"Kayla! What are you up to these days?"

"You're looking at it. What are you up to?"

"Oh, I'm a prostitute."

"What?"

"Just kidding. We should totally get together sometime."

"Sure, text me! Here's your food."

Before Olivia pulled out of the parking lot, she had already unwrapped the cheeseburger and taken a big bite, leaning over the foil so as not to get grease on her shirt. Benji's client probably wouldn't like it if his whore smelled like fast food. As she scarfed down the last of the burger, she navigated to a parking lot within walking distance of the Breakers, and took a long suck of the Coke Zero. She looked at her phone—10:15.

Olivia began to think that this was not such a good idea, and cursed herself for not considering this when she was back at Benji's house. The guy could be a weirdo—the guy could be violent. The only thing she knew about self-defense was to ram the attacker in the nose with the heel of her hand, driving it up into his brain. That would stun him, giving her time to escape. What if she didn't get paid—what would she tell Benji? Would she end up like the headless, armless, legless body, stranded on the beach in front of the Blue Hotel? It was too late to back out—or was it? She and Benji never exchanged numbers. But it was a small town—there was always a chance of running into him. There was a chance of running into the john, too, unless it was someone in town on vacation. She began to sweat profusely, her armpits dripping down her sides. *Fuck.*

She looked at her phone—10:45.

Time to go. She closed the car door behind her, setting off in the direction of the hotel.

She would, obviously, have to walk past the front desk. *Play it cool*, she thought, though she didn't know how cool she could play it with a roll of Saran Wrap around her leg. *Just pretend that you have a room there*, which meant that she would intuitively have to know where the elevators were, and not wander around the lobby looking for them. The automatic door opened, blasting her with air conditioning that was far too cold for this time of year. The front desk clerk, with his hairy arms, regarded her for a second, and went back to his computer. She saw the elevators in the distance, and hustled in that direction.

1404. Fourteenth floor. She pushed the button. There was no music in the elevator.

Room 1404 was off to the right. She hurried past the pink stucco and the window-unit air conditioners.

She stood at the door. She looked at her phone. 10:57.

What the hell. She knocked.

She heard a bed creak, then footsteps.

The door opened.

It was a man in his forties, in a pink-striped polo shirt, and khakis. Probably a golfer from the Dunes Club. He was wearing a Rolex Submariner.

"You aren't who I ordered."

Olivia stood speechless.

"You're even better. Come in."

Without ceremony, the golfer took off his shirt, revealing a wicked farmer tan, and hairy nipples.

"What's the Saran Wrap for?"

"I got a tattoo—you like it?"

"I guess."

In turn, Olivia began to lift her shirt over her head. "Stop!" he said. "Didn't they tell you? Leave your clothes on."

"Okay."

The golfer unbuckled his pants, and they fell to his ankles, revealing a pair of boxer briefs with a small sideways bulge. He doffed those too—they snagged the end of his penis, sending it boinging higher upon being freed. He kicked his pants to the side and sat down on the edge of the bed.

"Get on your knees."

Olivia complied.

He spit into his hand and began to stroke. "Humiliate me."

"What?"

"Humiliate me. Tell me how small it is." Olivia noticed that he was wearing a wedding ring.

"Um. You've got a small penis."

"You've got to do better than that."

Olivia really leaned into it. "Fucking married white guy with a tiny dick. Fucking pathetic."

The golfer began to stroke faster.

"Ridiculous. If only you could see what a loser you are."

The golfer began to pant audibly, his dick turning into an angry red throbber.

"I saw a cock three times as big two hours ago. This is a joke."

Golfer was turning purple. "Watch it! Watch it!"

Olivia looked at him.

"No, not me, this!" He pointed at his penis, which launched a few volleys of semen in her direction, landing on the carpet.

The golfer slumped back on the bed, exhausted from a few minutes of exertion. "That was awesome. Please tell Benji thanks." He pulled his pants back on, and handed her an envelope. "Here. Maybe we can do this again sometime?"

Olivia took the envelope, and peered inside. She didn't want to count it in front of him, but there looked to be roughly $2,000 in there. She shoved it in the pocket of her shorts.

"Goodbye," she said. She was in the elevator, through the lobby, and back out into the humid night air.

———

Olivia took a few steps towards the parking lot, and stopped. She looked at her phone: 11:27. Benji would likely be up all night—he could wait for the money a little longer. She would spend a few minutes sitting on the beach. She walked around the south side of the hotel, and onto the pathway that led to the sand. She took off her sneakers and socks, and held them in her left hand as she plowed through the sand, stumbling occasionally. The sand was dry—it was low tide, and it hadn't rained in a week.

She walked halfway down the beach, and dropped to her hindquarters. It was a new moon—all the stars were visible. The only constellation she knew was Orion. She found Betelgeuse in the left shoulder, the red supergiant—she learned about that in science class sophomore year—the only thing she remembered. She looked to the south, at the row of hotels, interspersed with a few carny rides, including the SkyWheel. A couple had filmed a porno in the giant, climate-controlled Ferris wheel two years ago—she was shocked at the effort law enforcement expended to track them down. But there was no likelihood that Olivia would be caught—there were no texts, no phone calls, no credit cards, no evidence that she spent a minute in that hotel room, unless there were cameras in the hallway. The hotel probably had better things to do.

Olivia took the envelope out of her pocket, removed the bills, counted them, and held them to her chest. She thought that if she made $1,000 a week for a year, she would have $52,000, plus what she made at Dunkin' Donuts. She would be able to afford an apartment, the penthouse in the hotel in winter, more tattoos, and a new car. It was the easiest money she had ever made, though she knew that it would not always be so easy. Maybe instead she could get a job as a dancer at the The DollHouse, and come home with a thick wad of cash in the mornings. A world of possibilities opened up to her, and she forgot momentarily about what she had seen, what she had done, and she almost forgot about giving the money to Benji.

THE WHITMAN
SCHOOL

———————

I RETRIEVED the bottle of Absolut from my nylon backpack, set it down on the tile floor, and smiled in expectation. Then I pulled out a ham-and-cheese sandwich in a triangular plastic box that I bought from the Sunoco station for $1.49.

This was my dinner.

The floor was chipped and broken; there was a bulletin board on the wall, filled with holes, and a few remaining thumbtacks holding torn pieces of yellowed paper in place. The desks and chairs had been moved out decades ago, sold for scrap or secondhand use. There was a chalkboard with a few remaining pieces of white chalk. NIGER had been scrawled on the blackboard in the upper-right hand corner, which amused me—I doubted that the scrawler knew anything about French colonies in West Africa. There were no lights, but lots of windows. It was getting dark. I laid out my half-body-size piece of cardboard and sat squarely on it, contemplating the vodka. I hadn't had any since last night, and I was detoxing a bit—I usually started my mornings with half a bottle just so I could feel normal. I unscrewed the cap, lifted the bottle to my mouth, and swallowed three times in succession. Just like the old days at the university, before I would head into class. There was a reason I had chosen this place—it was like home.

As it turns out, you can be fired even if you have tenure. My day-drinking was an open secret in the department for years, and it was tolerated, if not co-signed—I had the second-highest teacher evaluations in the college. Nobody got groped, I never puked in the trash can, and the status quo continued for some years until I pissed my pants while standing in front of the white board. I didn't even realize I had done it. One of the students called it in to the dean, and then began a series of legalese emails from the associate dean, which ultimately resulted in my termination. But I got to keep my pension, and the checks dutifully hit my account every month. I sold my house, which I had some equity in, and began my life as a backpacker. People in Rivertowne referred to me as homeless— *look at that poor alcoholic professor who lost everything and is now living in the woods*. As any backpacker will tell you, there is a fine line between backpacking and homelessness. If I was homeless, I was homeless by choice, worn down from years of paying cable and utility bills. I had no lawn to mow, no light bulbs to change, no carpets to vacuum. I had all the time in the world to think.

I have a PhD in mathematics from the University of Connecticut—topology, more specifically. The thing about having a PhD in math is that there are, at most, about fifty people in the world who care about the work that you are doing. There isn't even an academic association for topology. I authored a textbook in 1998, which, at last count, had sold seventy-eight copies. It took me a full eleven years to get my PhD, one of which I had taken off to hike the Appalachian Trail. I'd planned to do a lot of thinking about my thesis on the trail, but I ended up mostly thinking about finding water and food. That was in the pre-drinking days—I had abstained from alcohol into my thirties out of force of habit from my teenage years when I was straightedge, growing up in Red Lion, Pennsylvania, listening to Stryper. The drinking began when I got my PhD, figuring *what the hell*—I had accomplished everything I wanted to accomplish. And then it became a real handicap. I'd made a few attempts to quit, even going to Alcoholics Anonymous for a while, but found that it closely resembled religious conversion therapy, and in the world of mathematics, where the practitioners understand life's most fundamental truths, few believe in a higher power. They told me to take the cotton out of my ears and put it in my mouth, but I couldn't help but weigh in at the meetings, trying to prove the nonexistence of God. They sat there, smiling, and told me to keep coming back. It is easier for a camel to pass through the eye of a needle than for a professor to get sober. My students didn't like me much, anyway. It wasn't long before I was let go that I caught some differential equations students passing around a hobo/professor meme. I'm not a hobo, I'm a backpacker.

I'd been squatting in this old school since November; the winter is the rainy season in South Carolina. It hadn't been in use since the seventies, judging from the décor. It was on the black side of town, the other side of Fourth Street. I'd been wandering in and out of Blacktown for three months, down the main streets and through neighborhoods to get to the schools, and nobody had accosted me, not even once. A fifty-nine-year-old white man with a giant green backpack and a gray, flowing beard might attract attention elsewhere in Rivertowne, but not here. If I was on the white side of town, some busybody would call the cops on me in a half-second. I headed into downtown every once in a while, mostly to go to the ABC store, but the other businesses shooed me away if I darkened their door. Mostly, I'd lay out back behind Kimberly's and drink, leaning against the dumpster, until they called the cops on me. The first few times, I got thrown in the clink, but now they knew I was just the harmless town drunk, and made me move someplace else. Sometimes people give me food or money. The food I take; the money I refuse. I have money. I have $2,500 deposited into my bank account every two weeks. For me, living outside is a choice, and it is for a lot of other people as well.

Outside, I heard a car door slam, and heavy footsteps approaching the building. In the three months I'd been here, not once had someone approached the abandoned school, let alone in the middle of the night. I hauled my ass off the floor and made my way to the window. Two white men were walking toward the building, carrying gas cans. They were wearing jeans and blue windbreakers.

I rushed to the door and peeked down the hall. They were in the lobby. It was difficult to make out their faces, but I could tell that they were privileged men—their cheeks were fat and rosy, and they were each carrying an extra thirty pounds. They wore white sneakers. They started pouring gas all over the entrance to the school.

I quickly stuffed the bottle and the ham-and-cheese sandwich into the backpack and ran into the passageway, down the hall, and out the back of the school, slamming against the lever of the door. As I ran outside, I heard a *whoosh*, and felt a rush of air behind me. I ran into the woods, barreling through underbrush and poison ivy, and turned to look. The whole school was in flames.

Fuck. I forgot my cardboard. That was a good piece of cardboard.

The flames rose high into the night, and a Ford F-150 sped off in the distance.

———————

I slept in the woods, feeling the heat of the blaze, though I didn't drink much and I didn't sleep much. I finally drifted off to sleep as the sun was coming up, and the fire was mostly out, when I heard the *beep beep beep* of heavy machinery backing up. I sat up, and looked—a bulldozer was colliding with the charred remains of the building, smashing it into rubble.

This was all very unusual.

Why would anyone burn down a school that had been abandoned for over forty years in the middle of the night?

And why would someone bulldoze it the next morning?

I was pissed at the two rednecks—if they showed up one or two hours later, I would have been passed out on the floor, and would have burned to death. You'd think that if you were going to commit arson on an abandoned school, you should at least go through the building and see if anyone is there before burning the place down. Clearly, they were inexperienced criminals. Rich guys—that much I could tell. Though, nobody in Rivertowne was truly rich—they were $200,000-a-year guys, at best.

I sat and watched the demolition of the school from a distance, and when the bulldozer rumbled off down the driveway, I emerged from my hiding spot. The school was as flat as a pancake. I was going to have to find another place to live, and I did not know of any immediately available abandoned buildings. Back to the days of the Appalachian Trail.

I heaved my backpack on my shoulders and began the three-mile walk into town. It was a warm day for February. I already knew what would happen—any business I would try to enter would eighty-six me on account of my smell. I try to take a shower once every other week, at the Planet Fitness, where I have a membership, but that's six miles in the other direction, and there was no time for that. It occurred to me that I didn't have any vodka—I was going to be miserable in a few hours. But this I wanted to stay sober for.

Once I hiked out of Blacktown and into Whitetown, the catcalls picked up. *White people are more class-conscious than black people*, I observed. Black people never bothered me—

There but for the grace of God go I, was their attitude. Once I crossed Fourth Street, it began with a redneck yelling "Faggot!" out his car window. I ignored it; the guy undoubtedly had a gun in his car. I did not have a gun. A lot of the homeless people in Myrtle Beach are packing—they live in tent cities and are constantly getting robbed. I was, to my knowledge, the only backpacker in Rivertowne, and I preferred it that way. Myrtle Beach is heroin city, and I wanted nothing to do with that.

I made my way down Laurel Street and headed towards the Bistro, the one fancy restaurant in town. Amy, the owner, was always good for some gossip. I knew that I would be an unwelcome sight in my current condition. I opened the door, and made my way to the hostess stand, and Amy promptly appeared, yelling "*Out, out!*"

"I need to talk!"

"Herb, get the hell out of here."

"Well, come outside with me! It's important."

Amy and I stood on the sidewalk, eyeing ach other. She was pure, one-hundred percent Rivertowne, of Scotch-Irish descent, built like a wombat, squat, with a round ass and a Kate Gosselin haircut.

"Herb, what do you want?"

"Amy, I'm sober."

"That's nice, Herb. How long?"

"Twelve hours."

"Of course."

"What do you know about that school down on Pearl Street on the other side of town?"

"That's the Whitman School. It was an equalization school, for the black folks, in the 1950s, you know, so South Carolina could avoid integrating schools. During the whole separate-but-equal period. Why?"

"Someone burned it down last night."

"Oh."

"What does 'oh' mean? Sounds like you know something."

"Who told you it burned down?"

"I was *living* in it. Two guys came and poured gas all over it. I had to get the hell out of there."

"Hmm."

"Tell me what's going on."

"Well, the Whitman School has been the source of some controversy in town. The black folks wanted to restore it, and make it a historical landmark, and the city said it didn't have the money."

"How much would it have cost?"

"A few million. But number one, they had the money, because they built that new community center on the white side of town. And number two, they could have pretty much gotten it paid for with grants."

"So why didn't they do it?"

"You know: They don't want to put any resources towards that side of town."

"Well, the city definitely burned it down."

"Herb, you don't know that."

"Amy, you're telling me that the school was a big source of controversy, and suddenly two white guys pour gas all over it and set it on fire? And then a bulldozer shows up the next morning?"

"Someone bulldozed it?"

"Yes."

Amy paused. "This is bad."

"You know people on city council."

"Herb."

"You can get to the bottom of this."

"Herb, I don't want to be anywhere near this. I have a huge financial stake in what's going on here."

"Fine. *I'll* get to the bottom of it."

"I don't think that's a good idea."

"What do I have to lose? Absolutely nothing. They can't

take anything from me. I don't have anything. Also, those two hillbillies almost killed me. Imagine if they did? Imagine if they killed someone? Imagine if they found my body in there the next morning?"

"Are you really saying that someone from the city burned it down?"

"Either that, or they hired some goons to burn it down. There are no such things as coincidences."

Amy held her nose. "Herb, can I recommend you take a bath before you get involved in this? Maybe a change of clothes?"

"Who was leading the charge to save the school?"

"Talk to Pam. She has that farmstand up the road."

———————

I had walked by that farmstand on Laurel Street at least 200 times and never stopped—most of my food I got out of gas stations, because it was cheaper. I never was much interested in green peppers. But I always waved at the black woman when I walked by—I never knew her name. She would wave back and give me a friendly smile.

By this point, it was about seventy degrees. Perfect if you're sitting around on your front porch with an iced tea—not ideal if you're detoxing off alcohol and walking five miles with sixty pounds on your back. Amy was right—I smelled terrible. At least the farmstand was outside.

I saw Pam at the farmstand from a distance, a black woman with close-cropped gray hair, in her seventies. As I approached, I waved to her, and she waved back, smiling. She seemed surprised when I approached the farmstand.

"You must be Pam," I said.

"Yes, sir."

"I heard you were heading up the effort to turn the Whitman School into a historical monument."

"I was."

"So you know what happened to it?"

"I do."

"I was there. I saw two men burn it down."

Pam looked at me.

"Pam, I know you probably don't want to talk to a white person about this, but tell me why the school was so important."

Pam sighed and looked off in the distance. "We were *proud* of that school. You know, the equalization schools in those days were very modern, with the newest architecture, and the best teachers, but the only thing we didn't have money for was textbooks. We had hand-me-downs. But we got a better education there, better than the..."

"Go on."

"Better than the white kids. It was our way of proving we could do it. The students who went there did very well, and the teachers were dedicated. I actually was the last class, the class of 1971. The school was built in 1954."

"And in 1972, the schools were integrated, yes?"

"Yes. It's funny, because South Carolina was the only state with equalization schools—the government went to great lengths to keep the schools segregated."

"What did you do when you graduated?"

"I went to Duke."

"No kidding."

"Yes. I'm a minister at the Baptist church in town. My husband is a cardiologist. Most of the students from that school went on to do great things."

"Are you angry?"

Pam winced. "Who am I to say anything about it?"

"I will say something on your behalf.

"Where are you from, Mr. Herb?"

"Connecticut."

"Mr. Herb, this is *The South*. You're not going to change *The South*."

"Pam, two white men committed arson. In your neighborhood."

"Much worse things have been done in the past."

"Schools don't just spontaneously burn down. There was no electricity or gas."

"That's what they will say."

"Don't let the bad guys win."

"I appreciate your support, Mr. Herb."

"When is the next city council meeting?"

"Wednesday. And Mr. Herb—you look like hell."

———————

I had managed to stay sober a total of five days in a row. I had the shakes, intermittently. Every cell in my body wanted to go to the ABC store and get vodka, but I couldn't be drunk for the city council meeting. Though everyone would assume that I was drunk anyway.

The first order of business was to go to Goodwill and get some new clothes. I could afford nicer clothes—but no other store would let me in. I got a white-and-gray striped button-down shirt, size sixteen and a half, and a pair of charcoal slacks that were a bit too large. Buying dress shoes was impractical—I would just wear the pants over my hiking boots. There was no realistic place I could get my hair cut, so I did it myself—it didn't look too bad. I got a thing of pomade and patted it down. For a second, I considered shaving the beard, but decided against it. Too much work to grow it out again. I went to Planet Fitness and took the shower of a lifetime, and got some pizza on the way out. I didn't want to walk for two hours to get to City Hall, and get sweaty and filthy again, so I ordered an Uber. My passenger rating was abysmally low, but one eventually did pick me up, and I tipped the driver in cash at the end, hoping it would get my rating up. He eyed me suspiciously in the rear-view mirror throughout the ride.

When I got to City Hall, there was a small crowd milling about—mostly white women in floral-patterned dresses, and white men in pleated pants. There was a contingent of black folks wearing purple and gold—those must have been the colors of the Whitman School. I looked at my Casio watch—quarter to the hour. I wondered if security would give me a difficult time. Though, apart from the beard and the hiking boots, I was downright respectable at this point. The pomade had hardened on my forehead—I touched my hair to make sure it was still there. That shower at Planet Fitness had been otherworldly—I spent a full hour just standing under the water in a trance. It almost made me want to live in a house again.

The city council meeting had security, two police officers guarding the entrance, and a metal detector. I could see the cops eyeing me as I approached the entrance.

"You're going to have to leave the backpack outside," one of them said. I noticed that he did not call me *sir*.

"Everything I own is in this backpack."

"The backpack could have weapons in it. And it smells. Leave it by the entrance, we'll keep an eye on it. I doubt anyone is going to take it."

I reluctantly slid the backpack off my shoulders and set it next to the door, and walked through the metal detector, setting off a loud *beep*.

My pocketknife. I went back outside, put the pocketknife in my backpack, and went back through the metal detector without incident. I scanned the room—the black folks, in their purple and gold, were sitting on the left side. I spotted Pam; there was an empty seat next to her, and I took it.

"Good evening, Mr. Herb. How are you feeling?"

"I need a drink. It's been eight days. Are you nervous?"

"What is there to be nervous about?" she asked, smiling.

"Well, I'm nervous. I can feel everyone looking at me. I'm the town drunk."

"You have a right to be here as much as anyone."

I looked around the room. The South had long since been integrated, but not this room—the black people were on one side, and the white people were on the other. There was no overt animosity, but the white folks were smiling and gladhanding, talking about this or that oyster roast or church function, while the black folks were deadly serious, staring across the room at the white folks. They had forever lost a piece of their history. They weren't here to protest—there was no bringing the school back, but it was a show of solidarity. They had no voice—any black person who spoke would be dismissed out of hand. I hadn't intended to become a social justice warrior—I was more angry about the fact that two rednecks could have turned me into hobo fricassee.

And with that, the two men who burned down the school took a seat at the front of the room with the rest of the city council.

I stared at the two men, portly, with rosy cheeks. One of them reminded me of a character I had seen in a porno in the eighties, one of the only fat porn stars I had ever seen, ex-Ron Jeremy. He looked like a *sportsman*, someone who would traipse off in the woods to bag an alligator or a wild boar, and then call the local news station to take pictures of it. If he had more money, he'd be a trophy hunter, hunting lions in Kenya. The other one, better dressed, appeared as if he had come tumbling out of the womb looking like a banker. I wondered if I had seen him at Rivertowne National Bank on the occasions that I went in to get cash, sending all the other customers scurrying away. There was no doubt in my mind that these were the two men who had burned down the school that night. I looked at their nameplates—*Mr. Davis* and *Mr. Vaught*. Davis was a common name in these parts—I wondered if he was the Davis that owned the Ford dealership.

The mayor, Susan McCoy, took her seat in the center, a

petite woman in her late fifties, whose family had owned the beer distributor on the north end of town. I suddenly recalled that she was cousins with Amy, the proprietor of the Bistro, which explained her reticence to talk about the school with me. Rivertowne had a population of about 8,000, but was growing rapidly on account of economic refugees from the north, buying cheap property on the outskirts of town. This city council was all Rivertowne natives, families that had lived in the area for generations, before integration and in some cases all the way back to the antebellum South, but the demographics were soon to change in the coming years, as busybodies from New York and New Jersey took their places in city government. For now, this was small-town politics, and it became clear that everyone knew each other, everyone knew everything, and Davis and Vaught couldn't have acted without the blessing of the mayor.

Sue McCoy called the meeting to order.

"Thanks everyone for being here today—it's good to see so many people here engaged in city affairs. And thanks to our city council, who work tirelessly to make Rivertowne a better place."

I looked at Davis and Vaught. They were grinning.

"Now, onto old business. The first item is the Whitman School—as you have probably heard by now, the school inexplicably burned down earlier this week. It's a tragedy, and my heart goes out to the representatives of the Whitman School here tonight. But since it is no longer economically feasible to restore the school, we'll drop this item from city business and move onto new business." The mayor smiled all the while.

I felt myself standing up, almost against my will, and walking towards the microphone. I was detoxing still, and sweating.

They mayor glared at me. "Sir, there is a comment period at the end of the meeting."

"I'd like to speak now, if that's all right." My hands were shaking and bumped the microphone, sending feedback screeching around the room.

"Sir."

"Don't you think it's odd that an abandoned building with no electricity and no gas would suddenly, inexplicably burn down in the middle of the night? Doesn't that seem unusual to you?"

"Sir."

"Especially when that building was the focus of impassioned debate among the community about whether it should be restored and turned into a historical site?"

"Sir."

I went on, only pausing to look around the room—everyone was transfixed. "I was living in that building. I lived in that building the last three months, and I was there the night that Mr. Davis and Mr. Vaught burned it down," I said, pointing at them. The crowd gasped softly. "I saw them pull up in a Ford F-150, take out a few gas cans, pour gas all over the building, and set it on fire. I escaped, and I'm lucky to be alive. I was there when a bulldozer showed up the next morning, just a few hours later, to demolish the place. You ever stop and think about how the city knew that quickly that the school burned down that a bulldozer shows up to demolish it a few hours later?"

I looked over at Davis and Vaught. They were looking back at me, pie-eyed.

The mayor interjected. "Sir, you realize that you are accusing two city council members of arson, a felony?"

"I was there, I saw them do it."

She motioned towards the cops, and in one swift motion I was carried out of the room into the entryway, and handcuffed. The crowd buzzed.

"On what charge?" I yelled.

"Disturbing the peace," one of the cops said. He couldn't have been older than twenty-five.

"At least let me take my backpack, it has all my shit in it."

I'd been in the clink at least a dozen times, but usually they let me out after a night or two. This time, I was going to have to serve the full ninety days, and by then the fuss over the Whitman school would have blown over. At least I would get three squares and finish sobering up. I'd stopped drinking for eight days on my own—maybe this is what it would take to finally get clean. And I would have time to think, maybe about math and topology. I thought about taking my story to CNN or something like that, once I was released, but I had made my point. The whole town knew that the white city council burned down that black school on the black side of town. Sunlight is the best disinfectant.

It felt good to have a purpose again. I felt useful, though the prison guards treated me with complete indifference. I thought about what I would do once released. The unemployment rate for mathematics PhDs was close to zero. This was the most time I'd spent indoors in eight years. I could go back to work—but the thought of paying taxes and rent still weighed on me like ten encyclopedias. I could decide later. I ate a stale grilled cheese sandwich and baked beans and stared at the cinderblock wall, thinking of the future.

BEYOND LOVE

"You're beautiful."
          "You're married."
"I could not be."
"That's crazy talk."

Melanie Alexopoulos was a Greek fertility goddess, all breasts and hindquarters and flesh, flesh that would eventually succumb to gravity and be no good in a decade, but at age thirty-one, she was Robert's object of affection, his paramour, his *main squeeze*. She was working the fragrance counter at Saks Fifth Avenue when Robert swept in off the street with a very complex scarf knot and pea coat, and inquired about fragrances for his wife. He sampled fragrance after fragrance, Byredo, Le Labo, and Frédéric Malle, until the air had turned pungent and they were both intoxicated with sex potion. The final one, "The Promise," Robert sprayed on the inside of his forearm, and Melanie went in to smell it and brushed his arm with her nose. Robert bought it, thinking it might be good luck, and Melanie rang him up, in her tight black sweater. Robert made a pretense of perhaps coming back for more fragrance in the future, so asked for her business card—*aha!*—he had her email address, malexopoulos@s5a.com. Over the course of the coming months, Robert accumulated seven bottles of fragrance, some for his wife, Emily, and some for himself. Emily wondered about all the bottles accumulating on the bathroom counter, but figured it was just a phase. Robert did smell good, for a change.

Robert wanted to fuck Melanie in the pussy. But he had been married for seventeen years, and was careful to stay within the lines of the marriage—*flirting was okay, right*? It was after his fifth trip to Saks that he worked up the courage to ask her out for coffee. *Coffee was okay, right?* At Gregory's Coffee on 58 West 44th Street, he learned that Melanie was the sixth of seven children, practically an afterthought. She grew up in Astoria, went to school at Pace, and lived near Columbia. But she possessed none of the hard cynicism that most New Yorkers had, wide-eyed and innocent even in her thirties. He wondered how many times she had been fucked, and concluded, *not many*. They began touching on their coffee dates—*holding hands is okay, right*? But Robert knew that he was dangerously close to crossing an invisible line, and ending up in Melanie's apartment in a mess of bedsheets, Le Labo, drops of semen, and clots of blood. He knew that his conscience wouldn't be able to sustain the weight of that transgression.

"It's not crazy talk. I could divorce Emily. We could get married."

"Don't do that. It's not fair to her."

"I'm not happy. We could be together."

"I love you."

Emily was bored.

She counted—this was the nineteenth time she had taught 19th Century Architecture, a fact which she found somewhat amusing. But she was sleepwalking through it. She turned away from the white board, and counted, one, two, three students sleeping in her class. She thought she might not make it to a twentieth time.

After class, she gathered her things, logged out of the classroom computer, and collected her dry-erase markers—those things disappeared, and you had to have your own supply. When she turned around, all the students were already gone, no questions, no one to walk out of the building with. Loneliness descended. Emily slung her bag over her shoulder, went downstairs, and walked out of the building onto 8th Street. New York gets 110 days of sunlight a year. This was not one them.

Robert had always implored her to take a cab or an Uber home, thinking that the subways were too dangerous, but $50 each way to and from the Upper West Side would pretty much eat up all her salary as an adjunct. The 8th Street station was literally right across the street—she'd take the R train up to 42nd Street and switch to the 1, get off at 79th, and walk two blocks to 81st, where she shared a townhouse with her husband. The townhouse was her idea—it was a historic property, and in 2003, at the depths of the bear market, was only $4 million. Now, in 2014, it was worth $12 million. Robert had almost made more money on real estate than he had working at Twitter, a fact that Emily was keen to remind him of.

Robert was at the door. "We need to talk," he said.

Emily set down her bag with a crash. "Is something wrong?"

Robert motioned for her to come to the dining room. They sat down at the table.

He looked at her gravely. "I want a divorce."

Emily felt a numbness in her crotch. "What did I do?"

"You didn't do anything. It's me."

"Why?"

Robert prepared himself for the next sentence. "I'm in love with someone else."

Emily felt the heat rise in her face. "Who *is* she?"

"It's not important."

"Who is she?"

Robert pursed his lips. "She works the fragrance counter at Saks."

"Oh."

"Right."

"Seventeen years of marriage down the drain?"

"It's been wonderful. I need a fresh start."

"You're having a mid-life crisis. You're trading me in for a younger model. It's a terrible cliché. That's what you are: a cliché."

"Not false."

"How is the sex?"

"I haven't slept with her. I wouldn't, out of respect for you."

"Somehow that doesn't make me feel any better."

"It's my fault. I'll give you anything you want."

Emily thought about this for a second. "I want the house. And a little money to cover expenses. You can have everything else. You're not hooking up with another woman and kicking me out of the house."

"That's all?"

"That's all. Remember what we agreed upon seventeen years ago? If you cheat on me, I litigate this to infinity and take everything. If you don't, we part amicably. Thanks for not cheating on me. Just give me the fucking house. I like the house, I picked it out. I don't want to move."

"That's totally fair." He added: "I love you."

"That was a stupid thing to say. You love someone else. While you're at it, let me see a picture of her."

"Emily."

"I'm serious, I want to see what I was up against."

Robert reluctantly pulled out his phone, shuffled through his photos, and displayed one of Melanie Alexopoulos to Emily.

Emily shook her head. "I didn't stand a chance."

———

A month later, a small moving truck double parked outside to pick up the rest of Robert's belongings. There wasn't much. Emily was getting all of the furniture—Robert simply had to pack his clothes and personal effects. Robert and Melanie were moving into a substantial rental loft in Tribeca. Robert expressed concern that Emily would be rattling around the big house all by herself. Emily thought about getting cats to keep her company, but then *she* would be the cliché—frumpy middle-aged woman rattling around a house with a bunch of cats.

Emily thought she should have seen this coming. Robert always had been a bit of a *dude*, with his complex scarf knots and ironic mustaches. The preening had picked up in recent years. He had taken her on some of his shopping trips. With his trim frame and energetic waist, he could model just about anything. Emily dressed like a professor. Robert always teased her for wearing "dark, sweatery things," loose-fitting pullovers in shades of black, brown, gray, and forest green, paired with men's jeans. The longer they were together, the less they did together. While Robert was microdosing at his Twitter parties with the tech glitterati, Emily would be at home, reading e-books on her Kindle, free ones that she got from the library. But they had always been a team. They had no clothes in common, they had no friends in common, they had no work in common, but the relationship lasted as long as it did on deep, mutual respect. Robert sometimes thought he was making a mistake. Emily sometimes thought Robert was making a mistake, to trade away the safety and stability of a seventeen-year marriage for some strange. He would have to figure it out on his own.

After the moving truck left, Emily was in a 4,000-square-foot townhouse—alone. It was deathly quiet, except for the hum of city noise outside. Robert had taken his Bang & Olufsen stereo system, so there was no music to listen to. She went into the kitchen, reached into the cabinet, and pulled out a package of microwave popcorn, and stuck it in the microwave. She stood by the microwave through the crescendo and diminuendo of popping. She poured the popcorn in a large blue plastic bowl and came to rest on the sofa in front of the television, and pulled up *Amélie* on Amazon Prime, a movie she had always wanted to see but Robert had refused to put on because he wouldn't watch foreign films with subtitles. Emily found herself sobbing in parts of the movie—living alone was not off to a good start.

At the conclusion of the movie, she went upstairs, the steps creaking, doffed her pants, put on an oversized T-shirt, and crawled in bed, underneath the down comforter. Robert would always tease her by touching her feet with his in bed—she hated it; she thought feet were gross. It was their nightly routine. A few weeks ago, Robert said to her, after she had kicked him for the millionth time, *you'll miss this when I'm gone,* and now she did. Robert, at this moment, would be playing in titties and fur. Maybe she would get a cat.

———————

One difficult thing about teaching is that you have to do it even in times when you don't have the emotional energy. Teaching is a creative act, and it's difficult to do while distressed. The 19th Century Architecture class went worse than usual. Emily stood at the front of the class, in her forest green sweater, and was completely devoid of answers. She let them out early. The students, perhaps sensing trouble, avoided her and hurried out of the classroom, leaving her to log out of the classroom computer, wipe down the board, and collect her dry-erase markers in silence. It had been two weeks and a day since Robert left. She thought about dating, but her sexual capital had been mostly depleted. It had been a good while since a man had expressed interest in her. An introvert, she didn't have many friends outside of Robert's social circle of tech jerks; just Kathryn, another adjunct who taught public history. Her husband, Emmet, was a fantastically successful artist, a recovering alcoholic, who made huge, beautiful mobiles of birds out of chopped-up beer cans which he sold for $100,000 apiece. They also lived in Tribeca, and Emily wondered if Kathryn would bump into Robert and Melanie someday on the street. She concluded there was a good chance of that happening. Emily hadn't talked to Kathryn since Robert gave news of the divorce—it was too embarrassing. She would have to tell her eventually. Emily resolved to call Kathryn when she got home.

When Emily got on the R train, she found herself looking around the subway hopefully, wanting to make eye contact with someone, a man, in defiance of the unwritten rule that you should never make eye contact with another person on the subway. There was another professor on the train she recognized, who taught in the business school, and Emily looked at him for a full five minutes, hoping to get his attention. But he was buried in his phone. They both got off at the 42nd Street station in the mad rush of commuters, and Emily found herself following him all the way to the 1 train uptown, which coincidentally, was where she was going. Again, she stood across from him in a subway car, making eyes at him, and yet he stubbornly refused to return her gaze, completely oblivious to her presence. Defeated, Emily got off at the 79th Street Station.

Emily walked up to her house, grabbed the mail out of the mailbox—a property tax bill, Robert's responsibility—turned the key, and pushed the door. No cat to greet her. She set her bag down on the floor near the kitchen island, and removed her phone from her back pocket, intending to call Kathryn. But she thought she would drink some cranberry juice first. She opened the refrigerator and took the pitcher, but mishandled it, spilling a half-gallon of cranberry juice all over the refrigerator and the floor.

Dammit. This was bigger than a paper-towel job. Emily went upstairs to get a towel out of the bathroom, still holding her phone.

When she took the first step downstairs, she slipped—her

shoe was wet from the cranberry juice she had been standing in. She fell forward, smashing her face on the stairs, flipped over, landed on her back, and came to rest at the bottom of the stairs, face down, her phone sliding a few feet away from her.

How did I get down here? She looked around, at the refrigerator, the cranberry juice on the floor, the phone a few feet in front of her, and the frosted glass doors to the townhouse just beyond that.

How long was I out for? Judging from the position of the sun, Emily figured she might have been unconscious for about an hour.

Well, I'll just get up.

She couldn't. She couldn't feel her legs.

Well, I'll just pull myself over to the phone with my arms to call for help.

A sharp, shooting pain traveled down her side. She had broken something—ribs? Her arm? Her shoulder? She tried to get purchase from the palms of her hands and pull herself forward, even an inch, but it was too painful.

Robert will be coming home shortly.

No he won't.

Checkmate. *This couldn't be checkmate,* Emily thought. *This isn't how it ends.* She grunted and gasped as she tried to pull her body forward, but screamed from the pain. Out of breath, she put her forehead down on the wood floor and rested.

Ring! The singsong Apple ringtone cried out from her phone a few feet away. She raised her head and looked at the phone. *Robert.* She tried again to pull herself forward, screaming. The phone rang, and rang, and then it stopped. *Bloop!* Robert left a voicemail.

Emily wondered how many times he would call before he came to check on her. He would know that she was home this time of day, and he would know that it was unusual that she didn't pick up. She figured that, if she was lucky, he would call again tomorrow, and then he might take a train up from downtown to see what the hell was going on. If she could stay alive for that long. Robert was a fool, but he wasn't *evil*. She knew that he still cared about her. He was probably calling to ask about his favorite T-shirt that he left behind, or something inconsequentially stupid like that.

Or, maybe he would think that Emily was angry at him, and had stopped answering his calls. In that case, maybe he *wouldn't* check up on her, and would leave her at the bottom of the stairs to rot. Maybe he would cop a resentment at her—*Fuck her, I'll just hang out with my slam ham*, which would be something he was capable of. Emily tried to send energy out through the universe, a psychic message that she needed help. She couldn't tell if it was working.

It was getting dark. Foolishly, she hadn't turned on the lights when she came in the house—bright sun was coming through the windows then. Emily would be lying on the floor in abject darkness, alone with her thoughts. Emily and Robert met at a grad student party at Penn in 1995—a skinny, bearded compsci grad student with Morrissey hair who used an outrageously corny pick-up line on her while wearing a Big Johnson T-shirt. She thought he was an irresistible, entertaining goofball. He took off his pants, too, to reveal matching Big Johnson boxer shorts, and later told her that the corny pick-up lines *played*. Emily wondered if he had used one on Melanie. She couldn't get the image of Melanie out of her head, the dark curls, the perfect face, the huge bombs—and she was sorry that she had asked to see the picture. Emily was built like an ironing board—her hair, which was once a straight bob, had become unkempt, veering into crazy lady professor territory. She hadn't kept herself up. She remembered Robert commenting one time—she couldn't remember exactly what he said—but the essence of it was that what he really wanted was a beautiful woman to have on his arm for galas and formal events. Emily fell short, preferring to read books on the couch in her ugly sweaters.

Then she thought: *Why am I blaming myself for this? He's the one who ran off with another woman.* A marriage was *forever*— they should love each other unconditionally. Emily wasn't excited about hanging out with his tech bro friends, modern hippies who dabbled in left-wing politics but never read the underlying books, philistines, all of them. There was swinging culture, too, though thankfully Robert had never been attracted to that. She thought they were all a bunch of clueless hedonists with too much money, not knowing the value of it. But she tolerated them. She tolerated it all, because she had made a promise to Robert and she kept it. It was about keeping promises, not keeping promises until a better opportunity came along. *Fuck Robert*, she thought—but at this moment she needed him to come walking through that frosted glass door.

He still had a key.

He'll never want me now. I'm paralyzed.

Even if I survive this, I'll need constant care.

The room was pitch black.

In her contorted position, Emily went to sleep.

Emily awoke to the smell of shit.

She had defecated in the middle of the night, but since she was paralyzed, she couldn't control it or feel it. This indignity, on top of everything else, was too much.

Ring!

Emily lifted her head to look at her phone. *Mom.* The phone did its singsong Apple noise, then went silent after about thirty seconds.

Emily had told her mother about Robert's not-quite-infidelity when it happened, three weeks ago. Her mother was more upset than she was, on her behalf. Her mother also had a penchant for stuttering—saying the same word over and over again at the beginning of a sentence—and for always commenting on any background noise. Emily's mother had the hearing of a bat—she could hear birds chirping across the street, through the window. "That *asshole*," she had said, which is what mothers do when faced with an external threat to their children. Emily had tried to explain that she had a part in it, but her mother wouldn't have it. Emily didn't know what time it was—she figured about 8:30 a.m., and wondered why her mother was calling so early. She probably saw something on TV, perhaps Fox News. She wasn't a big Obama fan.

Emily tried once more to pull herself towards the phone, hoping that the pain had subsided. She managed to locate the pain—it was both in her right shoulder *and* her ribs. So she tried pulling herself forward using her left hand only, using the coefficient of friction between her skin and the wood floor—she managed to pull herself about a half-inch, with great effort. Encouraged, she rested for a minute and tried again. She couldn't tell if she was actually moving forward, or if it was just an illusion. She did this five times, and she seemed to be no closer to the phone, but her body had rotated counter-clockwise a bit. She decided this was progress, but she hadn't had anything to eat or drink in twenty-one hours. She thought she had probably peed on herself as well, but couldn't smell that.

Ring! It was a (212) 998-number. NYU. She had been a no-show for her first class, and the school was calling to check on her. There was no chance they would send someone after missing one class, or even a day's worth of classes. Emily thought about how long it would take for *anyone* to check on her—Robert, the school, anyone. Probably about three days. Could she survive three days without food and water, lying in a crumpled heap at the bottom of the stairs? Her thirst was growing unbearable— she looked over at the refrigerator, full of water and juice and soda. The cranberry juice had dried into a bright red stain on the floor.

Emily heard a clanking outside, and looked up to see a

moving shadow on the frosted glass window of the door. It was the mailman. "HELP!" she screamed, over and over again, but she was weak and not loud enough, and the glass was too thick. The mailman clanked the mailbox shut and walked down the stairs onto 81st Street.

I am not going to die here, she thought, and with every ounce of effort she could muster, she tried to pull herself forward with her left hand, grunting, screaming, until she was utterly exhausted. She looked up—she had traveled about an inch. *I am going to die here*, she thought—she needed a miracle. She needed Robert to urgently remember that he had left some important piece of paperwork in the house, and come back to retrieve it. She needed her mom to decide to visit. She needed someone at NYU to find it highly unusual that she had missed her classes, and head up to her house to check on her.

Ring! It was Kathryn. She had probably heard that Emily missed her classes, and was calling to check on her. Emily began to sob uncontrollably, thinking that the tears she shed were wasted water. She talked to the phone as it rang—"Please, please, *please* come here! *Help me*!" The sobbing turned into outright bawling, her chest heaving, which caused even more pain in her side. Emily came to terms with the fact that, yes, she was going to die alone, at the bottom of her stairs, in the house she had won in her divorce from her straying husband. There would be no more classes to teach. There would be no future or potential romance. There would be no more books to read. There would be nothing. Emily, an atheist, did not believe in an afterlife, which was inconvenient now. She would die, and it would end—there would be nothing afterwards. It just—ends.

Emily wondered about funeral plans—she guessed that her mother would take over and that she would be cremated and interred in the Northridge Cemetery in Upper Darby, Pennsylvania, where the rest of her family was. Perhaps there would be a memorial service in New York—Robert would arrange that. He would ensure that Melanie was not present; he had enough sense not to invite her. Some of Robert's coworkers and some NYU academics would attend, but it would be a small affair. Emily did not have an expansive life with lots of friends. Of course, Emily knew Robert would be wracked with guilt, leaving his wife alone in a huge house in order to get some afternoon delight while she fell down the stairs and died. He would never recover. Emily felt terrible for him for a moment.

Ring!

It was Robert. The phone rang for thirty seconds.

Ring!

It was Robert again.

Ring!

It was Robert again.

Then began a series of text messages—*ding ding ding ding ding ding*! The phone was too far away for Emily to read them. Either he was worried about her, and coming to check on her, or he was mad at her for ghosting him.

Emily waited for him to show up, for an hour—no Robert.

Another hour—no Robert.

It was getting dark.

Another hour—no Robert.

He's not coming.

Emily went to sleep at the bottom of the stairs.

———————

The phone was silent. Emily was lying in fresh shit.

There was no hope of reaching the phone. Emily was dying of thirst, and the pain from her shoulder and side had spread throughout the rest of her body—as much of it as she could feel. She couldn't move; she lay face down on the floor.

So this is what dying feels like, she thought. It hurt to open her eyes.

She heard the prattling of people on the sidewalk—people

talking on the phone, walking by, police sirens, the *beep beep beep* of construction equipment—everyone going about their day, while she died alone in the house.

She had a cat growing up—its name was Fred. Fred ate an astonishing amount of people food—peas, corn, lima beans, green beans, pancakes, spaghetti, bagels—and seemed to understand what she was feeling at any moment. She thought—a silly superstition—that maybe she would see Fred again after she died, and she would be able to tell him how much he helped her get through her parents' divorce, the yelling and screaming, the accusations, while Emily locked them in her bedroom. Out of anyone she knew in her life who she wanted to see again, she wanted to see Fred, with his green, iridescent eyes that looked into her soul.

Ring! It was Robert.

It was too late. She rested her head on the floor, took a breath, then another, then her last. Her heart stopped, and her brain began to die. Her spirit rose from her body, and she saw light—a light of indescribable, infinite beauty and love. She looked down—she could see Robert in a cab, frantically calling her, driving to their home on West 81st Street. He exited the cab, ran up to the door, and opened it, burst inside, and saw Emily's lifeless body on the floor. He got down on the floor, crying, and held her close. Emily turned to the light, knowing that they would be reunited, one day, in eternity.

ACKNOWLEDGMENTS

I want to thank my cats first—Stripe, Tars, Vesper, Wendy, Xenia, and Yellow for sitting next to me on the couch as I wrote these stories throughout 2023. And also Uma, who passed away on December 5, 2023—if I could dedicate this book to anyone, I would dedicate it to her, our seven-pound crabby tabby. And also, our new cat Zeus, though he wasn't around when I wrote the book.

Then I want to thank my wife, Carolyn, who read most of these stories and gave me practically no helpful feedback. But I'm sure she would have told me if I was crossing any lines—or maybe she wouldn't have.

I would like to thank Turney Duff, Carmela Caruso, and Amber Silverman, three professional writers who read practically all of the stories and gave me great suggestions—especially Turney, who is a master storyteller. The book simply would not have been as good without them.

I really want to thank my editor, Chris Parker, for his guidance throughout the process. I wisely asked Chris to read two of my stories while we were out in California for Future

Proof, and he was hooked. Chris also helped with the cover and page design, and I am in debt to him.

Thanks also go to my literary agent, Stephen Barr, who read the greatest hits from this collection, and came to the conclusion that no publisher would want them, for the reasons I described in the introduction. Even though he didn't help sell this book, I always appreciate his wise counsel.

I'd also like to thank Lee Griffith, professor at the Savannah College of Art and Design. I reluctantly took his fiction class in 2022; reluctantly, because I thought I was done writing fiction after *All the Evil of This World*. But his class, Techniques of Fiction, helped me find the inspiration that I had lost since 2016, and I went on to write several more stories with him in an independent study. I'd also like to thank Professor Jonathan Rabb, who gave me some feedback on "Amanda" in his class Writing About Place, though this version of the story turned out very different!

I want to thank in advance anyone who helps me promote this work of literary fiction written by a finance bro. If the literary people won't have me, at least my friends in finance will, and they can appreciate a good story.

And thank you, the reader, for making it all the way to the end.

MORE GREAT FICTION
by Jared Dillian

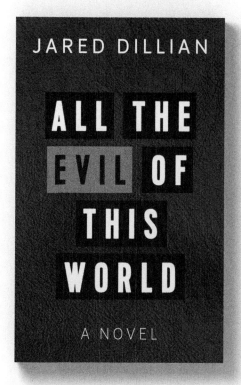

Reader reviews

"A wildly entertaining work of fiction."

"Exciting, thought provoking, cringe-inducing, and a lot of fun."

"Reads like a greased pig running through a chute to its eventual slaughter. Dillian is a great writer."

Printed in Great Britain
by Amazon

51899798R00158